D0209323

WORLD WAR II
OPPOSING VIEWPOINTS®

Other Books of Related Interest:

American History Series

African Americans
The American Frontier
The American Revolution
Asian Americans
The Bill of Rights
The Civil Rights Movement
The Civil War
The Cold War
The Creation of the Constitution
The Great Depression
Immigration
Isolationism
The 1960s
Puritanism
Reconstruction
Slavery
The Women's Rights Movement

Opposing Viewpoints in American History

Volume I: From Colonial Times to Reconstruction
Volume II: From Reconstruction to the Present

WORLD WAR II
OPPOSING VIEWPOINTS®

David L. Bender, *Publisher*
Bruno Leone, *Executive Editor*

William Dudley, *Series Editor*
John C. Chalberg, Ph.D., professor of history,
   Normandale Community College, *Consulting Editor*

William Dudley, *Book Editor*

AMERICAN HISTORY SERIES

Greenhaven Press, Inc.
San Diego, California

Cover photographs, clockwise from top: 1) President Franklin D. Roosevelt signing the declaration of war against Japan, December 8, 1941 (Library of Congress); 2) Pearl Harbor, Hawaii, being attacked by Japan, December 7, 1941 (National Archives); 3) Mary Josephine Farley working on a rebuilt Wright Whirlwind airplane engine (National Archives); 4) American soldiers displaying captured Nazi flag at Chambois, France, August 20, 1944 (National Archives).

Library of Congress Cataloging-in-Publication Data

World War II : opposing viewpoints / [edited by] William Dudley.
    p.   cm. — (American history series)
    Includes bibliographical references and index.
    ISBN 1-56510-527-3 (pbk.). — ISBN 1-56510-528-1 (lib. bdg.)
    1. World War, 1939–1945—United States—Sources. 2. World War, 1939–1945—Public opinion—Sources. 3. Public opinion—United States—Sources. I. Dudley, William, 1964– . II. Series: American history series (San Diego, Calif.)
D810.P85U68   1997   96-44978
940.54′09—dc20   CIP

"America was born of revolt, flourished in dissent, became great through experimentation."

Henry Steele Commager, American Historian

Contents

Chapter 3: The Home Front

Foreword

Aboard the *Arbella* as it lurched across the cold, gray Atlantic, John Winthrop was as calm as the waters surrounding him were wild. With the confidence of a leader, Winthrop gathered his Puritan companions around him. It was time to offer a sermon. England lay behind them, and years of strife and persecution for their religious beliefs were over, he said. But the Puritan abandonment of England, he reminded his followers, did not mean that England was beyond redemption. Winthrop wanted his followers to remember England even as they were leaving it behind. Their goal should be to create a new England, one far removed from the authority of the Anglican church and King Charles I. In Winthrop's words, their settlement in the New World ought to be "a city upon a hill," a just society for corrupt England to emulate.

A Chance to Start Over

One June 8, 1630, John Winthrop and his company of refugees had their first glimpse of what they came to call New England. High on the surrounding hills stood a welcoming band of fir trees whose fragrance drifted to the *Arbella* on a morning breeze. To Winthrop, the "smell off the shore [was] like the smell of a garden." This new world would, in fact, often be compared to the Garden of Eden. Here, John Winthrop would have his opportunity to start life over again. So would his family and his shipmates. So would all those who came after them. These victims of conflict in old England hoped to find peace in New England.

Winthrop, for one, had experienced much conflict in his life. As a Puritan, he was opposed to Catholicism and Anglicanism, both of which, he believed, were burdened by distracting rituals and distant hierarchies. A parliamentarian by conviction, he despised Charles I, who had spurned Parliament and created a private army to do his bidding. Winthrop believed in individual responsibility and fought against the loss of religious and political freedom. A gentleman landowner, he feared the rising economic power of a merchant class that seemed to value only money. Once Winthrop stepped aboard the *Arbella*, he hoped, these conflicts would not be a part of his American future.

Yet his Puritan religion told Winthrop that human beings are fallen creatures and that perfection, whether communal or individual, is unachievable on this earth. Therefore, he faced a paradox: On the one hand, his religion demanded that he attempt to live a perfect life in an imperfect world. On the other hand, it told him that he was destined to fail.

Soon after Winthrop disembarked from the *Arbella*, he came face-to-face with this maddening dilemma. He found himself presiding not over a utopia but over a colony caught up in disputes as troubling as any he had confronted in his English past. John Winthrop, it seems, was not the only Puritan with a dream of a heaven on earth. But others in the community saw the dream differently. They wanted greater political and religious freedom than their leader was prepared to grant. Often, Winthrop was able to handle this conflict diplomatically. For example, he expanded, participation in elections and allowed the voters of Massachusetts Bay greater power.

But religious conflict was another matter because it was grounded in competing visions of the Puritan utopia. In Roger Williams and Anne Hutchinson, two of his fellow colonists, John Winthrop faced rivals unprepared to accept his definition of the perfect community. To Williams, perfection demanded that he separate himself from the Puritan institutions in his community and create an even "purer" church. Winthrop, however, disagreed and exiled Williams to Rhode Island. Hutchinson presumed that she could interpret God's will without a minister. Again, Winthrop did not agree. Hutchinson was tried on charges of heresy, convicted, and banished from Massachusetts.

John Winthrop's Massachusetts colony was the first but far from the last American attempt to build a unified, peaceful community that, in the end, only provoked a discord. This glimpse at its history reveals what Winthrop confronted: the unavoidable presence of conflict in American life.

American Assumptions

From America's origins in the early seventeenth century, Americans have often held several interrelated assumptions about their country. First, people believe that to be American is to be free. Second, because Americans did not have to free themselves from feudal lords or an entrenched aristocracy, America has been seen as a perpetual haven from the troubles and disputes that are found in the Old World.

John Winthrop lived his life as though these assumptions were true. But the opposing viewpoints presented in the American History Series should reveal that for many Americans, these assumptions were and are myths. Indeed, for numerous Americans, liberty has not always been guaranteed, and disputes have been an integral, sometimes welcome part of their life.

The American landscape has been torn apart again and again by a great variety of clashes—theological, ideological, political, economic, geographical, and social. But such a landscape is not necessarily a hopelessly divided country. If the editors hope to prove anything during the course of this series, it is not that the United States has been destroyed by conflict but rather that it has been enlivened, enriched, and even strengthened by Americans who have disagreed with one another.

Thomas Jefferson was one of the least confrontational of Americans, but he boldly and irrevocably enriched American life with his individualistic views. Like John Winthrop before him, he had a notion of an American Eden. Like Winthrop, he offered a vision of a harmonious society. And like Winthrop, he not only became enmeshed in conflict but eventually presided over a people beset by it. But unlike Winthrop, Jefferson believed this Eden was not located in a specific community but in each individual American. His Declaration of Independence from Great Britain could also be read as a declaration of independence for each individual in American society.

Jefferson's Ideal

Jefferson's ideal world was composed of "yeoman farmers," each of whom was roughly equal to the others in society's eyes, each of whom was free from the restrictions of both government and fellow citizens. Throughout his life, Jefferson offered a continuing challenge to Americans: Advance individualism and equality or see the death of the American experiment. Jefferson believed that the strength of this experiment depended upon a society of autonomous individuals and a society without great gaps between rich and poor. His challenge to his fellow Americans to create—and sustain—such a society has itself produced both economic and political conflict.

A society whose guiding document is the Declaration of Independence is a society assured of the freedom to dream—and to disagree. We know that Jefferson hated conflict, both personal and political. His tendency was to avoid confrontations of any sort, to squirrel himself away and write rather than to stand up and speak his mind. It is only through his written words that we can grasp Jefferson's utopian dream of a society of independent farmers, all pursuing their private dreams and all leading lives of middling prosperity.

Jefferson, this man of wealth and intellect, lived an essentially happy private life. But his public life was much more troublesome. From the first rumblings of the American Revolution in the 1760s to the North-South skirmishes of the 1820s that ultimately produced the Civil War, Jefferson was at or near the center of American political history. The issues were almost too many—and too crucial—for one lifetime: Jefferson had to choose between supporting or rejecting the path of revolution. During and after the ensuing war, he was at the forefront of the battle for religious liberty. After endorsing the Constitution, he opposed the economic plans of Alexander Hamilton. At the end of the century, he fought the infamous Alien and Sedition Acts, which limited civil liberties. As president, he opposed the Federalist court, conspiracies to divide the union, and calls for a new war against England. Throughout his life, Thomas Jefferson, slaveholder, pondered the conflict between American freedom and American slavery. And from retirement at his Monticello retreat, he frowned at the rising spirit of commercialism he feared was dividing Americans and destroying his dream of American harmony.

No matter the issue, however, Thomas Jefferson invariably supported the rights of the individual. Worried as he was about the excesses of commercialism, he accepted them because his main concern was to live in a society where liberty and individualism could flourish. To Jefferson, Americans had to be free to worship as they desired. They also deserved to be free from an over-reaching government. To Jefferson, Americans should also be free to possess slaves.

Harmony, an Elusive Goal

Before reading the articles in this anthology, the editors ask readers to ponder the lives of John Winthrop and Thomas Jefferson. Each held a utopian vision, one based upon the demands of community and the other on the autonomy of the individual. Each dreamed of a country of perpetual new beginnings. Each found himself thrust into a position of leadership and found that conflict could not be avoided. Harmony, whether communal or individual, was a forever elusive goal.

The opposing visions of Winthrop and Jefferson have been at the heart of many differences among Americans from many backgrounds through the whole of American history. Moreover, their visions have provoked important responses that have helped shape American society, the American character, and many an American battle.

The editors of the American History Series have done extensive research to find representative opinions on the issues included in these volumes. They have found numerous outstanding opposing viewpoints from people of all times, classes, and genders in American history. From those, they have selected commentaries that best fit the nature and flavor of the period and topic under consideration. Every attempt was made to include the most important and relevant viewpoints in each chapter. Obviously, not every notable viewpoint could be included. Therefore, a selective, annotated bibliography has been provided at the end of each book to aid readers in seeking additional information.

The editors are confident that as this series reveals past conflicts, it will help revitalize the reader's views of the American present. In that spirit, the American History Series is dedicated to the proposition that American history is more complicated, more fascinating, and more troubling than John Winthrop or Thomas Jefferson ever dared to imagine.

John C. Chalberg
Consulting Editor

Introduction

"The debates over a peacetime military draft and national service legislation both illustrate a central concern of Americans during World War II—how to preserve American democracy at home while preparing for and fighting a war on its behalf."

World War II, which involved 60 million soldiers from forty nations, is perhaps the pivotal event of modern world history. It redrew the map of Europe and ended the era of European predominance in international politics; it ended Japan's attempt to become the dominant military power of Asia; and it introduced to warfare the fearsome powers of the atomic bomb. Approximately 17 million members of the armed forces of participating nations—including 322,000 Americans—were killed in the war; additional tens of millions of civilians (the exact total is unknown) perished from famine, bombing raids, epidemics, and other war-related causes. Approximately 11 million of the war's dead were victims of the Holocaust, including 6 million Jews.

The United States and World War II

The United States, as compared with other participating nations, suffered relatively little of the war's physical destructiveness. Except for the victims of Japan's December 7, 1941, attack on the Pearl Harbor naval base in Hawaii, most people in U.S. territory did not experience battles or air raids. Measured as a fraction of the total population, the number of American casualties was small compared with those of other countries. However, despite the fact that most of World War II was fought outside the United States, the conflict did effect profound changes in America. At the beginning of the conflict the United States was a neutral nation possessing the world's nineteenth largest army (with 190,000 personnel) and an economy still recovering from the Great Depression. By the end of the war the U.S. Army had grown to 12.1 million people in uniform, and the United States had become a leading member of the victorious Allies, a driving force behind the creation of the United Nations, and in many respects the world's most powerful nation.

During World War II, Americans disagreed over a wide variety of issues, ranging from questions of military tactics to the utilization of women in the labor force. Most of these controversies centered on how to preserve the American "way of life," which many Americans equated with the "four freedoms" (freedom of speech, freedom of worship, freedom from fear, and freedom from want) articulated by President Franklin D. Roosevelt in a 1940 speech. From September 1939, when war broke out in Europe, to December 1941, when Japan attacked Pearl Harbor, the United States was divided over whether declaring war against Germany and its partners would protect or jeopardize these freedoms. After the United States decided to enter the war following the Pearl Harbor attack, Americans continued to debate whether specific government measures would bolster the war effort or would endanger the very freedoms America was purportedly fighting to preserve.

Two specific issues can serve to illustrate the general debate over whether a democracy can wage "total war" and still maintain its essential freedoms: the 1940 controversy over the institution of a peacetime military draft and the 1944 debate over a proposal to draft civilians into essential wartime industries. Both measures were promoted as necessary for the nation's defense and for the preservation of American freedoms. Ironically, in both of these instances, restrictions on individual freedoms were proposed as a means of upholding those freedoms.

The Draft

In June 1940 Germany seemed unstoppable. Of the two major powers that opposed it, France had surrendered and Great Britain was under aerial attack and was apparently facing imminent invasion. Most Americans, including President Roosevelt, believed that a German victory would be disastrous for the United States. However, the U.S. Army then contained about 270,000 officers and soldiers—an insufficient number if the United States was to enter the war. The only practical way to create a larger army was through a system of military conscription.

America had never employed a system of compulsory military service during peacetime, relying instead on volunteers to serve in its armed forces (although temporary draft systems had been set up during the Civil War and World War I). Many Americans strongly opposed both large standing armies during peacetime and a system of military conscription. Because of potential public opposition, both Roosevelt and General George C. Marshall, the army chief of staff, hesitated to recommend a national draft.

The impetus for the institution of a draft came from a private group, the Emergency Committee of the Military Training Camps Association, led by corporate lawyer Grenville Clark. The group, consisting of prominent professionals, lobbied the president, Congress, and the military for a national draft law. They also launched a campaign to persuade the American public that the draft was needed.

Threats to Democracy

In their arguments for the draft, Clark and others stressed the threat posed to American democracy by the Axis nations, including Japan, Italy, and—especially—Germany. In the 1920s and 1930s these countries had come to be ruled by dictatorial governments and had embarked on ventures of military expansion. Japan had conquered the Chinese province of Manchuria in 1931 and had started an undeclared war on the rest of China in 1937; Italy had invaded and conquered Ethiopia in 1935; and Germany had invaded Poland in 1939, thereby beginning World War II. Clark and other supporters of the draft argued in speeches and newspaper articles that these nations, with their military aggression and antipathy for democracy, posed a clear danger to the United States. For example, in a radio broadcast on June 17, 1940, former secretary of state Henry L. Stimson stated:

> At the present moment the world today is divided into two irreconcilable groups of governments. One group is yet striving for justice and freedom . . . while the other group recognizes the rule of force. . . .
>
> In the light of this background, the military situation today is nothing less than appalling for our country. . . . We should at once adopt a system of universal compulsory military training and service.

However, other Americans opposed the peacetime military draft, viewing it as a step toward U.S. involvement in the war. Isolationists, who believed that America should stay out of conflicts taking place outside of the Western Hemisphere, were particularly vocal in their opposition. Many argued that U.S. involvement in World War I had been a mistake, and they feared that a peacetime draft and mobilization could lead to a similar error. The isolationist stance prior to Pearl Harbor was summed up by Hamilton Fish, a Republican member of the House of Representatives, in a January 6, 1939, speech. Fish insisted that the United States should not intervene in the affairs of other countries no matter how deplorable their governments were:

> As much as American citizens abhor racial and religious perse-
> cution and ruthless militarism, it is none of our business what
> form of government may exist in Soviet Russia, Fascist Italy, Im-
> perial Japan, or Nazi Germany any more than it is their busi-
> ness what form of government exists in our own country. We
> have our own problems to solve in America without becoming
> involved in the rotten mess in Europe or in the eternal wars of
> both Europe and Asia.

Isolationists held that U.S. participation in the war would be
more likely to undermine American democracy than would the
belligerent actions of European dictators. Some maintained that
going to war would itself be a major blow to democracy since the
majority of Americans opposed such an undertaking. Famed aviator Charles Lindbergh expressed this view in an April 23, 1941,
speech:

> If the principles of democracy mean anything at all, that is rea-
> son enough for us to stay out. If we are forced into a war
> against the wishes of an overwhelming majority of our people,
> we will have proved democracy such a failure at home that
> there will be little use of fighting for it abroad.

In addition, isolationists asserted that by creating a military capable of fighting the "total war" necessary to win, the American
government would inevitably grow larger and more repressive.
Many of these critics were longtime opponents of Roosevelt,
whom they accused of drifting toward dictatorship because he
had greatly expanded the powers of the presidency and the
American government in his New Deal programs during the
Great Depression.

Isolationists and other opponents argued that the compulsory
peacetime recruitment of civilians for military service would be a
near-dictatorial violation of the civil liberties of U.S. citizens. For
example, in an August 23, 1940, speech to Congress, Senator Gerald P. Nye of South Dakota warned that a peacetime military
draft would threaten American freedom and democracy by moving the country toward dictatorship and militarism:

> I see in peacetime conscription a response to hysteria that can
> so definitely lead to dictatorship. I see it adding to the fast-
> growing will to adopt the conclusion that an emergency con-
> fronts our country warranting a surrender of democratic pow-
> ers resting with the people and their representatives. . . .

> I see in this peacetime draft of men the fastening of a yoke of
> militarism upon us that will not be easily, if ever, cast off. . . .

> We are all agreed that there is no opposition to a proposed con-
> scription of manpower in time of war. But the drive for compul-
> sory peacetime conscription cannot be otherwise construed ex-
> cept as an insult, and a sharp one, to our American youth.

The fate of the draft legislation illustrates how evenly divided public opinion regarding World War II was prior to Pearl Harbor. Spurred by the work of Clark's group, both Roosevelt and Marshall eventually came out in support of the draft, and a draft law was passed in 1940. But because of the concerns of Nye and other isolationists, draftees were limited to one year of service, and that solely within the Western Hemisphere. In August 1941, with the war still raging in Europe and threatening to break out in Asia, the House of Representatives, by a vote of 203 to 202, barely managed to extend the terms of service of draftees by an additional eighteen months. By the time Japan attacked Pearl Harbor, the total number of people serving in the armed forces had grown to 2 million.

Pearl Harbor and Dissent

Opposition to the draft melted once America came under attack and entered the war in December 1941. Historian Richard Polenberg writes that "virtually all Americans believed the war was both just and necessary, fought for honorable purposes against a radically evil enemy." In fact, a number of prominent isolationists, including Lindbergh and Nye, publicly supported the war following Pearl Harbor. This public consensus was never unanimous, though, as attested by the fact that five thousand to six thousand men were imprisoned during the war as draft evaders, while an additional twenty-five thousand persons became conscientious objectors (although these were relatively small numbers compared to the 15 million men and women who served in the armed forces). However, while the Pearl Harbor attack had united most Americans in support of the war effort, concerns about how the war would affect America's democracy remained.

National Service

This concern found expression in the debate over legislation that would require national service—a civilian "draft" for war-industry workers. Those who called for a civilian draft were worried about the effectiveness of America's "home front"— specifically, the harnessing of the nation's industrial and agricultural resources to feed and equip its soldiers fighting abroad. In many respects the United States was successful in converting its economy to meet wartime needs. Military production rose 800 percent between 1941 and 1943; at one point the nation was building ships at the rate of one a day and airplanes at the rate of one every five minutes. Such production created a huge demand for labor. The total workforce in the United States grew from 56 million in 1940 to more than 65 million in 1945, as the increased employment of women, minorities, the young, and the elderly more than made up for the 15 million soldiers who were unavailable for the labor force. Despite this increase in the workforce, however, labor shortages existed in several areas. Some people thus advocated a "national service" system in which most civilians would register for defense work, allowing the government to assign workers to specific factories deemed essential for America's war effort.

Hoping to repeat his success in the draft debate, Grenville Clark again formed and led a private group—the Citizens' Committee for a National War Service Act—to mobilize public support for the idea. The group, like its 1940 predecessor, lobbied government officials and the American public, arguing in one of the group's reports that national service would be "a great constructive measure to do justice to our armed forces, to bring about more order and discipline on the home front, and to promote a greater degree of national unity, without which this war may be indefinitely prolonged." In a manner similar to his approach in the 1940 draft debate, Roosevelt let Clark and others take the lead before endorsing the idea and recommending it to Congress in 1944.

Despite the president's endorsement, however, and despite the fact that America was at war, many people strenuously opposed national service legislation. Their arguments against the proposals often resembled those used by draft opponents four years earlier. Such legislation constituted a system of "involuntary servitude," according to Matthew Woll, vice president of the American Federation of Labor. Senator C.W. Brooks of Illinois linked the debate over national service to the enormous growth in the reach and power of the federal government during World War II, believing it to be further evidence of the dictatorial ambitions of President Roosevelt: "Each pretended crisis in government has been marked by new evidences of this underlying mania for power—power over the states; power over private enterprise; power over resources; and now power over the rights of all our people." A civilian draft, opponents argued, would jeopardize American freedoms and would, in the words of George W. Gillie, a Republican representative from Indiana, "defeat the very principles we are fighting for in this war." Unlike the peacetime draft measure four years earlier, the national service legislation was never passed by Congress.

Preserving Democracy

The debates over a peacetime military draft and national service legislation both illustrate a central concern of Americans during World War II—how to preserve American democracy at home while preparing for and fighting a war on its behalf. In both cases, government policies limiting the freedoms of citizens were proposed as measures to protect those same freedoms. While the outcome of each debate differed, both were examples of the democratic process. The fact that these debates took place during wartime leads many people to conclude that American democracy successfully proved itself by functioning throughout the war. Whether this view is justified is just one of many questions raised by the collection of essays in this volume. *World War II: Opposing Viewpoints* examines the debates surrounding issues critical to America and its democracy during this turbulent time.

CHAPTER 1

Before Pearl Harbor

Chapter Preface

World War II began on September 1, 1939, when Germany invaded Poland, triggering declarations of war by Great Britain and France (the Allies). President Franklin D. Roosevelt's first response was to proclaim official U.S. neutrality. By June 1940 France had fallen and Italy had joined the war on the side of Germany. A year later the Soviet Union was attacked by Germany. Meanwhile, Japan (who had been at war with China since 1937) signed a military alliance with Germany and Italy in September 1940 and threatened to take over French, Dutch, and British colonies in Asia. While these developments occurred, the United States took gradual steps to aid the Allies but did not formally enter the conflict.

The issue of how the United States should respond to these foreign wars was hotly debated. "Isolationists" such as South Dakota senator Gerald P. Nye and famous aviator Charles Lindbergh argued that the United States, separated from the war by the Pacific and Atlantic Oceans, should concentrate on building up its defenses in the Western Hemisphere and should not expend resources or soldiers in battle in Europe and Asia. Many sympathized with pacifist views opposing all wars; some believed that U.S. involvement in World War I in particular was a tragic mistake that should not be repeated. A few isolationists openly supported the fascist nations. Others expressed the desire to see the Allies win, but not at the price of U.S. involvement.

"Interventionists," who included such figures as former secretary of state Henry L. Stimson, argued that the fascist and expansionist regimes of Germany, Italy, and Japan posed a deadly threat to worldwide peace and stability and that the United States should take any steps necessary to ensure their defeat. Robert Sherwood, a playwright who also wrote speeches for Roosevelt, published a political advertisement in the *New York Times* in June 1940 that stated:

> If Hitler wins in Europe . . . the United States will find itself alone in a barbaric world—a world ruled by Nazis, with "spheres of influence" assigned to their totalitarian allies. However different the dictatorships may be, racially, they all agree on one primary objective: *"Democracy must be wiped from the face of the earth."*

Most Americans fell somewhere between pure isolationism and interventionism. Public opinion polls taken in November 1939, for instance, revealed that two-thirds of Americans favored providing aid to England and France, but the same percentage believed that staying out of the war was more important than saving the Allies from defeat.

Even if Americans had wanted to immediately enter the war in 1939, the United States was ill prepared. The U.S. Army had less than 200,000 soldiers in active service (Germany had by then mobilized 2.7 million). Many of the guns, ships, tanks, and other equipment the United States possessed were outdated compared to those used by the Germans and the Japanese. In 1941 many American soldiers went through training using fake wooden rifles.

Following his initial proclamation of neutrality, President Franklin D. Roosevelt took steps both to build up America's military forces and to assist the Allies—steps his critics charged would lead the United States into war. In November 1939 Roosevelt called Congress into special session to modify neutrality laws to permit Britain and France to purchase munitions. In a speech on June 10, 1940, he announced a change in U.S. policy from "neutrality" to "nonbelligerency," by which he meant open support of the Allies short of war. In September 1940 he obtained congressional approval for the first peacetime military draft in U.S. history. Also in September, he authorized a "destroyers for bases" arrangement with Great Britain, in which America lent Britain fifty older destroyers in exchange for leases on British bases in the Western Hemisphere. In December 1940, following his reelection to a third term, Roosevelt proposed a "Lend-Lease" program to provide supplies to Great Britain. Lend-Lease, after much national debate, was enacted by Congress in March 1941. In July 1941 the United States extended Lend-Lease aid to the Soviets and began providing naval escorts to British cargo ships to protect them against attacks from German ships and submarines. In September 1941 Roosevelt announced that U.S. Navy escort ships would shoot German vessels "on sight." Despite increasing hostilities in the Atlantic, Congress remained deeply divided on the war question, and public opinion polls showed that barely a quarter of Americans favored entering the war. Waiting in vain for Germany to declare war, Roosevelt refrained from asking Congress for a war declaration.

Ironically, it was not Germany but Japan that provided the impetus for America's entry into World War II. Relations between Japan and the United States had been deteriorating since Japan's invasions of Manchuria in 1931 and China in 1937. With the fall of France and the Netherlands to Germany in 1940, Japan's military-dominated government began to covet French and Dutch colonial possessions in Asia, especially for their rubber, tin, petroleum, and other raw materials. In an effort both to limit Japan's reach and to punish that nation for its war against China, the United States imposed an embargo of aviation fuel and scrap metal on Japan in July 1940. It broadened these sanctions in July 1941 when it froze Japanese assets in America and halted exports of petroleum products to Japan. Negotiations between the two countries foundered when America insisted that Japan relinquish all of its territorial gains in China and Southeast Asia. Determined to maintain its new order in Asia and running short on supplies (due in part to American economic sanctions), Japan made the fateful decision to preemptively wipe out America's Pacific fleet stationed in Pearl Harbor, Hawaii. One day after Japan's surprise attack on December 7, 1941, Congress passed a declaration of war on Japan with just one dissenting vote. Three days later, Germany declared war on the United States in support of its Asian ally. At that point, Americans no longer debated whether to enter the war but, instead, how best to win it.

VIEWPOINT 1

"Let no man or woman thoughtlessly or falsely talk of America sending its armies to European fields. At this moment there is being prepared a proclamation of American neutrality."

The United States Should Remain Neutral

Franklin D. Roosevelt (1882–1945)

In September 1939, a little more than two decades after World War I ended, Europe again plunged into war when France and Great Britain declared war on Germany following Germany's invasion of Poland. The following two-part viewpoint consists of excerpts from two important speeches by President Franklin D. Roosevelt in response to the war's outbreak. Part I is from one of Roosevelt's "fireside chats"—his informal radio addresses to the public in which he discussed major issues facing the nation. In his radio address of September 3, 1939, Roosevelt announces that America will officially proclaim itself neutral (as required by law), expresses his personal hatred for war, and argues that American policy will focus on keeping the war out of the Western Hemisphere.

Part II of this viewpoint is taken from a September 21, 1939, speech by Roosevelt to Congress calling for the modification of America's neutrality laws. Passed in 1935 and revised in 1937, these laws were designed to preclude America from taking sides in foreign wars in order to prevent direct U.S. involvement in such conflicts. Under these laws, when Roosevelt formally proclaimed American neutrality on September 5, the United States was forbidden to export arms and munitions to any nation engaged in the conflict, regardless of whether such countries were aggressors or victims. Roosevelt proposed that the laws be modi-

Part I: From Franklin D. Roosevelt's "fireside chat" radio broadcast, September 3, 1939. Part II: From Roosevelt's speech to Congress, September 21, 1939.

fied to permit some arms exports, and he recommended a limited "cash-and-carry" program that required all supplies bought in America to be paid for in cash and carried by the Allies' own ships. The practical upshot of his proposal would have been to permit the selling of American arms to Great Britain and France. In his speech to Congress, however, Roosevelt argues that the proposed changes would preserve American neutrality and keep the United States out of war.

I

Tonight my single duty is to speak to the whole of America. Until four-thirty this morning I had hoped against hope that some miracle would prevent a devastating war in Europe and bring to an end the invasion of Poland by Germany.

For four long years a succession of actual wars and constant crises have shaken the entire world and have threatened in each case to bring on the gigantic conflict which is today unhappily a fact.

It is right that I should recall to your minds the consistent and at times successful efforts of your Government in these crises to throw the full weight of the United States into the cause of peace. In spite of spreading wars I think that we have every right and every reason to maintain as a national policy the fundamental moralities, the teachings of religion and the continuation of efforts to restore peace—for some day, though the time may be distant, we can be of even greater help to a crippled humanity.

It is right, too, to point out that the unfortunate events of these recent years have, without question, been based on the use of force and the threat of force. And it seems to me clear, even at the outbreak of this great war, that the influence of America should be consistent in seeking for humanity a final peace which will eliminate, as far as it is possible to do so, the continued use of force between nations.

It is, of course, impossible to predict the future. I have my constant stream of information from American representatives and other sources throughout the world. You, the people of this country, are receiving news through your radios and your newspapers at every hour of the day.

You are, I believe, the most enlightened and the best informed people in all the world at this moment. You are subjected to no censorship of news, and I want to add that your Government has no information which it withholds or which it has any thought of withholding from you.

At the same time, as I told my press conference on Friday, it is of the highest importance that the press and the radio use the utmost caution to discriminate between actual verified fact on the one hand, and mere rumor on the other.

I can add to that by saying that I hope the people of this country will also discriminate most carefully between news and rumor. Do not believe of necessity everything you hear or read. Check up on it first.

You must master at the outset a simple but unalterable fact in modern foreign relations between nations. When peace has been broken anywhere, the peace of all countries everywhere is in danger.

It is easy for you and for me to shrug our shoulders and to say that conflicts taking place thousands of miles from the continental United States, and, indeed, thousands of miles from the whole American Hemisphere, do not seriously affect the Americas—and that all the United States has to do is to ignore them and go about its own business. Passionately though we may desire detachment, we are forced to realize that every word that comes through the air, every ship that sails the sea, every battle that is fought, does affect the American future.

Proclaiming American Neutrality

Let no man or woman thoughtlessly or falsely talk of America sending its armies to European fields. At this moment there is being prepared a proclamation of American neutrality. This would have been done even if there had been no neutrality statute on the books, for this proclamation is in accordance with international law and in accordance with American policy.

This will be followed by a Proclamation required by the existing Neutrality Act. And I trust that in the days to come our neutrality can be made a true neutrality.

It is of the utmost importance that the people of this country, with the best information in the world, think things through. The most dangerous enemies of American peace are those who, without well-rounded information on the whole broad subject of the past, the present and the future, undertake to speak with assumed authority, to talk in terms of glittering generalities, to give to the nation assurances or prophesies which are of little present or future value.

I myself cannot and do not prophesy the course of events abroad—and the reason is that, because I have of necessity such a complete picture of what is going on in every part of the world, I do not dare to do so. And the other reason is that I think it is honest for me to be honest with the people of the United States.

I cannot prophesy the immediate economic effect of this new war on our nation, but I do say that no American has the moral right to profiteer at the expense either of his fellow citizens or of the men, the women and the children who are living and dying in the midst of war in Europe.

Some things we do know. Most of us in the United States believe in spiritual values. Most of us, regardless of what church we belong to, believe in the spirit of the New Testament—a great teaching which opposes itself to the use of force, of armed force, of marching armies and falling bombs. The overwhelming masses of our people seek peace—peace at home, and the kind of peace in other lands which will not jeopardize our peace at home.

Certain Ideals

We have certain ideas and certain ideals of national safety, and we must act to preserve that safety today, and to preserve the safety of our children in future years.

That safety is and will be bound up with the safety of the Western Hemisphere and of the seas adjacent thereto. We seek to keep war from our own firesides by keeping war from coming to the Americas. For that we have historic precedent that goes back to the days of the Administration of President George Washington. It is serious enough and tragic enough to every American family in every State in the Union to live in a world that is torn by wars on other continents. Those wars today affect every American home. It is our national duty to use every effort to keep them out of the Americas.

And at this time let me make the simple plea that partisanship and selfishness be adjourned; and that national unity be the thought that underlies all others.

This Nation will remain a neutral Nation, but I cannot ask that every American remain neutral in thought as well. Even a neutral has a right to take account of facts. Even a neutral cannot be asked to close his mind or his conscience.

I have said not once, but many times, that I have seen war and that I hate war. I say that again and again.

I hope the United States will keep out of this war. I believe that it will. And I give you assurance and reassurance that every effort of your Government will be directed toward that end.

As long as it remains within my power to prevent, there will be no black-out of peace in the United States.

II

I have asked the Congress to reassemble in extraordinary session in order that it may consider and act on the amendment of certain legislation, which, in my best judgment, so alters the historic foreign policy of the United States that it impairs the peaceful relations of the United States with foreign nations.

At the outset I proceed on the assumption that every member of the Senate and of the House of Representatives, and every member of the executive branch of the government, including the President and his associates, personally and officially, are equally and without reservation in favor of such measures as will protect the neutrality, the safety and the integrity of our country and at the same time keep us out of war.

Because I am wholly willing to ascribe an honorable desire for peace to those who hold different views from my own as to what those measures should be, I trust that these gentlemen will be sufficiently generous to ascribe equally lofty purposes to those with whom they disagree.

Let no man or group in any walk of life assume exclusive protectorate over the future well-being of America—because I conceive that regardless of party or section the mantle of peace and of patriotism is wide enough to cover us all.

Let no group assume the exclusive label of the peace "bloc." We all belong to it. . . .

Past American Policy

Beginning with the foundation of our constitutional government in the year 1789, the American policy in respect to belligerent nations, with one notable exception, has been based on international law. Be it remembered that what we call international law has had as its primary objectives the avoidance of causes of war and the prevention of the extension of war.

The single exception was the policy adopted by this nation during the Napoleonic wars, when, seeking to avoid involvement, we acted for some years under the so-called Embargo and Non-Intercourse Acts. That policy turned out to be a disastrous failure—First, because it brought our own nation close to ruin, and second, because it was the major cause of bringing us into active participation in European wars in our own War of 1812. It is merely reciting history to recall to you that one of the results of the policy of embargo and non-intercourse was the burning in 1814 of part of this Capitol in which we are assembled.

Our next deviation by statute from the sound principles of neutrality and peace through international law did not come for one hundred and thirty years. It was the so-called Neutrality Act of 1935—only four years ago—an act continued in force by the joint resolution of May 1, 1937, despite grave doubts expressed as to its wisdom by many Senators and Representatives and by officials charged with the conduct of our foreign relations, including myself. I regret that the Congress passed that act. I regret equally that I signed that act.

On July 14 of this year I asked the Congress in the course of peace and in the interest of real American neutrality and security to take action to change that act. I now ask again that such action be taken in respect to that part of the act which is wholly inconsistent with ancient precepts of the law of nations—the embargo provisions. I ask it because they are, in my opinion, most vitally dangerous to American neutrality, American security and American peace.

These embargo provisions, as they exist today, prevent the sale to a belligerent by an American factory of any completed implements of war but they allow the sale of many types of uncompleted implements of war, as well as all kinds of general material and supplies. They, furthermore, allow such products of industry and agriculture to be taken in American-flag ships to belligerent nations. There in itself—under the present law—lies definite danger to our neutrality and our peace.

From a purely material point of view, what is the advantage to us in sending all manner of articles across the ocean for final processing there, when we could give employment to thousands by doing it here? Incidentally, and again from the material point of view, by such employment we automatically aid our own national defense. And if abnormal profits appear in our midst even in time of peace, as a result of this increase of industry, I feel certain that the subject will be adequately dealt with at the coming regular session of the Congress.

Let me set forth the present paradox of the existing legislation in its simplest terms: If, prior to 1935, a general war had broken out in Europe, the United States would have sold to and bought from belligerent nations such goods and products of all kinds as the belligerent nations, with their existing facilities and geographical situations, were able to buy from us or sell to us. This would have been the normal practice under the age-old doctrines of international law. Our prior position accepted the facts of geography and of conditions of land power and sea power alike as they existed in all parts of the world.

If a war in Europe had broken out prior to 1935, there would have been no difference, for example, between our exports of sheets of aluminum and airplane wings; today there is an artificial legal difference. Before 1935 there would have been no difference between the export of cotton and the export of gun cotton. Today there is. Before 1935 there would have been no difference between the shipment of brass tubing in piece form and brass tubing in shell form. Today there is. Before 1935 there would have been no difference between the export of a motor truck and an armored motor truck. Today there is.

Let us be factual and recognize that a belligerent nation often needs wheat and lard and cotton for the survival of its population just as much as it needs anti-aircraft guns and anti-submarine depth charges. Let those who seek to retain the present embargo position be wholly consistent and seek new legislation to cut off cloth and copper and meat and wheat and a thousand other articles from all of the nations at war.

I seek a greater consistency through the repeal of the embargo provisions, and a return to international law. I seek reenactment of the historic and traditional American policy which, except for the disastrous interlude of the Embargo and Non-Intercourse Acts, has served us well for nearly a century and a half. . . .

The Road to Peace

Repeal of the embargo and a return to international law are the crux of this issue. The enactment of the embargo provisions did more than merely reverse our traditional policy. It had the effect of putting land powers on the same footing as naval powers, so far as sea-borne commerce was concerned. A land power which threatened war could thus feel assured in advance that any prospective sea-power antagonist would be weakened through denial of its ancient right to buy anything anywhere.

This, four years ago, gave a definite advantage to one belligerent as against another, not through his own strength or geographic position, but through an affirmative act of ours. Removal of the embargo is merely reverting to the sounder international practice, and pursuing in time of war as in time of peace our ordinary trade policies. This will be liked by some and disliked by others, depending on the view they take of the present war, but that is not the issue. The step I recommend is to put this country back on the solid footing of real and traditional neutrality. . . .

To those who say that this program would involve a step toward war on our part, I reply that it offers far greater safeguards than we now possess or have ever possessed to protect American lives and property from danger. It is a positive program for giving safety. This means less likelihood of incidents and controversies which tend to draw us into conflict, as they did in the last World War. There lies the road to peace.

"To repeal the arms embargo is to strike down a great, indispensable, insulating defense against our involvement in this war."

Roosevelt's Policies Jeopardize American Neutrality

Arthur H. Vandenberg (1884–1951)

In his September 3, 1939, radio address, President Franklin D. Roosevelt called for U.S. neutrality in the war in Europe. However, for most of the next two years critics of the Roosevelt administration accused the president of forsaking American neutrality and of pursuing policies that would lead the United States into war. From September 1939 to December 1941 Congress and the nation were divided by fierce debates over war and American neutrality.

The following viewpoint is taken from one of the earliest of such debates. On September 21, 1939, Roosevelt called Congress into a special session to revise America's neutrality laws and relax its strict ban on the selling of arms to any warring nation. In his September 21 speech to Congress, Roosevelt defended the proposed change as a way of ultimately keeping the United States out of war.

The following viewpoint is excerpted from a speech by Arthur H. Vandenberg, a Republican senator from Michigan from 1928 until his death in 1951. Vandenberg was one of the nation's isolationists—those in Congress and the public who strongly believed that the United States should stay out of foreign entanglements, especially European politics and wars. Many believed that American participation in World War I had been a mistake. While not

Arthur H. Vandenberg, *Congressional Record*, 76th Cong., 2nd sess., October 4, 1939, pp. 95–103.

accusing Roosevelt of insincerity in his avowed objectives of peace and neutrality, Vandenberg in his address argues that the effect of revising the neutrality laws would be to increase the risk of U.S. entry into war. Such a result would be disastrous for the United States, he argues.

Congress ultimately did pass Roosevelt's recommendations into law. Vandenberg and other isolationists continued to question many of Roosevelt's policies over the next two years. The Michigan senator supported the war effort after the Japanese attack on Pearl Harbor in 1941, and he later provided crucial support for the formation of the United Nations and for President Harry S. Truman's foreign policies following World War II.

Mr. President [of the Senate], I believe this debate symbolically involves the most momentous decision, in the eyes of America and of the world, that the United States Senate has confronted in a generation. In the midst of foreign war and the alarms of other wars, we are asked to depart basically from the neutrality which the American Congress has twice told the world, since 1935, would be our rule of conduct in such event. We are particularly asked to depart from it through the repeal of existing neutrality law establishing an embargo on arms, ammunition, and implements of war. We are asked to depart from it in violation of our own officially asserted doctrine, during the [first] World War, that the rules of a neutral cannot be prejudicially altered in the midst of a war. We are asked to depart from international law itself, as we ourselves have officially declared it to exist. Consciously or otherwise, but mostly consciously, we are asked to depart from it in behalf of one belligerent whom our personal sympathies largely favor, and against another belligerent whom our personal feelings largely condemn. In my opinion, this is the road that may lead us to war, and I will not voluntarily take it.

Mr. President, millions of Americans, including many Members of the Congress, believe—rightly or wrongly—this action not only breaks down our will to peace but also relatively faces toward our involvement in this war. Therefore millions of Americans and many Members of the Congress, regardless of their belligerent sympathies, earnestly oppose the inauguration of such a trend. The proponents of the change vehemently insist that their steadfast purpose, like ours, is to keep America out of the war, and their sincere assurances are presented to our people. But the motive is obvious, and the inevitable interpretation of the change, inevitably invited by the circumstances, will be that we have officially taken sides. Somebody will be fooled—either the America which is assured that the change is wholly pacific, or the foreigners who believe it is the casting of our die. Either of these disillusionments would be intolerable. Each is ominous. Yet someone will be fooled—either those at home who expect too much, or those abroad who will get too little.

There is no such hazard, at least to our own America, in preserving neutrality in the existing law precisely as we almost unanimously notified the world was our intention as recently as 1935 and 1937. There is no such jeopardy, at least to our own America, in maintaining the arms embargo as it is. No menace, no jeopardy, to us can thus be persuasively conjured. Therefore millions of Americans and many Members of the Congress can see no reason for the change, but infinite reason to the contrary, if neutral detachment is our sole objective. I am one who deeply holds this view. If I err, I want to err on America's side. I oppose the change and I present the reasons for my view. . . .

Peace and Politics

Mr. President, at the outset I want to subscribe myself in agreement with the President of the United States in his message of September 21, that the issue transcends any thought or phase of domestic politics. To prostitute the peace of America to politics would be sheer treason. On the other hand, I am certain that the President equally would agree that those of us who fear the unleashed consequences of the major proposal in the pending bill—the repeal of the arms embargo—should say so in candor, conscience, and conviction. . . .

At the outset again I concur in the President's defense of the principles of liberty, religion, morality, and international good faith, and in his condemnation of military conquest. I hate these latter things. So does America. There is no doubt about our overwhelming personal attitude upon these subjects nor toward today's belligerents. Yes; and if America is ever challenged upon this malignant score—either here or elsewhere on this continent—there can be no doubt of our uncompromising answer. We shall invincibly answer with our lives and fortunes. Any alien tyrant who might reckon otherwise would be tragically disillusioned. We are not too proud to fight. But I am not voting upon that issue now. It has not arisen. I am not speaking upon that issue now. My external sympathies are not involved. In my view, they have no right to be involved. This is a problem in neutrality, not in unneutrality. I must think solely of the welfare of our own America. I believe that welfare is inseverably linked to immunity to any foreign war which does not come to us. "America first" is now a literal necessity. The single, paramount question is Shall America stay out of this war, and how? . . . I quote the President:

> Our acts must must be guided by one single, hard-headed thought—keeping America out of this war.

Hard-headedly I applaud the objective. Hard-headedly I dissent from the proposed method of reaching it.

Thus it appears that both sides in this controversy say that we must stay out of this war. The split comes over the formula to keep us out. The chief split—the one issue that overshadows all others—comes over the proposed repeal of the existing embargo on arms, ammunition, and implements of war to all belligerents. You, upon the other side of this debate, assert with the President that it is the embargo itself which endangers peace, though I cannot for the life of me understand it is if it is our peace you are discussing. We, on the contrary, are guided by the one, single, hard-headed thought that to repeal the arms embargo is to strike down a great, indispensable, insulating defense against our involvement in this war; that the repeal, though labeled otherwise, is in its essence a deliberately unneutral act which may too easily be the forerunner of others when once the habit starts; that the substitution of so-called cash and carry as respects munitions is the inauguration of relatively dangerous and complicating factors which seriously hamper if they do not finally destroy our detachment. We are guided by the one, single, hard-headed thought that the retention of the arms embargo cannot possibly involve us in any of these compromising factors; that repeal is not relatively the surest road to peace; that it may finally be the road to war. I oppose repeal because I believe repeal makes us relatively vulnerable while the embargo leaves us relatively immune. And there the major issue lies. . . .

Rival Emotions

Since we all start with an apparent agreement that all of our objectives are pacific in intent—passing for the moment the question of their actual effect—it is perhaps unnecessary to labor the stupendous importance of keeping America out of this war. But unfortunately there are rival emotions in most American hearts—upon the one hand, a deeply sympathetic urge to help one belligerent against the other; upon the other hand, an urge to keep ourselves bombproof and aloof. Again, there is a school of thought which conscientiously promotes the persuasive but, I believe, utterly treacherous doctrine that we can do many unneutral things short of war to help our favorites—as though we might successfully be half in this war and yet safely stay half out. Yet, again, there are those who would mend our faltering economy—even the

President's recent message plaintively touched the rim of this cash-register suggestion—by reaching for war orders and war profits behind a shield of technical but highly transparent and fictitious neutrality. And, again, there is the group that is so righteously sensitized to the cause of one belligerent against the other—feeling that its cause is our own, which feeling I can fully understand—that they do not wholly reject the hazards of our own involvement if worst unexpectedly comes to worst in Europe's mystifying cabinets and on Europe's mystifying battle fields.

Roosevelt's Foreign Policy

Charles A. Beard, one of America's leading historians, was a frequent commentator on foreign and political affairs. In this passage from his small book Giddy Minds and Foreign Quarrels, *published just prior to the outbreak of war in Europe in 1939, he argues that the foreign policy of President Franklin D. Roosevelt will inevitably lead to war.*

President Roosevelt's foreign policy is clear as daylight. He proposes to collaborate actively with Great Britain and France in their everlasting wrangle with Germany, Italy, and Japan. He wants to wring from Congress the power to throw the whole weight of the United States on the side of Great Britain and France in negotiations, and in war if they manage to bungle the game. That using measures short of war would, it is highly probable, lead the United States into full war must be evident to all who take thought about such tactics.

In view of all these competing, collateral emotions—each one of which tends to dull the tenacity of our resolution completely to insulate America against involvement in this war—a little time is not misspent if we linger for a brief moment upon the consequences if, through the omission of any act of effective neutrality or through the commission of any act of entangling unneutrality, America once more finds herself pulled into Europe's wars. It may serve to steel our dominating purpose to keep out, regardless of these other considerations; and keep out we must, unless our own American sovereignty and our own American security are challenged. Against the possibility of such a challenge, Mr. President, I will join in a national defense which shall be as impregnable and as invincible as we can make it—a frontier of democracy in this western world which never can be successfully assailed. But I do not believe it is necessary that the challenge should ever come.

There are many who are not too earnest in their fears about our involvement in this war, and I do not speak of them invidiously.

Suppose this thing should happen. Let us look at the net result.

The last war cost us 40,000 American boys killed in action. Their crosses dot the skyline of futility. This present one, says Colonel [Charles] Lindbergh, would cost us a million boys. The last war cost us 192,000 wounded, 76,000 who died of disease, and 350,000 more who now deserve and receive disability allowances. The next war, if Lindbergh is remotely right, would infinitely multiply this sacrifice. . . .

The Consequences of War

To those Americans who are not too unwilling to believe it may be necessary or wise for us not only to scrap the arms embargo, but even to go further in support of one belligerent today against the other, I ask, what would we, what could we get out of participation in this new war, even on the assured presumption that we would emerge victorious? What would we get?

First, we would get such a regimentation of our own lives and livelihoods, 20 minutes after we entered the war, that the Bill of Rights would need a gas mask, and individual liberty of action would swiftly become a mocking memory. This is not hyperbole. Scan the Army's industrial mobilization plan, for example. We have previewed it here in Congress. I quote a few typical sentences from a recent authentic newspaper review:

> Labor and business would be regimented. . . . Strikes would be outlawed. . . . Employers would be told by Government what wages to pay and hours to work; what prices to charge; what profits to make. . . . The Government would dictate costs, prices, interest rates, rents, etc. . . . Light, heat, food will be rationed—

And so forth. Another columnist says:

> It is the complete disappearance of an individual's or a corporation's liberty of choice and action—social and economic—which reveals how closely the United States will resemble a Fascist country controlled by a Mussolini or a Hitler.

Let no one distort what I am saying. Specifically I am not charging, even by remotest inference, that this administration has some malignant purpose to chain our freedom through its abuse of war powers. I am simply saying that these chains are inherent in the new war technique all around the globe, and that our own official expectations, in some quarters, anticipate this mold. What has already happened in England? Here is a headline from last week: "British Find Liberties Vanish With War; Traditional Freedom is 'Blacked-out.'" We should not avoid these blackouts here. In the name of another war "to save democracy," we should have to strangle democracy in our own land and erect an American paraphrase of the cooperative state—the very plan of life against which we universally rebel and against which presumably we would be making war. One step in this direction inevitably invites another. It requires little imagination to conjure the ultimate picture. If the war went long enough, I doubt whether we should ever get the Republic back. When we head for war in its contemporary version we head for chains.

Second, we should come out of the victory with an infinitely pyramided debt. If the war dragged on, the debt would not be long in staggering toward $100,000,000,000. It never could be carried or repaid. Repudiation or ruinous inflation would be inevitable. Our economic values would collapse. Nothing but all-powerful central government could save the pieces. We should ultimately understand what old King Pyrrhus meant when he said, "Another such victory and we are lost." We should win another war and lose another peace. Nobody can win anything else.

Discount as you please, Mr. President, this prospectus and its dread casualty rolls, nevertheless, it approximates the outline of our destiny in some degree if we go to Europe to fight another European war. We shall be ready to face even these extremities if ever it is honorably necessary in defense of America and her institutions and her security. But before we dare to think of any other obligation or any other objective than our own security and the security of this Western Hemisphere, before we dilute our own grim determination to stay out of this war and not to yield to any other motives, no matter how nobly meditated, let us frankly count the cruel cost. Let us face it with hardheaded thought.

Before we dream of war booms, let us remember the devastating boom deflations which irresistibly follow as gloomy night pursues departing day.

Before we speculate with measures short of war, let us remember that this equivocal phrase inherently defines a nearer approach to the thing we unitedly say we propose to avoid. Let us learn our lesson, as the British Winston Churchill wrote some years ago:

> Never, never, never believe that any war will be smooth and easy, or that anyone who embarks on the strange voyage can measure the tides and hurricanes he will encounter; and the statesman who yields to war fever must realize that once the signal is given he is no longer the master of policy but the slave of unforeseeable and uncontrollable events.

Let us not see how close we can squirm toward these unforeseeable and uncontrollable events by so-called measures short of war, comforted by the blind infatuation that we shall always be able to pull back from the tides and hurricanes. . . .

Not Our War

It is entirely human—and a credit to our sensibilities—to give vent to our outraged emotions from time to time in the presence of broken liberties and broken lives beneath other flags. But surely our paramount responsibility—every minute of every hour in every day—is so to maintain our national attitudes that the wars of others do not needlessly come to us, and that whatever destruction happens elsewhere may not needlessly happen here. This is not our war. We did not start it. We have no control over its course. We cannot dictate its conclusion. We cannot order Europe's destiny, not even if we took it as a permanent assignment. It is not our war, despite our devotion to democracy. It need not—it should not—become our war. We should deliberately and consciously stay all the way out unless and until we are deliberately and consciously ready to go all the way in. . . .

No one, I hope, will attempt to read me as charging deception or distortion to the authors of this bill. Again and again I pay tribute to the effort they have made to give us adequate protective compensation for the loss of the arms embargo. But they fail before they start—when they start with the repeal of the arms embargo because it is the key to the whole situation. It is our expectations that are distorted and our hopes that are deceived when we try to be neutral and unneutral in the same breath.

If we ever reach the point where the American people are substantially convinced that American destiny is unavoidably dependent upon and inseverably linked with the fate of one side or the other in a European war—which, in spite of my predilections, I strongly deny—or if we ever find one of these belligerents invading essential democracy in the United States or in this Western World, then let us not be content merely to edge our way toward war in the disguise of a neutral, but let us go all the way in with everything we have got. But God forbid the arrival of such a zero hour. Meanwhile, let us stay all the way out.

VIEWPOINT 3

"The dangers of conscription far outweigh its utility for a country possessing the peculiar defense advantages of the United States."

A Military Draft Should Be Opposed

Maxwell S. Stewart (1900–1990)

Events in Europe in 1940 prompted increasing preparations for war in the United States. Following a period of relative inactivity, German forces conquered Norway and Denmark in April and swept into Holland and Belgium in May. In what many viewed as shocking developments, France surrendered to Germany in June 1940 and Britain was forced to evacuate 338,000 British and French troops from the French seaport of Dunkerque (Dunkirk), leaving behind most of their equipment and supplies. In the following months the Battle of Britain raged as Germany sought to bomb Great Britain into submission. Responding to these events, President Roosevelt proposed increases in military spending; by October Congress appropriated $17 billion. To further bolster American defense, Senator Edward R. Burke of Nebraska and Representative James W. Wadsworth of New York, both Republicans, introduced legislation on June 20, 1940, to establish the first peacetime military draft in U.S. history.

The draft measure was decried by many isolationists and others who viewed it as an unacceptable step toward war. Other opponents of the draft included liberals and leftists who worried about the growing militarization of American society. In the following viewpoint, taken from an article published in the *Nation*, Maxwell S. Stewart opposes the proposed Burke-Wadsworth bill. Stewart, a New York–based writer who served in World War I, argues that

Maxwell S. Stewart, "Conscripting America," *Nation*, August 3, 1940. Reprinted with permission from the *Nation* magazine; © The Nation Company, L.P.

subjecting America's youth to the "monotony" of military life would produce undesirable social consequences, and that America's defense needs would not be met by a conscripted army. The Burke-Wadsworth bill passed Congress and was signed into law by Roosevelt on September 16, 1940.

The brutal logic of events during the past few weeks has swept away many illusions long cherished by those who call themselves liberals or progressives. Pacifism has become a luxury which we dare no longer enjoy; few of us who fought armament bills in the past have come out against the President's recent unprecedented defense program. The fate of France with its Popular Front reforms has even raised the question of how far we dare go in ameliorating working conditions when faced by potential enemies whose strength is based on a slave economy.

This revision of judgments has not been wholly free of hysteria. In the rush to secure our national defense, in the shortest possible time, we have taken action that would have seemed fantastic a year ago and that may seem equally so a year hence. Some of it has little relation to a rational defense plan. The gravest example of this mass hysteria, to my mind, is the general support which has been given to proposals for peace-time compulsory military service. Conscription in war time is regrettable but necessary; it also may be necessary for a country with hostile armies on its borders. But the dangers of conscription far outweigh its utility for a country possessing the peculiar defense advantages of the United States.

That these dangers have not been more clearly pointed out is probably due to the fact that they are largely intangible, and are recognizable chiefly to those who have had the misfortune to pass through a period of rigorous military service. My protest against conscription grows out of personal experience and observation in the last war; prior to my enlistment in the marine corps in 1918 I shared most of the popular misconceptions regarding the value of military training. (The training given to marines during the last war, however, was in every way superior to that given the conscript army.)

Theoretically, compulsory military service offers certain advantages. It is said to develop strong bodies, a valuable sense of discipline, self-reliance, and a worthy spirit of patriotism. There is a tendency to idealize it as a means of building citizens. On the first point there is little room for argument. Military training, like any

42

other form of organized exercise, is beneficial physically. The more intensive the training, the greater, under most circumstances, are the physical benefits. Sloppy, half-hearted training which leaves the recruit with hours of time hanging on his hands may actually be detrimental physically. As to the other supposed gains, the effects of military service are the reverse of those claimed.

Harms of Military Training

Take, for example, the matter of discipline. No one will deny that intensive military training involves strict discipline. Discipline is indispensable for effective military operations. A certain type of discipline is also valuable in civil life. But American army discipline as enforced in the last war was a far better training for life under a dictatorship than in a democracy. It was anything but a conscious, self-imposed discipline. No effort was made to explain its purpose. Obedience was expected to be unquestioning. Every detail of the soldier's life, including much of his recreation, was controlled from above. Individual initiative of any type was distinctly not encouraged in the ranks. It was a prerogative of officers. Absolute discipline is of course necessary in war. But I maintain that the efficiency it creates is gained at the expense of those qualities of human personality most essential to a democracy. It is sheer hypocrisy to pretend, as do the military-minded, that discipline "builds men." It's purpose is to create not men but robots.

Nor does military training build self-reliance. A soldier may be accustomed to hardships, but he is not practiced in bearing responsibility. His food, clothing, shelter, and employment are provided by the government. As a result, civilian life with its uncertainties and lack of security becomes rather terrifying. I have known able young men who have reenlisted in the army year after year because they lacked confidence in their ability to cope with civilian problems. And I can testify from personal experience to the deadly, enervating effect of having all decisions made by superiors. It is particularly unfortunate that military training should usually come just at the period when boys are attempting to escape from the sheltered life of childhood and take their places in the world. For it definitely impedes, if it does not altogether block, that process.

Equally demoralizing for the developing personality is the dull routine of military life. Wholesome recreation is almost completely lacking. To be sure, there is a certain amount of supervised athletics, and some "uplift" recreation is provided by the Y.M.C.A. and the Salvation Army. But the average young soldier wants to get away from supervision and uplift in his free time. He wants, if possible, to use his scant leisure as he chooses. He would like, above all, the companionship of young women of his own kind. This is rarely possible. So, at best, the average soldier idles away his spare hours in desultory talk or in playing cards or shooting dice; at worst, he spends his time, at least before payday is too far in the past, in bars or brothels. Often he can literally find nothing else to do. Good current books or magazines are rarely available. Nothing is provided to appeal to the intellectual or artistic interests of youth. The effect is particularly bad in the case of pampered youngsters who have never learned to stand on their own feet. And how many young men of eighteen to twenty-one are really fortified against the dull monotony of military life?

For years our jingoes have lauded military training as a means of developing a sound patriotism. Pacifists have opposed it on the ground that it tends to create a military mind-set, that it makes killers out of otherwise normal young men. Actually, it develops neither patriotism nor militarism, as millions of former service men can testify. The average soldier in the ranks comes to dislike or despise his officers, and soon his resentment is extended to the government which is responsible for the injustices and petty inconveniences of military life. Our conscript is not patriotic; he is cowed and submissive though inwardly seething with rebellion. This attitude may, as military men insist, make a good soldier. It does not make a good citizen.

I have reserved for the last what seems to me to be the most serious indictment of military training, especially in peace time, namely, that such training conduces to inefficiency and sloth. Nowhere in civil life would inefficiency be so generally tolerated, or rather encouraged, as it is in the army. This is quickly realized by the soldier in the ranks. Seeing inefficiency on all sides of him, he rapidly becomes cynical regarding his own duties. Finding that only suckers work, he shirks at every opportunity. This is distinctly not the attitude that I should like to see inculcated in American youth.

The inefficiency which characterized our war-time preparations in 1917–18 is sometimes blamed on the necessity for speed. It is pointed out that nearly five million men were trained, fed, and equipped within about eighteen months. Under such circumstances little attention could be given to standards of efficiency. Most of the officers were either uneducated army men from the ranks or inexperienced men drawn hastily from civil life. But I suspect that conditions would be even worse if an extensive program of military training were launched today. Control would rest in the same military caste as before, and my experience with this caste suggests that without the compulsion of war, morale would probably be lower than it was in 1918. Moreover, the peace-time conscript is not likely to take his job as seriously as the man seeking knowledge that may save his life. In the last war it was difficult to make the average soldier see the value of close-order drill. In peace time the traditional routine makes even less sense.

Some sober-minded persons who advocate universal military training in spite of its dangers give two arguments more weight than they deserve. One is that conscription is a means of getting rid of the military caste that has held the services in its grasp for many generations. Only a draft army, it is asserted, can be truly democratic, because it alone allows no distinction of class. The idea appears on the surface to make sense, but unfortunately if finds little support in the experience of the democratic countries of Europe which have had conscription. The Swiss army has frequently been held up as a model of democratic efficiency. Yet a recent study shows that even in Switzerland a highly disproportionate number of the officers come from well-to-do families with rightist political leanings. The same seems to have been true in France. In this country conscription would probably only place more power in the hands of the present military caste.

Drift Toward Militarism

Republican Gerald P. Nye of North Dakota was one of the leading isolationist members of the Senate. In a speech in Congress on August 23, 1940, he assailed proposals for military conscription.

For my own part I see this proposed peacetime conscription of men in the Military Establishment as a borrowing of foreign tools the use of which by others we condemn. I see it a challenge and an insult to American boys. I see it as a serious departure from the American way. I see it as a thing that can easily lead to other adoptions which will help to crack our democracy, shelve it, and prove that democracy does not and cannot work. . . .

I sense in this peacetime draft of men the fastening of a yoke of militarism upon us that will not be easily, if ever, cast off.

Even more persuasive is the argument that universal military training is necessary if we are to avoid the slaughter of untrained youths in the next war. This belief seems to me to be based on a misreading of history. Insufficient training was not responsible for American young men being sent to certain death during the last war. Few men were sent to the front without an adequate number of weeks of training. It was simply the wrong kind of training. Practically the entire period in camp in this country was given over to close-order drill and parades. Little or no attention was paid to maneuvers simulating actual combat conditions. Many a man was sent to France before he had ever handled a rifle, but this was not for lack of time but for lack of rifles.

American Defense Requirements

The experiences of the last war, moreover, can scarcely be used to illuminate America's present defense problem. For under any conditions that can be foreseen today man-power is of relatively little importance. Experts are generally agreed that a rational defense program for the United States requires (1) a two-ocean navy, (2) an enlarged air force together with greatly improved anti-aircraft defenses, and (3) a small but highly mobile land force. A well-equipped, well-trained army of 300,000, with a National Guard of about the same size in reserve, could meet any conceivable defense demands. Such a force would have to be highly trained technically. The doughboy of the last war must give way to the technician, skilled in one specialized duty. This implies a professional army with a relatively long period of enlistment. Conscript armies may still have their place in the land fighting of Europe, but they are ill suited to the peculiar defense needs of this country.

In the light of these facts Senator Burke's plan for universal military service seems fantastic. His bill looks forward to the training of all men between the ages of eighteen and sixty-four, men between twenty-one and forty-five being subject to call for active service. To provide these tens of millions of men with even the most fragmentary training would place an enormous strain on our military equipment and personnel. And in modern warfare poor training is little better than none.

If war comes, conscription may become necessary as a means of mobilizing the entire force of the nation against the enemy—conscription of economic resources as well as of man-power. The nature of the training to be given will depend on the source of the attack. Presumably more attention would have to be paid to education in industrial techniques than to purely military training. Let us arm to the limit against Nazi aggression. But let us not think that we are safeguarding ourselves against attack by teaching our men and boys to do "squads right" and "squads left" under the totalitarian discipline of an army clique.

VIEWPOINT 4

"If . . . a conscript army is required in case of war, it should most certainly be created before the actual fighting begins."

A Military Draft Should Be Supported

Freda Kirchwey (1894–1976)

In June 1940, Senator Edward R. Burke of Nebraska and Representative James W. Wadsworth of New York introduced legislation creating the first peacetime military draft in U.S. history. The Burke-Wadsworth bill, which was created largely in response to pressure by a private lobbying group headed by corporate lawyer Grenville Clark, was endorsed by President Franklin D. Roosevelt on August 2. It was supported by those who argued that America should be doing more to stop Hitler's Germany, but was opposed by many who viewed it as an unnecessary and dangerous step toward American participation in Europe's war.

The following viewpoint in support of the draft is taken from an article by Freda Kirchwey that was published in the *Nation* on August 3, 1940. Kirchwey was editor and publisher of the left-liberal magazine from 1937 to 1955 and was a member of many leftist political groups, including the Woman's International League for Peace and Freedom. Kirchwey takes issue with the arguments against the draft made by Maxwell S. Stewart in the same issue of the magazine. She contends that conscription is an undesirable necessity that was forced on the United States by Germany's aggression in Europe. The Burke-Wadsworth bill passed Congress in September 1940.

Almost every sentence in Maxwell Stewart's attack on conscription in this issue of *The Nation* is, by itself, convincing. The trouble with his argument lies in its premises. He analyzes the proposal for universal military service today in terms of the draft army of 1917, and in those terms he opposes it—cogently. If our army is to be only the A.E.F. [American Expeditionary Force] over again, its value is certainly to be questioned. But the very circumstances in which it is being created insure important differences.

The conscript army of 1917 was improvised after war had been declared. With surprising efficiency considering the pressure of events, but hastily none the less, two million men were selected, trained, and put under arms. The raising of this army was a temporary break in a normal national life in which military affairs were happily remote from the ordinary citizen. After the war armament expenditures were sharply reduced, the army was remobilized, and the United States washed its hands of the affairs of Europe.

Contrast the situation today: France disastrously defeated in the field and Hitler lord over continental Europe; Britain, with no unconquered allies except its colonies and the dominions, facing imminent assault. No one knows whether Britain will be able to resist or will be overwhelmed with the loss of empire and fleet. But, at best, we cannot realistically hope for an early defeat of Hitler. Churchill's warning after Dunkerque that a successful withdrawal must not be confused with a victory applies to England's present situation. A successful resistance will also not be a victory. The political and military dominance of Nazi Germany, together with the spreading power of Japan in Asia—these are the controlling characteristics of the world of 1940. The creation of a strong army is not a temporary emergency measure; it is part of a long-range program necessitated by a world situation which is likely to grow worse.

A period of peace preceded the war of 1914. It was a period pricked with warnings for those who chose to see them; but few did. The world awoke to war with a start. The present war is different. It began—where? In the Rhineland or in Ethiopia? Or before that in the bare hills of Manchuria? It is not an event that can be pinned down with a date, but this much is sure: Hitler did not defeat France in forty days of invasion; he defeated France in the years that went before—years of deliberate, implacable preparation. Britain and France were at peace during those years, but Germany was at war. Britain and France approached the final showdown in much the same mood that characterized the years leading up to 1914—the same old diplomatic maneuvers, the conventional pre–World War military preparations. They believed that they were at peace until they found themselves fighting, but all the time they were in process of being conquered.

A State of War

It is this error that the United States should avoid. As long as Nazi despotism rules Europe and threatens the world, so long must the word and hope of peace be banished from our minds. Even today the United States is no longer at peace. It is living in a state of war preparation which will last until fascism has been defeated. Hitler's successes and further ambitions have thrust upon us an unwelcome but inescapable job of total preparation. Out of nothing—speaking relatively—we must create a war machine, not as an emergency improvisation but as an integral part of our national life in the years to come.

Maxwell Stewart opposes conscription for two reasons. First, he contends, we need no large army; a two-ocean navy, an expanded air force, together with anti-aircraft defenses, and a well-equipped army of about 300,000 men are all that is required. For such an army conscription is unnecessary. Second, American experience with conscription in 1917 was not the sort to recommend the system today.

Even in his own terms Mr. Stewart is not wholly consistent. At the start of his essay he says, "Conscription in war time is regrettable but necessary." But why? If a small, well-equipped army were sufficient, conscription would never be necessary. On the other hand, if, as Mr. Stewart admits, a conscript army is required in case of war, it should most certainly be created before the actual fighting begins. That is the real lesson of 1917. For such an army must not be improvised. Its construction and equipping are a long job, especially today, when, as Mr. Stewart points out, the intricate machines of modern warfare demand a high proportion of technically trained soldiers.

It is quite true that the final size and disposition of the army cannot be determined exactly until we know the issue of the struggle over England. As long as the British fleet is intact, we have a two-ocean navy. If it is lost to Hitler, we have far less than a one-ocean navy. If it is lost, we must rush our preparations in order to be able to occupy by land and air forces any threatened area near our coasts or within striking distance of the Panama Canal. A two-ocean navy takes longer to build than even a modern army: during the next few years, years in which Hitler will be making his bid for world dominion, our newly authorized navy will still be under construction. Today we must act on the assumption that Britain may be defeated and that we may be faced with an early threat to the security of the hemisphere. It will be easier later on to limit our program, if fate permits, than to try, in

The Need for Compulsory Military Service

Henry L. Stimson, soon to be named secretary of war by President Franklin D. Roosevelt, supported the creation of a military draft in a June 18, 1940, radio address.

At the present moment the world today is divided into two irreconcilable groups of governments. One group is yet striving for justice and freedom . . . while the other group recognizes only the rule of force. . . .

Thus an emergency exists today which strikes at the very existence of all that our country has cherished and fought for for over 160 years. . . .

In the light of this background, the military situation today is nothing less than appalling for our country . . . we should at once adopt a system of universal compulsory military training and service which would not only be the most potent evidence that we are in earnest but which is at the present moment imperative if we are to have men ready to operate the planes and other munitions the creation of which Congress has just authorized by a practically unanimous vote.

the face of threat, to reach the level of totalitarian preparation in one desperate leap.

Mr. Stewart's second main argument against compulsory military service rests on two sets of facts—his experiences in the American army during the [first] World War, and the reactionary influence of the conscript armies of Europe. With many of his points I agree. At a time when a reasonable chance existed of maintaining our independence and our democratic way of life without a big army, his insistence on the social dangers of militarism and on the deadening effect of army discipline would have bespoken a radical and militant attitude. Today that chance is gone. We have no choice between civilian virtues and military vices, between good and evil, between an army and no army. The choice lies between an army based on universal service and a greatly expanded professional army. That is the issue under debate in Washington this week. Admittedly a conscript army holds many potential dangers of reaction; admittedly, even in democratic nations, the armies are more reactionary than the general political level of the countries; at the same time the dangers of reactionary control in a volunteer professional army are even greater.

Democraticizing the Army

By and large, in every nation, the progressive groups in the community have shunned the army. This is due partly to a sensible objection to military life and military ideals, partly to the lack of professional inducements to take up an army career. The result is that a volunteer army is largely populated with able-bodied ne'er do-wells and misfits, officered by reactionaries and bureaucrats. An army based on universal service will not be democratic *per se*, but it offers all the elements out of which a democratic institution can be built. To reject universal service out of fear of its potentially reactionary results would be to deliver the army to the reactionaries without a struggle. The very dangers to which Mr. Stewart points lead me to the opposite conclusion. An army is at best a favorable breeding-ground for reaction. We must fight for its democratization; and success in that fight is only possible if we have an army in which all elements of the population are represented.

American liberals should recognize before it is too late what the British working class and its leaders realized only after the war had started—that the left must take a positive position on the question of national defense. It must make the struggle against Hitler an honest fight for the faith it lives by. And it can do this in only one way—by working not against the army but for the army. It must help to create it and man it and then to control it—by democratic methods and for democratic ends.

VIEWPOINT 5

"Let us say to the democracies, 'We Americans are vitally concerned in your defense of freedom. . . .We shall send you, in ever-increasing numbers, ships, planes, tanks, guns. This is our purpose and our pledge.'"

The United States Should Aid the Allies

Franklin D. Roosevelt (1882–1945)

After the fall of France in June 1940, Great Britain, the remaining major European power at war with Germany, continued to purchase U.S. arms and supplies on a "cash and carry" basis—paying for its purchases without American loans or American shipping. Wishing neither to see Germany victorious nor to declare war on Germany, and forbidden by American neutrality laws to provide monetary loans to Great Britain, President Franklin D. Roosevelt sought various ways to aid Great Britain short of direct military intervention. In September 1940, Roosevelt exchanged fifty older American destroyers for lease rights on British overseas bases. In December, Roosevelt and his advisers conceived the idea of "Lend-Lease." Under this proposal, which would need congressional approval, the United States would lend arms and other materials of war to nations deemed by the president to be vital to U.S. interests, with decisions concerning repayment deferred to the end of the war.

Roosevelt introduced the policy in a press conference on December 17 and elaborated on the idea in a radio "fireside chat" on December 29, in which he called on the United States to "become the great arsenal of democracy." On January 6, 1941, in his annual message to Congress, he calls for U.S. aid for countries fighting "dictator nations," defending such aid as being necessary to de-

Franklin D. Roosevelt, *Congressional Record*, 77th Cong., 1st sess., January 6, 1941, pp. 44–47.

fend freedom at home and abroad. Within the speech, excerpted here, he first listed the "four freedoms" (freedom of speech, freedom of religion, freedom from want, and freedom from fear of armed aggression) that were later repeatedly cited as America's war aims after the United States formally entered the war in December 1941.

I address you, the Members of the Seventy-seventh Congress, at a moment unprecedented in the history of the Union. I use the word "unprecedented," because at no previous time has American security been as seriously threatened from without as it is today.

Since the permanent formation of our Government under the Constitution, in 1789, most of the periods of crises in our history have related to our domestic affairs. Fortunately, only one of these—the 4-year War between the States—ever threatened our national unity. Today, thank God, 130,000,000 Americans, in 48 States, have forgotten points of the compass in our national unity.

It is true that prior to 1914 the United States often had been disturbed by events in other continents. We had even engaged in two wars with European nations and in a number of undeclared wars in the West Indies, in the Mediterranean, and in the Pacific for the maintenance of American rights and for the principles of peaceful commerce. In no case, however, had a serious threat been raised against our national safety or our independence. . . .

Even when the World War broke out in 1914 it seemed to contain only small threat of danger to our own American future. But as time went on the American people began to visualize what the downfall of democratic nations might mean to our own democracy.

We need not overemphasize imperfections in the peace of Versailles. We need not harp on failure of the democracies to deal with problems of world reconstruction. We should remember that the peace of 1919 was far less unjust than the kind of "pacification" which began even before Munich and which is being carried on under the new order of tyranny that seeks to spread over every continent today. The American people have unalterably set their faces against that tyranny.

Democracy Under Attack

Every realist knows that the democratic way of life is at this moment being directly assailed in every part of the world—assailed either by arms or by secret spreading of poisonous propaganda by those who seek to destroy unity and promote discord in nations still at peace.

During 16 months this assault has blotted out the whole pattern of democratic life in an appalling number of independent nations, great and small. The assailants are still on the march, threatening other nations, great and small.

Therefore, as your President, performing my constitutional duty to "give to the Congress information of the state of the Union," I find it necessary to report that the future and the safety of our country and of our democracy are overwhelmingly involved in events far beyond our borders.

Armed defense of democratic existence is now being gallantly waged in four continents. If that defense fails, all the population and all the resources of Europe, Asia, Africa, and Australasia will be dominated by the conquerors. The total of those populations and their resources greatly exceeds the sum total of the population and resources of the whole of the Western Hemisphere—many times over.

In times like these it is immature—and incidentally untrue—for anybody to brag that an unprepared America, single-handed, and with one hand tied behind its back, can hold off the whole world.

No realistic American can expect from a dictator's peace international generosity, or return of true independence, or world disarmament, or freedom of expression, or freedom of religion—or even good business.

Such a peace would bring no security for us or for our neighbors. "Those who would give up essential liberty to purchase a little temporary safety deserve neither liberty nor safety."

As a Nation we may take pride in the fact that we are soft-hearted; but we cannot afford to be soft-headed.

We must always be wary of those who, with sounding brass and a tinkling cymbal, preach the "ism" of appeasement.

We must especially beware of that small group of selfish men who would clip the wings of the American eagle in order to feather their own nests.

I have recently pointed out how quickly the tempo of modern warfare could bring into our very midst the physical attack which we must expect if the dictator nations win this war.

There is much loose talk of our immunity from immediate and direct invasion from across the seas. Obviously, as long as the British Navy retains its power, no such danger exists. Even if there were no British Navy, it is not probable that any enemy would be stupid enough to attack us by landing troops in the United States from across thousands of miles of ocean, until it had acquired strategic bases from which to operate.

But we learn much from the lessons of the past years in Europe—particularly the lesson of Norway, whose essential seaports were captured by treachery and surprise built up over a series of years.

The first phase of the invasion of this hemisphere would not be the landing of regular troops. The necessary strategic points would be occupied by secret agents and their dupes, and great numbers of them are already here, and in Latin America.

As long as the aggressor nations maintain the offensive, they, not we, will choose the time and the place and the method of their attack.

That is why the future of all American republics is today in serious danger.

That is why this annual message to the Congress is unique in our history.

That is why every member of the executive branch of the Government and every Member of the Congress face great responsibility—and great accountability.

The Great Emergency

The need of the moment is that our actions and our policy should be devoted primarily—almost exclusively—to meeting this foreign peril. For all our domestic problems are now a part of the great emergency.

Just as our national policy in internal affairs has been based upon a decent respect for the rights and dignity of all our fellowmen within our gates, so our national policy in foreign affairs has been based on a decent respect for the rights and dignity of all nations, large and small. And the justice of morality must and will win in the end.

Our national policy is this:

First, by an impressive expression of the public will and without regard to partisanship, we are committed to all-inclusive national defense.

Second, by an impressive expression of the public will and without regard to partisanship, we are committed to full support of all those resolute peoples, everywhere, who are resisting aggression and are thereby keeping war away from our hemisphere. By this support, we express our determination that the democratic cause shall prevail, and we strengthen the defense and security of our own Nation.

Third, by an impressive expression of the public will and without regard to partisanship, we are committed to the proposition that principles of morality and considerations for our own security will never permit us to acquiesce in a peace dictated by aggressors and sponsored by appeasers. We know that enduring peace cannot be bought at the cost of other people's freedom.

In the recent national election there was no substantial difference between the two great parties in respect to that national policy. No issue was fought out on this line before the American electorate. Today it is abundantly evident that American citizens everywhere are demanding and supporting speedy and complete action in recognition of obvious danger.

Therefore, the immediate need is a swift and driving increase in our armament production.

Leaders of industry and labor have responded to our summons. Goals of speed have been set. In some cases these goals are being reached ahead of time; in some cases we are on schedule; in other cases there are slight but not serious delays; and in some cases—and I am sorry to say very important cases—we are all concerned by the slowness of the accomplishment of our plans.

The Army and Navy, however, have made substantial progress during the past year. Actual experience is improving and speeding up our methods of production with every passing day. And today's best is not good enough for tomorrow.

I am not satisfied with the progress thus far made. The men in charge of the program represent the best in training, ability, and patriotism. They are not satisfied with the progress thus far made. None of us will be satisfied until the job is done. . . .

To change a whole nation from a basis of peacetime production of implements of peace to a basis of wartime production of implements of war is no small task. And the greatest difficulty comes at the beginning of the program, when new tools and plant facilities and new assembly lines and shipways must first be constructed before the actual matériel begins to flow steadily and speedily from them.

The Congress, of course, must rightly keep itself informed at all times of the progress of the program. However, there is certain information, as the Congress itself will readily recognize, which, in the interests of our own security and those of the nations we are supporting must of needs be kept in confidence.

New circumstances are constantly begetting new needs for our safety. I shall ask this Congress for greatly increased new appropriations and authorizations to carry on what we have begun.

Supplying Other Nations

I also ask this Congress for authority and for funds sufficient to manufacture additional munitions and war supplies of many kinds, to be turned over to those nations which are now in actual war with aggressor nations.

Our most useful and immediate role is to act as an arsenal for them as well as for ourselves. They do not need manpower. They do need billions of dollars' worth of the weapons of defense.

The time is near when they will not be able to pay for them in ready cash. We cannot, and will not, tell them they must surrender merely because of present inability to pay for the weapons which we know they must have.

I do not recommend that we make them a loan of dollars with which to pay for these weapons—a loan to be repaid in dollars.

I recommend that we make it possible for those nations to continue to obtain war materials in the United States, fitting their orders into our own program. Nearly all of their matériel would, if the time ever came, be useful for our own defense.

Facing the Facts

James F. Byrnes, then a senator from South Carolina, was one of the leading congressional defenders of Lend-Lease. The following is excerpted from a January 17, 1941, radio address.

Over the radio and from platforms, it is argued that it is none of our business whether Britain stands or falls. If this be true, then it was inexcusable for the Congress to draft men for the Army in time of peace, and unanimously to appropriate millions of dollars for equipment and for a two-ocean Navy.

Let us face the facts. The reason we are feverishly working to provide an Army and Navy is to defend ourselves against the Axis powers. If we could be certain that Britain would defeat Hitler we could and would stop appropriating money for military purposes. But we cannot be certain of it. We are certain only that each day Britain holds Hitler we are better able to defend America. If Britain can hold Hitler for a year, we can hold him forever. Self preservation, therefore, demands that we now give Britain aid instead of sympathy.

Taking counsel of expert military and naval authorities, considering what is best for our own security, we are free to decide how much should be kept here and how much should be sent abroad to our friends who, by their determined and heroic resistance, are giving us time in which to make ready our own defense.

For what we send abroad we shall be repaid, within a reasonable time following the close of hostilities, in similar materials or, at our option, in other goods of many kinds which they can produce and which we need.

Let us say to the democracies, "We Americans are vitally concerned in your defense of freedom. We are putting forth our energies, our resources, and our organizing powers to give you the strength to regain and maintain a free world. We shall send you, in ever-increasing numbers, ships, planes, tanks, guns. This is our purpose and our pledge."

In fulfillment of this purpose we will not be intimidated by the threats of dictators that they will regard as a breach of international law and as an act of war our aid to the democracies which dare to resist their aggression. Such aid is not an act of war, even if a dictator should unilaterally proclaim it so to be.

When the dictators are ready to make war upon us, they will not wait for an act of war on our part. They did not wait for Norway or Belgium or the Netherlands to commit an act of war.

Their only interest is in a new one-way international law, which lacks mutuality in its observance and, therefore, becomes an instrument of oppression.

The happiness of future generations of Americans may well depend upon how effective and how immediate we can make our aid felt. No one can tell the exact character of the emergency situations that we may be called upon to meet. The Nation's hands must not be tied when the Nation's life is in danger.

We Must Make Sacrifices

We must all prepare to make the sacrifices that the emergency—as serious as war itself—demands. Whatever stands in the way of speed and efficiency in defense preparations must give way to the national need.

A free nation has the right to expect full cooperation from all groups. A free nation has the right to look to the leaders of business, of labor, and of agriculture to take the lead in stimulating effort, not among other groups but within their own groups.

The best way of dealing with the few slackers or trouble makers in our midst is, first, to shame them by patriotic example; and if that fails, to use the sovereignty of government to save government.

As men do not live by bread alone, they do not fight by armaments alone. Those who man our defenses, and those behind them who build our defenses, must have the stamina and courage which come from an unshakable belief in the manner of life which they are defending. The mighty action which we are calling for cannot be based on a disregard of all things worth fighting for.

The Nation takes great satisfaction and much strength from the things which have been done to make its people conscious of their individual stake in the preservation of democratic life in America. Those things have toughened the fiber of our people, have renewed their faith and strengthened their devotion to the institutions we make ready to protect.

Certainly this is no time to stop thinking about the social and economic problems which are the root cause of the social revolution which is today a supreme factor in the world.

There is nothing mysterious about the foundations of a healthy and strong democracy. The basic things expected by our people of their political and economic systems are simple. They are:

Equality of opportunity for youth and for others.

Jobs for those who can work.

Security for those who need it.

The ending of special privilege for the few.

The preservation of civil liberties for all.

The enjoyment of the fruits of scientific progress in a wider and constantly rising standard of living.

These are the simple and basic things that must never be lost sight of in the turmoil and unbelievable complexity of our modern world. The inner and abiding strength of our economic and political systems is dependent upon the degree to which they fulfill these expectations.

Many subjects connected with our social economy call for immediate improvement.

As examples:

We should bring more citizens under the coverage of old-age pensions and unemployment insurance.

We should widen the opportunities for adequate medical care.

We should plan a better system by which persons deserving or needing gainful employment may obtain it.

I have called for personal sacrifice. I am assured of the willingness of almost all Americans to respond to that call.

A part of the sacrifice means the payment of more money in taxes. In my Budget message I recommend that a greater portion of this great defense program be paid for from taxation than we are paying today. No person should try, or be allowed, to get rich out of this program; and the principle of tax payments in accordance with ability to pay should be constantly before our eyes to guide our legislation.

If the Congress maintains these principles, the voters, putting patriotism ahead of pocketbooks, will give you their applause.

The Four Freedoms

In the future days, which we seek to make secure, we look forward to a world founded upon four essential human freedoms.

The first is freedom of speech and expression everywhere in the world.

The second is freedom of every person to worship God in his own way everywhere in the world.

The third is freedom from want, which, translated into world terms, means economic understandings which will secure to every nation a healthy peacetime life for its inhabitants everywhere in the world.

The fourth is freedom from fear—which, translated into world terms, means a world-wide reduction of armaments to such a point and in such a thorough fashion that no nation will be in a position to commit an act of physical aggression against any neighbor—anywhere in the world.

That is no vision of a distant millennium. It is a definite basis for a kind of world attainable in our own time and generation. That kind of world is the very antithesis of the so-called new order of tyranny which the dictators seek to create with the crash of a bomb.

To that new order we oppose the greater conception—the moral order. A good society is able to face schemes of world domination and foreign revolutions alike without fear.

Since the beginning of our American history we have been engaged in change—in a perpetual peaceful revolution—a revolution which goes on steadily, quietly adjusting itself to changing conditions—without the concentration camp or the quicklime in the ditch. The world order which we seek is the cooperation of free countries, working together in a friendly, civilized society.

This Nation has placed its destiny in the hands and heads and hearts of its millions of free men and women; and its faith in freedom under the guidance of God. Freedom means the supremacy of human rights everywhere. Our support goes to those who struggle to gain those rights or keep them. Our strength is in our unity of purpose.

To that high concept there can be no end save victory.

VIEWPOINT 6

"How can the United States better serve suffering humanity everywhere: by going into this war, or by staying out? I hold that the United States can better serve . . . by staying out."

The United States Should Not Aid the Allies

Robert M. Hutchins (1899–1977)

President Franklin D. Roosevelt's proposal for Lend-Lease aid to Great Britain and other nations (authorizing the president to transfer war goods to countries without payment) was heatedly debated by Congress in the early months of 1941. Many people both in and out of Congress opposed Lend-Lease on the grounds that it would eventually lead to direct American military intervention and the sending of American troops to Europe.

Robert M. Hutchins, the source of the following viewpoint, was president of the University of Chicago from 1929 to 1945 and its chancellor from 1945 to 1951. In a January 23, 1941, speech, which was broadcast nationwide on radio, he questions Roosevelt's Lend-Lease proposal. He argues that the United States under Roosevelt has "abandoned all pretense of neutrality" and that the president's policies have left America "drifting into war." He maintains that the four freedoms Roosevelt outlined in his January 6, 1941, address to Congress (freedom of speech, freedom of worship, freedom from want, and freedom from fear) should be secured through internal reforms rather than by supporting and entering war in Europe.

Robert M. Hutchins, radio address, January 23, 1941.

I speak tonight because I believe that the American people are about to commit suicide. We are not planning to. We have no plan. We are drifting into suicide. Deafened by martial music, fine language, and large appropriations, we are drifting into war.

I address you simply as an American citizen. I do not represent any organization or committee. I do not represent the University of Chicago. I am not a military expert. It is true that from the age of eighteen to the age of twenty I was a private in the American Army. I must have somewhere the very fine medal given me by the Italian government of that day in token of my cooperation on the Italian front. But this experience would not justify me in discussing tactics, strategy, or the strength to which our armed forces should now attain.

I wish to dissociate myself from all Nazis, Fascists, Communists, and appeasers. I regard the doctrine of all totalitarian regimes as wrong in theory, evil in execution, and incompatible with the rights of man. I wish to dissociate myself from those who want us to stay out of war to save our own skins or our own property. I believe that the people of this country are and should be prepared to make sacrifices for humanity. National selfishness should not determine national policy.

President Roosevelt's Policies

It is impossible to listen to Mr. Roosevelt's recent speeches, to study the Lease-Lend Bill, and to read the testimony of Cabinet officers upon it without coming to the conclusion that the President now requires us to underwrite a British victory, and apparently a Chinese and a Greek victory, too. We are going to try to produce the victory by supplying our friends with the materials of war. But what if this is not enough? We have abandoned all pretense of neutrality. We are to turn our ports into British naval bases. But what if this is not enough? Then we must send the navy, the air force, and, if Mr. Churchill wants it, the army. We must guarantee the victory.

We used to hear of "all aid short of war." The words "short of war" are ominously missing from the President's recent speeches. The Lease-Lend Bill contains provisions that we should have regarded as acts of war up to last week. The conclusion is inescapable that the President is reconciled to active military intervention if such intervention is needed to defeat the Axis in this war.

I have supported Mr. Roosevelt since he first went to the White House, I have never questioned his integrity or his goodwill. But under the pressure of great responsibilities, in the heat of controversy, in the international game of bluff, the President's speeches and recommendations are committing us to obligations abroad which we cannot perform. The effort to perform them will prevent the achievement of the aims for which the President stands at home.

If we go to war, what are we going to war for? This is to be a crusade, a holy war. Its object is moral. We are seeking, the President tells us, "a world founded on freedom of speech, freedom of worship, freedom from want, and freedom from fear." We are to intervene to support the moral order. We are to fight for "the supremacy of human rights everywhere."

With the President's desire to see freedom of speech, freedom of worship, freedom from want, and freedom from fear flourish everywhere we must all agree. Millions of Americans have supported the President because they felt that he wanted to achieve these four freedoms for America. Others, who now long to carry these blessings to the rest of the world, were not conspicuous on the firing line when Mr. Roosevelt called them, eight years ago, to do battle for the four freedoms at home. But let us agree now that we want the four freedoms; we want justice, the moral order, democracy, and the supremacy of human rights, not here alone but everywhere. The question is whether entrance into this war is likely to bring us closer to this goal.

Staying Out of War

How can the United States better serve suffering humanity everywhere: by going into this war, or by staying out? I hold that the United States can better serve suffering humanity everywhere by staying out.

But can we stay out? We are told it is too late. The house is on fire. When the house is on fire, you do not straighten the furniture, and clean out the cellar, or ask yourself whether the house is as good a house as you would like. You put out the fire if you can.

The answer is that the house is not on fire. The house next door is on fire. When the house next door is on fire you do not set fire to your own house, throw the baby on the floor, and rush off to join the fun. And when you do go to quench the fire next door, you make sure that your bucket is full of water and not oil.

But, we are told, we are going to have to fight the Axis sometime. Why not fight it now, when we have Britain to help us? Why wait until we have to face the whole world alone?

Think of the mass of assumptions upon which this program rests. First, we must assume that in spite of its heroic resistance and in spite of the enormous supplies of munitions which it is yet to receive from America the British Empire must fall.

Second, we must assume that the present rulers of totalitarian states will survive the conflict.

Third, we must assume that if these regimes survive they will want to attack us.

Fourth, we must assume that they will be in a position to attack us. This involves the assumptions that they will have the resources to do so, that their people will consent to new and hazardous ventures, that their task of holding down conquered nations will be easily completed, and that the ambiguous attitude of Russia will cause them little concern.

Next, if Britain falls, if the totalitarian regimes survive, if they want to attack us, if they are in a position to do so, we must further assume that they will find it possible to do so. The flying time between Africa and Brazil, or Europe and America, does not decide this question. The issue is what will be at the western end of the line? This will depend on our moral and military preparedness. A lone squadron of bombers might conquer a continent peopled with inhabitants careless of safety or bent on slavery. We cannot assume that any combination of powers can successfully invade this hemisphere if we are prepared to defend ourselves and determined to be free.

On a pyramid of assumptions, hypotheses, and guesses, therefore, rests a decision to go to war now because it is too late to stay out. There is no such inevitability about war with the Axis as to prevent us from asking ourselves whether we shall serve suffering humanity better everywhere by going into this war or by staying out.

The chances of accomplishing the high moral purposes which the President has stated for America, even if we stay out of war, are not bright. The world is in chaos. We must give our thought and energy to building our defenses. What we have of high moral purpose is likely to suffer dilution at home and a cold reception abroad. But we have a chance to help humanity if we do not go into this war. If we do go into it, we have no chance at all.

We Are Not Prepared

The reason why we have no chance to help humanity if we go into this war is that we are not prepared. I do not mean, primarily, that we are unprepared in a military sense. I mean that we are morally and intellectually unprepared to execute the moral mission to which the President calls us.

A missionary, even a missionary to the cannibals, must have clear and defensible convictions. And if his plan is to eat some of the cannibals in order to persuade the others to espouse the true faith, his convictions must be very clear and very defensible indeed. It is surely not too much to ask of such a missionary that his own life and works reflect the virtues which he seeks to compel others to adopt. If we stay out of war, we may perhaps some day understand and practice freedom of speech, freedom of worship, freedom from want, and freedom from fear. We may even be able to comprehend and support justice, democracy, the moral order, and the supremacy of human rights. Today we have barely begun to grasp the meaning of the words.

Those beginnings are important. They place us ahead of where we were at the end of the last century. They raise us, in accomplishment as well as in ideals, far above the accomplishment and ideals of totalitarian powers. They leave us, however, a good deal short of that level of excellence which entitles us to convert the world by force of arms.

Have we freedom of speech and freedom of worship in this country? We do have freedom to say what everybody else is saying and freedom of worship if we do not take our religion too seriously. But teachers who do not conform to the established canons of social thought lose their jobs. People who are called "radicals" have mysterious difficulties in renting halls. Labor organizers sometimes get beaten up and ridden out of town on a rail. [Socialist politician] Norman Thomas had some troubles in Jersey City. And the Daughters of the American Revolution refused to let Marian Anderson sing in the national capital in a building called Constitution Hall.

If we regard these exceptions as minor, reflecting the attitude of the more backward and illiterate parts of the country, what are we to say of freedom from want and freedom from fear? What of the moral order and justice and the supremacy of human rights? What of democracy in the United States?

Words like these have no meaning unless we believe in human dignity. Human dignity means that every man is an end in himself. No man can be exploited by another. Think of these things and then think of the sharecroppers, the Okies, the Negroes, the slumdwellers, downtrodden and oppressed for gain. They have neither freedom from want nor freedom from fear. They hardly know they are living in a moral order or in a democracy where justice and human rights are supreme.

We have it on the highest authority that one-third of the nation is ill-fed, ill-clothed, and ill-housed. The latest figures of the National Resources Board show that almost precisely 55 percent of our people are living on family incomes of less than $1,250 a year. This sum, says *Fortune* magazine, will not support a family of four. On this basis more than half our people are living below the minimum level of subsistence. More than half the army which will defend democracy will be drawn from those who have had this experience of the economic benefits of "the American way of life."

We know that we have had till lately 9 million unemployed and that we should have them still if it were not for our military preparations. When our military preparations cease, we shall, for all we know, have 9 million unemployed again. In his speech on December 29, Mr. Roosevelt said, "After the present needs of our defense are past, a proper handling of the country's peacetime needs will require all of the new productive capacity—if not still more." For ten years we have not known how to use the productive capacity we had. Now suddenly we are to believe that by some miracle, after the war is over, we shall know what to do with our old productive capacity and what to do in addition with the tremendous increases which are now being made. We have want and fear today. We shall have want and fear "when the present needs of our defense are past."

As for democracy, we know that millions of men and women are disfranchised in this country because of their race, color, or condition of economic servitude. We know that many municipal governments are models of corruption. Some state governments are merely the shadows of big city machines. Our national government is a government by pressure groups. Almost the last question an American is expected to ask about a proposal is whether it is just. The question is how much pressure is there behind it or how strong are the interests against it. On this basis are settled such great issues as monopoly, the organization of agriculture, the relation of labor and capital, whether bonuses should be paid to veterans, and whether a tariff policy based on greed should be modified by reciprocal trade agreements.

To have a community men must work together. They must have common principles and purposes. If some men are tearing down a house while others are building it, we do not say they are working together. If some men are robbing, cheating, and oppressing others, we should not say they are a community. The aims of a democratic community are moral. United by devotion to law, equality, and justice, the democratic community works together for the happiness of all the citizens. I leave to you the decision whether we have yet achieved a democratic community in the United States.

In the speech in which Mr. Roosevelt told us, in effect, that we are headed for war, he said, "Certainly this is no time to stop thinking about the social and economic problems which are the root cause of the social revolution which is today a supreme factor in the world." But in the same speech he said, "The need of the moment is that our actions and our policy should be devoted primarily—almost exclusively—to meeting this foreign peril. For all our domestic problems are now a part of the great emergency." This means—and it is perfectly obvious—that if any social objective interferes with the conduct of the war, it will be, it must be instantly abandoned. War can mean only the loss of "social gains" and the destruction of the livelihood of millions in modest circumstances, while pirates and profiteers, in spite of Mr. Roosevelt's efforts to stop them, emerge stronger than ever.

This 1939 cartoon by Carey Orr of the Chicago Tribune *was captioned "The Only Way We Can Save Her."*

The four freedoms must be abandoned if they interfere with winning a war. In the ordinary course of war most of them do interfere. All of them may. In calmer days, in 1929, the *New York Times* said, "War brings many collateral disasters. Freedom of speech, freedom of the press suffer. We think we shall be wiser and cooler the next time, if there is one; but we shan't." The urge to victory annihilates tolerance. In April 1939, Alfred Duff-Cooper said that "hatred of any race was a sign of mental deficiency and of lack of a broad conception of the facts of the world." In April 1940, Mr. Duff-Cooper said that the crimes of the German militarists were the crimes of the whole people and that this should be kept in mind when the peace treaty was written.

We cannot suppose, because civil liberties were restricted in the last war and expanded after it, that we can rely on their revival after the next one. We Americans have only the faintest glimmering of what war is like. This war, if we enter it, will make the last one look like a stroll in the park. If we go into this one, we go in against powers dominating Europe and most of Asia to aid an ally who, we are told, is already in mortal danger. When we remember what a short war did to the four freedoms, we must recognize that they face extermination in the total war to come.

We Americans have hardly begun to understand and practice the ideals that we are urged to force on others. What we have, in this country, is hope. We and we alone have the hope that we can actually achieve these ideals. The framework of our government was designed to help us achieve them. We have a tremendous continent, with vast resources, in a relatively impregnable position. We have energy, imagination, and brains. We have made some notable advances in the long march toward justice, freedom, and democracy.

If we go to war, we cast away our opportunity and cancel our gains. For a generation, perhaps for a hundred years, we shall not be able to struggle back to where we were. In fact the changes that total war will bring may mean that we shall never be able to struggle back. Education will cease. Its place will be taken by vocational and military training. The effort to establish a democratic community will stop. We shall think no more of justice, the moral order, and the supremacy of human rights. We shall have hope no longer.

What, then, should our policy be? Instead of doing everything we can to get into the war, we should do everything we can to stay at peace. Our policy should be peace. Aid to Britain, China, and Greece should be extended on the basis most likely to keep us at peace and least likely to involve us in war.

At the same time we should prepare to defend ourselves. We should prepare to defend ourselves against military or political penetration. We should bend every energy to the construction of an adequate navy and air force and the training of an adequate army. By adequate I mean adequate for defense against any power or combination of powers.

In the meantime, we should begin to make this country a refuge for those who will not live without liberty. For less than the cost of two battleships we could accommodate half a million refugees from totalitarian countries for a year. The net cost would not approach the cost of two battleships, for these victims, unlike battleships, would contribute to our industry and our cultural life, and help us make democracy work.

But most important of all, we should take up with new vigor the long struggle for moral, intellectual, and spiritual preparedness. If we would change the face of the earth, we must first change our own hearts. The principal end that we have hitherto set before ourselves is the unlimited acquisition of material goods. The business of America, said Calvin Coolidge, is business. We must now learn that material goods are a means and not an end. We want them to sustain life, but they are not the aim of life. The aim of life is the fullest development of the highest powers of men. This means art, religion, education, moral and intellectual growth. These things we have regarded as mere decorations or relaxations in the serious business of life, which was making money. The American people, in their own interest, require a moral regeneration. If they are to be missionaries to the world, this regeneration must be profound and complete.

A New Moral Order

We must try to build a new moral order for America. We need moral conviction, intellectual clarity, and moral action: moral conviction about the dignity of man, intellectual clarity about ends and means, moral action to construct institutions to bring to pass the ends we have chosen.

A new moral order for America means a new conception of security. Today we do not permit men to die of starvation, but neither do we give them an incentive to live. Every citizen must have a respected place in the achievement of the national purpose.

A new moral order for America means a new conception of sacrifice, sacrifice for the moral purposes of the community. In the interest of human dignity we need a rising standard of health, character, and intelligence. These positive goals demand the devotion and sacrifice of every American. We should rebuild one-third of the nation's homes. We must provide adequate medical care in every corner of the land. We must develop an education aimed at moral and intellectual growth instead of at making money.

A new moral order for America means a new conception of mastery. We must learn how to reconcile the machine with human dignity. We have allowed it to run wild in prosperity and war and to rust idly in periodic collapse. We have hitherto avoided the issue by seeking new markets. In an unstable world this has meant bigger and bigger collapses, more and more catastrophic war. In Europe and Russia the efforts to master the machine are carried out by methods we despise. America can master the machine within the framework of a balanced democracy, outdistance the totalitarian despotisms, and bring light and hope to the world. It is our highest function and greatest opportunity to learn to make democracy work. We must bring justice and the moral order to life, here and now.

If we have strong defenses and understand and believe in what we are defending, we need fear nobody in the world. If we do not understand and believe in what we are defending, we may still win, but the victory will be as fruitless as the last. What did we do with the last one? What shall we do with this one? The government of Great Britain has repeatedly refused to state its war aims. The President in his foreign policy is pledged to back up Great Britain, and beyond that, to the pursuit of the unattainable. If we go to war, we shall not know what we are fighting for. If we stay out of war until we do, we may have the stamina to win and the knowledge to use the victory for the welfare of mankind.

The path to war is a false path to freedom. A new moral order for America is the true path to freedom. A new moral order for America means new strength for America and new hope for the moral reconstruction of mankind. We are turning aside from the true path to freedom because it is easier to blame Hitler for our troubles than to fight for democracy at home. As Hitler made the Jews his scapegoat, so we are making Hitler ours. But Hitler did not spring full-armed from the brow of Satan. He sprang from the materialism and paganism of our times. In the long run we can beat what Hitler stands for only by beating the materialism and paganism that produced him. We must show the world a nation clear in purpose, united in action, and sacrificial in spirit. The influence of that example upon suffering humanity everywhere will be more powerful than the combined armies of the Axis.

"If his [Hitler's] defeat is of desperate, deadly, importance then . . . we have got to go all-out and whole-hog to defeat him."

The United States Should Use All Means to Defeat Hitler

Stanley High (1895–1961)

Debate over U.S. policy continued after Congress passed the Lend-Lease Act in March 1941. Some argued that if the defeat of Germany under its Nazi leader Adolf Hitler justified massive U.S. aid to Great Britain, it also justified U.S. entry into war. In the following viewpoint, writer and lecturer Stanley High argues for a complete American commitment to the defeat of Nazi Germany, even if such a commitment means war for America.

Either Hitler's defeat is of desperate, deadly importance to us or it's of no importance whatsoever. If his defeat is of desperate, deadly, importance then—now, immediately and at once—we have got to go all-out and whole-hog to defeat him. If his defeat is of no importance to us—then we've got to stop slapping his wrists, let him devour Britain and stock its bones in the New Order mausoleum where the remains of his other victims are lodged. Its one or the other. To say we want Hitler's defeat and to try a delicate side-step at the all-out job of defeating him is, first, a guarantee that he'll win; it's second, a guarantee that, having

Stanley High, remarks on *American Forum of the Air* radio broadcast, May 4, 1941.

won, he'll hate us with a hatred backed up by the resources of four-fifths of the world; and, third, it's a doctrine of turn-tail defeatism that's a travesty on everything American and an insult to the memory of those who—in blood and toil and tears and sweat—gave us America.

I think that Hitler's defeat is of desperate, deadly importance to us and that the time has come to stop aiming at his wrists and aim for his chin—and do it with the total armed might of the United States of America.

To do that may take us to war. Granted. But not to do it won't keep us at peace; not, that is, the kind of peace in which decency has elbowroom and the free spirit of man can go to work mending the torn fabric of our civilization. In this world there isn't any of that peace.

Two Kinds of Peace

In this world there is peace of two sorts: There is the kind of peace that's come to the Poles, the Czechs, the Norwegians, and now the Greeks. If all you mean by peace is an absence of fighting—then those people have it. But if by peace you mean the defense and nurture of those inalienable rights among which are life, liberty and the pursuit of happiness—then the peace of those peoples is the peace of the dead.

There's another kind of peace we can have. We're getting it already. It's the peace of an armed camp—in which, for the indefinable future, our resources, our energies and our skills will be of use only as fuel for the engines of war and our lives of use only if they're bound and shackled to the war machine. That's the kind of peace the isolationists prescribe. That's why with almost one accord in Congress, they vote to load down our democracy with multiplied military billions and our nation with a wholly alien, completely militarized way of life. They're willing to do that because they know that, if we don't beat Hitler today, we've got to keep ready to beat him tomorrow—any tomorrow.

That kind of peace—for a grim interlude—may have no fighting in it. But neither will it have in it any room for those creative ventures, those civilized dreams and undertakings by which man, one day, may redeem himself from beastliness. That's the other kind of peace—the only other kind—we can have. It means a world—and a United States of America—whose moral climate will be fixed, not by the aspirations of free men, but by the blood-lusting ambitions of Adolf Hitler.

That becomes more sure with every Nazi victory. Today can be ours. Tomorrow certainly will be Hitler's. Today we've got Allies. Tomorrow we'll have none. Today, the British control the seas. Tomorrow they won't. Today Hitler has the continent of Europe. Tomorrow he and his associate plunderers will control four-fifths of the earth and its resources. Today our production can be decisive. Tomorrow in every war-making asset Hitler will out-match us five, ten, twenty, to one. Today—there's hope and, therefore, resistance among the people he has conquered. Tomorrow, hope having died, these people will not only be conquered, they'll be subdued. Today his ideological missionaries in South America are making headway against odds. Tomorrow—as emissaries of an unbeatable, world-conquering regime there'll be a wholesale flocking to their banners? Today Hitler's American kinsmen work under cover or wrapped in the flag. Tomorrow, they'll strut their foul stuff in the open.

We Must Decide

James B. Conant, president of Harvard University, argued in a November 20, 1940, radio address that the United States should make every commitment, including war if necessary, to ensure the defeat of the Axis nations.

It seems clear that a large majority of the country is determined to give material aid to Great Britain. But we must now answer a fundamental question which lies deeper. Do we as a free people agree that the Axis powers must be defeated? If we answer yes, then the words, "all possible aid to the Allies," mean exactly what they say. Then there are no reservations in our pledge. It then becomes a matter of strategy and strategy only when, if ever, material aid must be supplemented by direct naval and military assistance. It then becomes purely a matter of strategy whether at some later time active belligerency is required. Having settled the fundamental issue we must be ready to follow the advice of those military experts who have access to all relevant information. But until the fundamental question has been answered, military experts cannot settle those detailed problems which now disturb the country.

The citizens of 1940 are the trustees of the future of these United States. We shall be rightly condemned by posterity if we needlessly become involved in war and squander life and treasure. But we shall be yet more guilty in the eyes of our descendants if we fail to preserve our heritage of freedom—if we fail because of timidity or lack of farsighted resolution. The decision is momentous. Those who feel as I do believe the future of human liberty is at stake.

With that Nazi noose round our necks, what chance will there be for that working democracy for which men like Norman Thomas so long have labored? Our social gains, our civil liberties and the dreams and ambitions of our younger generation will be swallowed up in the dire needs of a nation with its back to the wall. Give our youth five-ten years of that and at the end—the ways and the fruits of freedom will be as strange to them as they are to the youth of Germany.

Never Surrender

The people of the United States aren't of a surrendering breed. They won't surrender now. They won't surrender—because what's at stake is more than a place on the map which we can call our own. What's at stake is the chance for us and for our children to call our lives our own. We can either beat Hitler now—or we can deliver into his hands the power to fashion our future.

VIEWPOINT 8

"The reaction to an unpopular and bitterly costly war will make for an indefinite continuance of conditions wholly unsuitable to democracy."

The United States Should Not Risk War to Defeat Hitler

Norman Thomas (1884–1968)

Norman Thomas, at one time a Presbyterian minister, was the Socialist Party's presidential candidate in all elections from 1928 to 1948. He was also a member of the America First Committee, the largest private organization to emerge in opposition to American intervention in World War II. The following viewpoint is taken from a May 4, 1941, radio debate about World War II and U.S. policy. By this time the United States had deployed U.S. Navy ships as convoys to protect British ships from German submarines. Private groups such as the Fight for Freedom Committee were openly calling on the United States to declare war. Thomas agrees with those who argue that the United States cannot take any more steps to aid Great Britain without declaring war, but he argues entering the war poses greater dangers to the United States than staying out of the conflict.

How far should the United States go to insure the defeat of Hitler? Well, after all, it isn't Hitler the man, but Hitlerism that is the disease, and there is a great deal too much emphasis on one

Norman Thomas, remarks on *American Forum of the Air* radio broadcast, May 4, 1941.

mortal man, and Hitlerism isn't born of the devil; it is born of a bad system. I believe we should go not so far as to insure the triumphs of an American Hitlerism, and that would be the probable consequence of our entry into total war far more probably than under any other circumstances. The issue we are discussing in reality is war, total war, of indefinite duration which will have to be fought on the Atlantic, the Pacific, in Asia, Africa and Europe. To continue wishful and unrealistic thinking or desperate gambling on anything else but war is intellectual stupidity and moral hypocrisy. We cut a sorry figure telling other people that they must fight on and on unless we are willing to fight. Our present tactics are hurtful to our own morale and our reputation. I disagree with this new Fight for Freedom Committee but have a respect for it that I do not feel for these who believe we can take further steps short of war.

To be specific it is still as true as when the President stated the fact that convoys mean shooting and shooting almost certainly means war. Even if it doesn't, I do not suppose there are five advocates of convoys in all Washington who will not admit, if they are honest, that naval convoys alone cannot guarantee complete British victory. If that is our goal the cry for convoys will be just one more maneuver to get an unwilling people into war. Against dive bombers convoys don't mean much unless we send out fighter planes to protect them. Thus do we stumble towards war.

The question is, ought we to go to war? It is not a question to be answered simply by contemplating the undeniable crimes of the Nazi regime or by asserting what I have always admitted, namely that British Imperialism offers fewer dangers to America than German and is less of a curse to the earth.

The Dangers of War

The question is whether the means of full entry into this war by America will gain the end of peace and freedom for mankind or, to put it in another form, whether the dangers which our entry into war will bring upon us are not greater than any conceivable dangers which may come upon us if we stay out of war.

A wise Government policy must face probabilities. It must deal with them as scientifically as it can in the spirit of the engineer, the scientist or the surgeon who recognizes the limits to what can be done by wishful thinking and the impossibility of achieving the desirable simply because it is desirable.

The possibilities serious enough to deserve attention are these: (1) a German victory, before an America unprepared for aggressive long range war, can make her weight felt; (2) a complete Anglo-American victory over the Axis and probably Japan, after a long and costly struggle; (3) some degree of stalemate with

Americans Want Peace with Japan

Although Germany was the focus of most of America's attention in 1940 and 1941, some people were concerned about American policy towards Japan as well. In an October 17, 1940, radio address, Rush D. Holt, senator from West Virginia, argues that the United States should not go to war against Japan to protect the British Empire.

We are told Japan is an aggressor. But when did we become the "policeman of the world?" By what authority were we given the special privilege to pass upon the actions of other nations? They may not like our lynchings and our past activities in Nicaragua and Haiti but we are to protect the English Empire in Asia. And I ask, where did England get her territory in Asia? Was it by aggression? The Burma Road, as you probably know, was opened today. War profits will increase as a result. How was Burma acquired by Great Britain? Have you forgotten the three wars of England in the 19th century over Burma? The English people did not originate in Burma or Singapore. How did they get there? Oh—but they say, England has reformed. She is now purified. We recall the stories of her purification preceding our entrance in the last World War when we were asked "to make the world safe for democracy." We were told to forget the Boer Wars, to forget the atrocities in Ireland, to forget the incidents of India. Again—we are supposed to forget. They say this is another war for civilization and democracy. My mind goes to the great fight made by India for her freedom and how the democracy of England is used in India. . . . We are told we must protect our trade. This may interest you to know that our exports to Asia, excluding Japan, are approximately three hundred and thirty million dollars for an entire year. That amount alone would not begin to pay the cost of a few weeks' war. Shall your son be killed for the tin and rubber of the Dutch East Indies? Shall your brother be shot to protect the oil business in China? Shall your husband be shell shocked to protect the Malay Peninsula? . . .

I believe every possible defense should be made against our possible attack from any source. Let us have the world's best air force, over American land; the world's best navy, in American waters; the world's best army, on American land. But, do not send any American soldiers or sailors to protect the English Empire in Asia or require them to die for Singapore, Burma or Indo-China, because some governmental official may have secretly agreed to parallel action.

The great danger in America today is that the President through the handling of foreign affairs can enter into secret alliances or promote acts of undeclared war that would involve America. This means war whether declared by Congress or not. We must watch these actions if we are to remain at peace and the American people want peace. They do not want war with Japan.

exhaustion and then perhaps Stalin as the final victor. It is this third possibility which seems to me, on the evidence, the most probable. Any of these possibilities, given the realities of war, America's own unsolved problems, and the American temperament, will require us to lose our internal democracy for the duration of the war. The reaction to an unpopular and bitterly costly war will make for an indefinite continuance of conditions wholly unsuitable to democracy. On the other hand, victory would be accompanied, not by the achievement of the noble purposes which a minority of the interventionists profess, but by an American or Anglo-American imperialism which would perpetuate armaments, and for which Fascism at home in this generation must be the inevitable accompaniment. Against this there is a far better possibility of our blessing ourselves and ultimately mankind by making our own democracy work in the relative security of this continent, yes, and of a hemisphere which we can make friendly by the right sort of statesmanship. The real question is how far should the United States go to preserve and increase democracy rather than to spread fascism by spreading the area of total war?

CHAPTER 2

Military and Diplomatic Controversies

Chapter Preface

The December 7, 1941, attack on Pearl Harbor unified Americans to a remarkable degree on the question of the necessity for war. Between that day and the end of the war, however, there remained much disagreement over America's military strategy, tactics, and diplomacy.

World War II was, to a greater degree than World War I, a truly global conflict. America's main adversaries, Germany and Japan, were situated on opposite sides of the globe. American forces fought in China, Southeast Asia, the Pacific and Atlantic Oceans, North Africa, and Europe. Because their resources were limited, American military strategists were compelled to prioritize areas and campaigns. Furthermore, in deploying forces and planning strategy, America needed to cooperate with a wide array of allies, including Great Britain and the British Empire, the Soviet Union, the Free French movement, a China divided between Chiang Kai-shek's regime and communist revolutionaries, and others. Because World War II was not a unilateral American war, diplomatic and political considerations weighed heavily on military strategic decisions. In addition to defeating Germany and Japan, President Franklin D. Roosevelt and his lieutenants sought to maintain good relations with their wartime allies, minimize casualties, preserve national morale, and plan the shape of the postwar world order.

The complex interplay of military and diplomatic factors that lay behind wartime decisions is illustrated by the debates over whether the Allies should launch a massive cross-Channel invasion of Nazi-occupied France. Almost as soon as the United States entered the war, the Soviet Union pressed Great Britain and America to open a "second front" against Germany, arguing that the Soviets were bearing the main burden of fighting Hitler. Military planners of the War Plans Division (later renamed the Operations Division) of the U.S. Army, commanded by General George C. Marshall, insisted that a direct invasion of France would be the quickest and best way to open such a second front and to thus engage and defeat Germany. In April 1942 President Roosevelt endorsed their strategic blueprint that provided for the buildup of American forces in Great Britain and a 1943 invasion of France (or 1942 emergency assault if collapse of the Soviet Union seemed imminent). Roosevelt, seeking to promote trust between the United

States and the Soviet Union and worried that the Soviet Union might make a separate peace with Germany, went so far as to promise Soviet foreign minister V. M. Molotov in May 1942 that "we expect the formation of a second front this year."

However, British opposition helped delay a cross-Channel invasion through 1942 and 1943. Great Britain and the United States had agreed to make the war in Europe their first priority over the war in Asia. But many British leaders, including Prime Minister Winston S. Churchill, were leery of the idea of a direct invasion. Historian Robert James Maddox writes in *The United States and World War II* that they were instead

> committed to what became known as the "peripheral" strategy, which meant attacking Hitler around the borders of Germany's sphere and forcing him to commit men and resources to several places at the same time. They believed that such harassment, together with strategic bombing (stressed especially by the airmen) and the demands of the eastern front, would erode Germany's strength. A direct thrust should be made only when it became clear that Germany was already crumbling.

Some American military leaders also opposed a cross-Channel invasion. Some, such as Henry H. Arnold, asserted that Germany could be defeated with airpower and strategic bombing. Ernest J. King, naval chief of staff, consistently argued that the war against Japan should take precedence and resisted diverting resources to Europe. At one point, frustrated by British objections to a cross-Channel invasion, Marshall joined King in presenting to Roosevelt a proposal to abandon the "Germany first" strategy and to concentrate on Japan; Roosevelt rejected their scheme.

Nonmilitary factors influenced discussions of a cross-Channel invasion as well. One of the most important considerations was the debate over the postwar boundaries of Europe. Roosevelt made his 1942 promise to Molotov in part to compensate for his refusal to agree to Soviet postwar territorial demands. In order to prevent Soviet military forces from occupying much of Europe, some advisers to Roosevelt recommended an early cross-Channel invasion or, alternatively, military drives up Italy or the Balkan nations from the south. (These proposals were not followed; by the time of Germany's surrender Soviet forces were occupying much of Europe—a development that left Eastern Europe under Soviet control for decades to come.)

Because of British proposals for invasions of North Africa and Italy (to which Roosevelt agreed in order to get the United States actively involved in the war in Europe), and in part because the war against Japan continued to consume resources, a cross-Channel invasion of France was delayed until June 6, 1944. D-Day, when it finally came, was a success for the Allies and a key turning point of World War II. Whether a 1943 invasion could have shortened the war and resulted in a different postwar Europe is still debated by historians.

As the debate over the cross-Channel invasion reveals, wartime decisions were influenced by both military concerns and diplomatic considerations. The viewpoints in this chapter examine some of the arguments surrounding the second front issue and other important political and military controversies of World War II.

"Only by massing the immense . . . power of the American and British nations under the . . . mastery of the air, . . . which can be made to cover our subsequent advance in France . . . , can Germany be really defeated."

A Cross-Channel Invasion of Western Europe Is Necessary

George C. Marshall (1880–1959)
and Henry L. Stimson (1867–1950)

A central strategic and diplomatic issue facing the United States almost from the day it entered World War II was the opening of a "second front" against Germany (the first front being the German-Soviet frontier). The timing, location, and planning of a U.S.-British attack on Germany were a cause of division not only between the United States, Great Britain, and the Soviet Union, but also between different officers and branches of the U.S. military. Military planners and other public officials in the United States and Great Britain disagreed about whether such an invasion was necessary and timely, with some arguing that Germany could instead be defeated by naval blockade, strategic bombing, and continued Soviet pressure.

The following two-part viewpoint presents excerpts from advice President Franklin D. Roosevelt received from two of his top wartime officials: George C. Marshall, chief of staff for the U.S. Army from 1939 to 1945, and Henry L. Stimson, secretary of war from 1940 to 1945. Both were supporters of a large cross-Channel invasion of German-occupied France; the two memoranda describe both the military reasons for and diplomatic concerns sur-

Part I: George C. Marshall, memorandum to President Roosevelt, April 1, 1942. Part II: Henry L. Stimson, letter to President Roosevelt, August 10, 1943.

rounding this plan. Part I is from a memorandum Marshall presented to Roosevelt on April 1, 1942, calling for Roosevelt to endorse the strategy of defeating Germany through a direct and massive invasion of France across the English Channel, using American and British forces transported to and based in Great Britain. Marshall gives several strategic reasons why this plan, which had been prepared by Marshall and his staff (including Dwight D. Eisenhower), makes military sense, including the argument that such an invasion would greatly help the Soviet Union, which until then had been bearing the brunt of the German attack. Roosevelt approved the plan and sent Marshall and presidential aide Harry Hopkins to London to gain Britain's endorsement.

Part II is from a letter Stimson wrote to Roosevelt, dated August 10, 1943, which describes some of the diplomatic complexities of the invasion. By then Operation Bolero (the buildup of American forces in Great Britain) was proceeding, but the invasion itself was likely to be postponed at least until 1944, in part because Allied troops and resources were committed to large operations against North Africa and Italy. Stimson describes his concerns, which were shared by other Americans, that British prime minister Winston S. Churchill and other officials did not fully support a plan to conduct a cross-Channel invasion, despite growing pressure from Soviet leader Joseph Stalin. He attributes this reluctance in part to British leaders' memories of prior costly defeats in Europe, including the Battle of Passchendaele (the Third Battle of Ypres) in World War I, in which thousands of British soldiers perished, and the forced evacuation of entrapped British soldiers from the French seaport of Dunkerque (Dunkirk) in 1940. Stimson argues that the United States should assume the responsibility of leadership in planning the invasion.

In November 1943, Roosevelt, Stalin, and Churchill met at Tehran, Iran, where the three countries reached a firm agreement in support of a large-scale invasion of France. Shortly afterward Roosevelt named Dwight D. Eisenhower to the supreme command of what was now called Operation Overlord.

I

Western Europe has been selected as the theatre in which to stage the first great offensive of the United Powers because:

It is the only place in which a powerful offensive can be prepared and executed by the United Powers in the near future. In any other locality the building up of the required forces would be much more slowly accomplished due to sea distances. Moreover, in other localities the enemy is protected against invasion by natural obstacles and poor communications leading toward the seat of the hostile power, or by elaborately organized and distant outposts. Time would be required to reduce these and to make the attack effective.

General George C. Marshall and Secretary of War Henry L. Stimson confer in January 1942 in Washington, D.C. Both supported a cross-Channel invasion of France.

It is the only place where the vital air superiority over the hostile land areas preliminary to a major attack can be staged by the United Powers. This is due to the existence of a network of landing fields in England and to the fact that at no other place could massed British air power be employed for such an operation.

Can Concentrate Forces

It is the only place in which the bulk of the British ground forces can be committed to a general offensive in cooperation with United States forces. It is impossible, in view of the shipping situation, to transfer the bulk of the British forces to any distant region, and the protection of the British islands would hold the bulk of the divisions in England.

The United States can concentrate and use larger forces in Western Europe than in any other place, due to sea distances and the existence in England of base facilities.

The bulk of the combat forces of the United States, United Kingdom and Russia can be applied simultaneously only against Germany, and then only if we attack in time. We cannot concentrate against Japan.

Successful attack in this area will afford the maximum of support to the Russian front.

II

In my memorandum of last week, which was intended to be as factual as possible, I did not include certain conclusions to which I was driven by experiences of my trip. For a year and a half they have been looming more and more clearly through the fog of our successive conferences with the British. The personal contacts, talks, and observations of my visit made them very distinct.

British Doubts

First: We cannot now rationally hope to be able to cross the Channel and come to grips with our German enemy under a British commander. His Prime Minister and his Chief of the Imperial Staff are frankly at variance with such a proposal. The shadows of Passchendaele and Dunkerque still hang too heavily upon the imagination of these leaders of his government. Though they have rendered lip service to the operation, their hearts are not in it and it will require more independence, more faith, and more vigor than it is reasonable to expect we can find in any British commander to overcome the natural difficulties of such an operation carried on in such an atmosphere of his government. There are too many natural obstacles to be overcome, too many possible side avenues of diversion which are capable of stalling and thus thwarting such an operation.

Second: The difference between us is a vital difference of faith. The American staff believes that only by massing the immense vigor and power of the American and British nations under the overwhelming mastery of the air, which they already exercise far into the north of France and which can be made to cover our subsequent advance in France just as it has in Tunis and Sicily, can Germany be really defeated and the war brought to a real victory.

On the other side, the British theory (which cropped out again and again in unguarded sentences of the British leaders with whom I have just been talking) is that Germany can be beaten by a series of attritions in northern Italy, in the eastern Mediterranean, in Greece, in the Balkans, in Rumania and other satellite countries. . . .

To me, in the light of the postwar problems which we shall face, that attitude . . . seems terribly dangerous. We are pledged quite as clearly as Great Britain to the opening of a real second front. None of these methods of pinprick warfare can be counted on by us to fool Stalin into believing that we have kept that pledge.

We Must Assume Leadership

Third: I believe therefore that the time has come for you to decide that your government must assume the responsibility of leadership in this great final movement on the European war which is now confronting us. We cannot afford to confer again and close with a lip tribute to BOLERO which we have tried twice and failed to carry out. We cannot afford to begin the most dangerous operation of the war under halfhearted leadership which will invite failure or at least disappointing results. Nearly two years ago the British offered us this command. I think that now it should be accepted—if necessary, insisted on.

VIEWPOINT 2

"It is . . . hoped that those in power in England and the United States will appreciate that a frontal attack on the continent is out of the question."

A Cross-Channel Invasion of Western Europe Would Be a Mistake

Charles Sweeny (1881–1963)

One of the largest and most significant military operations carried out by the United States during World War II was Operation Overlord, or D-Day. This massive amphibious assault of Normandy, France, which was launched on June 6, 1944, was the product of several years of planning and the subject of much debate. Some observers prior to the Normandy invasion questioned whether such a direct assault against entrenched German defenses in "Fortress Europe" was the best war strategy.

The following viewpoint is taken from a 1943 book on military strategy by Charles Sweeny, a professional soldier who, after attaining the rank of lieutenant colonel in the U.S. Army, served for many years in North Africa for France and Morocco. Sweeny, citing military principles of noted German generals of the past, including Carl von Clausewitz and Count von Schlieffen, argues that a direct invasion from England to France would be unlikely to succeed and should not be attempted.

We have in face of us two groups of enemies—the Japanese Group in Eastern Asia, the German Group in Europe. The first can put 8 million men in the field, the second 26 million. Our task is to defeat these forces. . . .

To meet this force of 26 million Germans in Europe and 8 million Japanese in Asia we have 26 million men likewise:

Russia	12,000,000
England	2,500,000
South Africa	300,000
Australia	500,000
New Zealand	150,000
Canada	600,000
United States	10,000,000
	26,050,000

China is not considered here because we can hardly count on its forces to intervene on any important battlefield in the immediate future.

One of the most sacred principles of war is to build up the general reserves as quickly and as solidly as possible. When they are thoroughly organized, trained and equipped, the commander-in-chief has at his disposal a force which in military parlance is called a "mass of manoeuvre" or a "striking force."

The English, the South Africans, the Australians can not be counted on to furnish large contingents to this mass of manoeuvre. They are, all of them, living under the menace of invasion. Their troops are needed at home. Russia is engaged up to her limit. Canada and ourselves are left. We can, between us, create and maintain a mass of manoeuvre of ten million men. We can also implement, supply and transport it when ready. Upon it rests our hope of victory. When it will be ready only our General Staff can know even approximately; though others, including the German and Japanese General Staffs, can make a shrewd guess.

It is not likely that the geographical "Battle Front" will have changed a great deal between now and the time when we shall be ready to undertake an offensive operation. So before considering and adopting any solution to the problem of utilizing our striking force of ten million it would be wise to make a careful study of the possible battlefields. When we shall have rejected a certain number of theoretical ones, we shall have rejected certain hypothetical solutions at the same time.

Principles of War

But first let us study the principles of war:

1. "Pursue *one* great decision with force and determination"

counsels [Carl von] Clausewitz in his *Principles of War*. And he continues:

2. "We must select for our attack *one* point of the enemy's position . . . and attack it with great superiority, leaving the rest of his army in uncertainty but keeping it occupied. This is the only way that we can use an equal or smaller force to fight with advantage and thus with a chance of success."

Many American troops who landed on the coast of France on June 6, 1944, faced heavy machine-gun fire.

3. "We should choose as object of our offensive that section of the enemy's army whose defeat will give us decisive advantages."

4. And to these [Count] von Schlieffen adds: "The attack against the flank is essentially the sum and substance of the entire history of war."

Now to apply these principles to the specific war we are fighting. The above table shows our probable forces. Russia alone among our allies is capable of putting great armies into the field, now and in the future. We can match her in manpower. We can also fill the hole in her production of munitions and supplies caused by the German occupation of her richest industrial regions. We can at the same time supply our own needs. We, the

United States and Russia, are the principal adversaries of Japan and Germany. Together we stand, divided we fall.

Any battlefield on which we two can join our forces is at least three thousand miles across submarine-infested seas from the nearest ports in the United States. To arrive at these battlefields we must cross these seas—men, munitions and supplies. This is, therefore, first a TRANSPORTATION WAR.

Transport is by three means: transport by ship, transport by rail and transport by road. On the horizon awaiting development is transport by plane. Transport by ship is far and away the most efficient and economical of these means. Rail comes second and should be preferred to road. In our search for a battlefield this should never be lost sight of. Nor should we forget that a military operation of any description and importance is absolutely impossible without *secure lines of communications*. From now on we shall call them *"life lines."*

Which Second Front?

Now that we have decided *how* we are going to use our military and naval forces let us try to decide *where* to use them. In other words let us search for a battlefield. When this question is raised—a "Second Front" it is called for the moment—several are suggested. Mr. Roosevelt even promises us many. Mr. Churchill goes farther and suggests many. Clausewitz strongly advises to find one—only one. A landing on the Continent from England seems to engage the popular fancy. . . .

Let us recall, before all else, that Germany is mistress of the continent. Also that she can mobilize 26 million men of whom 20 million—the German, Italian and Hungarian contingents—can be considered her "Mass of Manoeuvre" or "Striking Force." The other six million would be required to garrison conquered countries, to meet unexpected attacks and to keep open the life lines. In letters of fire above the desk of every person in any way responsible for United Nations strategy should be written: "Any attack on Europe will be met by 20 million fully organized and trained Germans and their Allies."

Those in favor of the English base and the Continental field of manoeuvre propose that we transport our mass of manoeuvre—10 million men—to England and then throw them on the continent against Hitler's 20 million.

Observations

First observation: to transport, supply and munition this force—with all its artillery, tanks, trucks, airplanes, etc.—would require a minimum of five tons of shipping per man—fifty million tons of shipping. Where can it be found or built? The transport of this mass across the Channel, let us say to Brittany in France, under the mass bombardment of the Luftwaffe and the never ceasing attack of the entire German submarine force, without even mentioning the fire of the coast batteries and the German surface ships, will not be pictured. It is too painful. Dieppe [a French town raided by six thousand Allied troops in August 1942] with its more than fifty per cent loss, was child's play in comparison.

Second observation: suppose Hitler allows us to land and even to establish a base on the Brittany coast or farther south on the Vendean coast. Brest or St. Nazaire, the two bases created by the American Army in 1917–18, are the most likely. Once firmly established we would have to come out from behind our fortifications and attempt an advance into the country in search of the German Army. Otherwise the landing would be without reason or logic.

Suppose Hitler enticed us into the open country as he did the French and the English in 1940. Or suppose we rejected all his blandishments and advanced slowly along the coast. In either case as our lines of communications grew longer our difficulties would increase and, by continual detachment of guards for our communications and our stores, our force would decrease. When finally we were in up to our necks, Hitler would strike with a superiority of effectives and matériel of at least three to one. Suppose under these conditions we were defeated, what would be the consequence? Our Army destroyed, England would fall. We would be thrown back to our own shores with whatever remnants of our force we succeeded in withdrawing from the ambush. There, while licking our wounds, we would be powerless to prevent Germany from conquering Africa and South America. We would have risked much for little.

But to all this it will be replied that millions and millions of French, Belgians, Dutch, etc., will spring to arms to receive us. Where will they get the arms? Who will organize and train them? How will the millions in Paris, Lyons, Marseille, Brussels, Rotterdam and Amsterdam join us across German occupied territory? Soldiers—trained soldiers—win battles, not mobs that "spring to arms."

It is to be hoped that those in power in England and the United States will appreciate that a frontal attack on the continent is out of the question. Frontal attacks are foolish. Common sense is to be preferred to commandos.

VIEWPOINT 3

"[The committee] recommends, because of the importance of ultimate German reconciliation with the peace settlement, that the [occupation] measures be kept to the minimum."

Germany Should Not Be Partitioned and Punished After the War

The State Department Interdivisional Country Committee on Germany

While military officials were devising plans for the defeat of Germany and the other Axis nations, diplomatic officials, in anticipation of Allied victory, were attempting to plan the postwar future. Among the concerns that had to be addressed were the terms of surrender, the postwar balance of power, and the reconstruction of occupied Europe and Asia. Germany, the nation that had been defeated in World War I and had reemerged to start World War II, was a special focus of attention. Government officials and others disagreed on whether the Versailles treaty following World War I had been too lenient or too harsh toward Germany and whether the goal of U.S. policy should be Germany's punishment or rehabilitation.

The following viewpoint is taken from a 1943 memorandum composed by a committee of State Department officials charged with recommending postwar U.S. policy toward Germany. The officials argue that the best way to secure future peace would be to encourage democracy in Germany. To prevent the future rise of militarism, they recommend that Allied occupation of Germany be undertaken in a manner that provokes "a minimum of bitter-

From "The Political Reorganization of Germany," a memorandum of the State Department Interdivisional Country Committee on Germany, in U.S. Department of State, *Postwar Foreign Policy Preparation, 1939–1945*, Harley Notter, ed. (Washington, DC: GPO, 1949).

ness" from the German people. In addition, they contend that Germany should not be partitioned or dismembered.

Following the war, Germany was initially carved into military districts occupied by the Allied powers. Although the subsequent Cold War between the Soviet Union and the United States left Germany divided into East and West Germany for more than four decades, much of American policy toward Germany following World War II reflected the sentiments expressed in this document.

I. Partition

The Departmental Committee on Germany unanimously recommends that the United States Government oppose the enforced break-up of Germany as a part of the peace settlement.

The committee bases its recommendation on the following considerations

1. The crucial means of attaining security against further German aggression for some time to come will be controls to insure military and economic disarmament. If these controls are effectively enforced Germany will be incapable of waging war.

2. These measures will have to be maintained whether Germany is partitioned or left intact. Partition would make no useful contribution either to occupation or to the administration of the basic controls; it might, on the contrary, complicate the administration and, by setting up separate zones, lead to friction between the victor powers over the character of the occupation and the treatment of the several regions.

3. Because of the high degree of economic, political and cultural integration in Germany it is to be anticipated that partition would have to be imposed and maintained by external force and that such action would evoke a greatly increased resentment on the part of the German people to the serious detriment of their ultimate reconciliation with the peace settlement.

4. An imposed partition would require the enforcement of sweeping measures, over and above the basic military and economic controls, to prevent surreptitious collaboration of the partite states and to restrain the nationalistic drive for reunification. The victor powers would consequently impose on themselves through partition a burden unnecessary for the attainment of security and would give to the Germans, equally without necessity, a ready-made program of national resurgence at the expense of the peace.

5. By the tests of effectiveness, enforceability and continued acceptability to both victors and vanquished, partition would make

no contribution to security and would, on the contrary, create such bitterness and require such rigorous methods of enforcement that it would constitute a grave danger to future world order.

II. DEMOCRACY

The Departmental Committee on Germany believes that it would be unwise for the United Nations to disinterest themselves in the kind of government which will be established in Germany after the war. The potentialities for evil on the part of a revived aggressive state point to the desirability of every feasible effort to prevent the resurgence of a government and people dominated by excessive nationalism. The committee anticipates that there will be strong incentives for individual states to exercise influence and suggests that the best means of forestalling such a dangerous procedure would be an agreement among the principal United Nations for a common policy in so far as it can be achieved.

The committee is of opinion that, in the long run, the most desirable form of government for Germany would be a broadly-based democracy operating under a bill of rights to protect the civil and political liberties of the individual.

The committee is under no illusions as to the difficulties in the way of creating an effective democracy in Germany. It suggests that there are three conditions under which a new democratic experiment might survive:

1. A tolerable standard of living.

2. A minimum of bitterness against the peace terms in order, in so far as possible, to avoid an appealing program for future nationalistic upheavals at home and disturbances abroad. The committee is aware that the occupation and the permanent security controls which it deems imperative will give offense to many Germans, but it recommends, because of the importance of ultimate German reconciliation with the peace settlement, that the measures be kept to the minimum in number and in severity which will be compatible with security.

3. A harmony of policy between the British and American Governments on the one hand and the Soviet Government on the other. In case of friction Germany would be in a position to hold the balance of power with disastrous results both for treaty limitations and for political stability at home. The Soviet Government, in turn, would be in a position to use the Communist strength in Germany to the great disadvantage of the internal political peace of Germany and to the comparably great advantage of Russian interests.

The Assimilation of Germany

The committee therefore recommends that the United States Government adopt, in the interest of fostering moderate government in Germany, the principle of a program looking to the economic recovery of Germany, to the earliest possible reconciliation of the German people with the peace, and to the assimilation of Germany, as soon as would be compatible with security considerations, into the projected international order. The committee further recommends that the Soviet Government be invited to give its support to a new democratic experiment and to the principle of the suggested program.

The committee believes that there is a marked disadvantage, both from the viewpoint of political warfare against National Socialism and from the viewpoint of preparing the democratic forces of Germany for action, in the failure of the United States and British Governments to announce their support of future German democracy. The committee likewise believes that the recent appearance of a democratic German program under tacit Russian patronage might serve to give the Communists control of the democratic movement, and therefore establish a Russian hegemony in Germany, unless Anglo-American support encourages the moderates to participate and make the movement genuinely democratic.

III. DECENTRALIZATION

The committee is of opinion that the potential threat of Germany might be reduced by a decentralization of political structure that would deprive the government of the means of conducting a strong policy internally and abroad. Such a weakening might be accomplished by assigning to the federal units such functions as police power, the major taxation powers, the right to ratify international commitments, control over education, etc.

The committee believes that the victorious powers should give all the support that is prudent and possible to any internal movement for decentralization that might arise from the living tradition of federalism and from a reaction to Nazi centralization. It has doubts, however, of the ultimate wisdom of coercing the Germans, as would be necessary if a sweeping devolution of political authority were desired. An imposed weakening of the governmental structure would place a premium, in the minds of the nationalistic groups, on flouting the constitution, a practice ultimately detrimental to any political stability. There would likewise exist, in the form of a political party, or parties, an extra-constitutional but unattackable means of integrating the various political agencies and of securing rapid decision and action. . . .

It would point out that the economic and social necessities of modern life have everywhere imposed a progressive abandonment of federal devolution and that an extensive decentralization of Germany would probably make it impossible for the German people adequately to meet the present-day need for governmental participation in social and economic activities. One of the factors contributing to the discredit of the Weimar Republic was its weakness in the face of the problems the German people expected it to solve.

The committee therefore feels that the major emphasis in political reorganization should be placed on securing a democracy that will be able to withstand the attacks of some new version of Pan-Germanism or National Socialism. The character of the political outlook of the German people and their elected leaders will be more important than the machinery of government.

VIEWPOINT 4

"It should be the aim of the Allied Forces to accomplish the complete demilitarization of Germany in the shortest possible period of time."

Germany Should Be Partitioned and Punished After the War

Henry Morgenthau Jr. (1891–1967)

In 1944 Henry Morgenthau Jr., President Franklin D. Roosevelt's secretary of the treasury from 1934 to 1945 (and Roosevelt's longtime friend and neighbor), presented the president with a plan for the future occupation of Germany that was far different from proposals and ideas then being discussed in the U.S. State Department. Developed by Morgenthau and his staff, the Morgenthau Plan, as it came to be known, sought to punish Germany and prevent it from reemerging as a military threat by placing it under tight military and economic control, dividing it into two separate states, and deindustrializing its economy. Morgenthau's ideas were tentatively approved by Roosevelt and Winston Churchill at the second Quebec Conference in September 1944, but within weeks Roosevelt disavowed the plan in the face of criticism from other cabinet officials and negative public reaction following the plan's publication.

From "Program to Prevent Germany from Starting World War III," by Henry Morgenthau Jr., in U.S. Department of State, *American Foreign Policy: Current Documents, 1941–1949* (Washington, DC: GPO, 1950).

1. Demilitarization of Germany

It should be the aim of the Allied Forces to accomplish the complete demilitarization of Germany in the shortest possible period of time after surrender. This means completely disarming the German Army and people (including the removal or destruction of all war material), the total destruction of the whole German armament industry, and the removal or destruction of other key industries which are basic to military strength.

2. New Boundaries of Germany

a. Poland should get that part of East Prussia which doesn't go to the U.S.S.R. and the southern portion of Silesia.

b. France should get the Saar and the adjacent territories bounded by the Rhine and the Moselle Rivers.

c. As indicated in 4 below an International Zone should be created containing the Ruhr and the surrounding industrial areas.

3. Partitioning of New Germany

The remaining portion of Germany should be divided into two autonomous, independent states, (1) a South German state comprising Bavaria, Wuerttemberg, Baden and some smaller areas and (2) a North German state comprising a large part of the old state of Prussia, Saxony, Thuringia and several smaller states.

There shall be a custom union between the new South German state and Austria, which will be restored to her pre-1938 political borders.

4. The Ruhr Area

(The Ruhr, surrounding industrial areas, including the Rhineland, the Keil Canal, and all German territory north of the Keil Canal.)

Here lies the heart of German industrial power. This area should not only be stripped of all presently existing industries but so weakened and controlled that it cannot in the foreseeable future become an industrial area. The following steps will accomplish this:

a. Within a short period, if possible not longer than 6 months after the cessation of hostilities, all industrial plants and equipment not destroyed by military action shall be completely dismantled and transported to Allied Nations as restitution. All equipment shall be removed from the mines and the mines closed.

b. The area should be made an international zone to be governed by an international security organization to be established by the United Nations. In governing the area the international organization should be guided by policies designed to further the above stated objective.

5. Restitution and Reparation

Reparations, in the form of future payments and deliveries, should not be demanded. Restitution and reparation shall be effected by the transfer of existing German resources and territories, e.g.,

a. by restitution of property looted by the Germans in territories occupied by them;

b. by transfer of German territory and German private rights in industrial property situated in such territory to invaded countries and the international organization under the program of partition;

c. by the removal and distribution among devastated countries of industrial plants and equipment situated within the International Zone and the North and South German states delimited in the section on partition;

Germany Must Be Punished

In an August 1944 memorandum to his secretary of war, President Franklin D. Roosevelt expresses his view that the German people must be punished for the war.

It is of the utmost importance that every person in Germany should realize that this time Germany is a defeated nation. I do not want them to starve to death, but, as an example, if they need food to keep body and soul together beyond what they have, they should be fed three times a day with soup from Army soup kitchens. That will keep them perfectly healthy and they will remember that experience all their lives. . . .

Too many people here and in England hold to the view that the German people as a whole are not responsible for what has taken place—that only a few Nazi leaders are responsible. That unfortunately is not based on fact. The German people as a whole must have it driven home to them that the whole nation has been engaged in a lawless conspiracy against the decencies of modern civilization.

---

d. by forced German labor outside Germany; and

e. by confiscation of all German assets of any character whatsoever outside of Germany.

6. Education and Propaganda

a. All schools and universities will be closed until an Allied Commission of Education has formulated an effective reorganization program. It is contemplated that it may require a considerable period of time before any institutions of higher education are reopened. Meanwhile the education of German students in foreign universities will not be prohibited. Elementary schools will be reopened as quickly as appropriate teachers and text books are available.

b. All German radio stations and newspapers, magazines, weeklies, etc. shall be discontinued until adequate controls are established and an appropriate program formulated.

7. Political Decentralization

The military administration in Germany in the initial period should be carried out with a view toward the eventual partitioning of Germany. To facilitate partitioning and to assure its permanence the military authorities should be guided by the following principles:

a. Dismiss all policy-making officials of the Reich government and deal primarily with local governments.

b. Encourage the reestablishment of state governments in each of the states (Lander) corresponding to 18 states into which Germany is presently divided and in addition make the Prussian provinces separate states.

c. Upon the partition of Germany, the various state governments should be encouraged to organize a federal government for each of the newly partitioned areas. Such new governments should be in the form of a confederation of states, with emphasis on states' rights and a large degree of local autonomy.

8. Responsibility of Military for Local German Economy

The sole purpose of the military in control of the German economy shall be to facilitate military operations and military occupation. The Allied Military Government shall not assume responsibility for such economic problems as price controls, rationing, unemployment, production, reconstruction, distribution, consumption, housing, or transportation, or take any measures designed to maintain or strengthen the German economy, except those which are essential to military operations. The responsibility for sustaining the German economy and people rests with the German people with such facilities as may be available under the circumstances.

9. Controls over Development of German Economy

During a period of at least twenty years after surrender adequate controls, including controls over foreign trade and tight restrictions on capital imports, shall be maintained by the United Nations designed to prevent in the newly-established states the establishment or expansion of key industries basic to the German military potential and to control other key industries.

10. Agrarian Program

All large estates should be broken up and divided among the peasants and the system of primogeniture and entail should be abolished.

11. Punishment of War Crimes and Treatment of Special Groups

A program for the punishment of certain war crimes and for

the treatment of Nazi organizations and other special groups is [advised].

12. Uniforms and Parades

a. No German shall be permitted to wear, after an appropriate period of time following the cessation of hostilities, any military uniform or any uniform of any quasi military organizations.

b. No military parades shall be permitted anywhere in Germany and all military bands shall be disbanded.

13. Aircraft

All aircraft (including gliders), whether military or commercial, will be confiscated for later disposition. No German shall be permitted to operate or to help operate any aircraft, including those owned by foreign interests.

14. United States Responsibility

Although the United States would have full military and civilian representation on whatever international commission or commissions may be established for the execution of the whole German program, the primary responsibility for the policing of Germany and for civil administration in Germany should be assumed by the military forces of Germany's continental neighbors. Specifically, these should include Russian, French, Polish, Czech, Greek, Yugoslav, Norwegian, Dutch, and Belgian soldiers.

Under this program United States troops could be withdrawn within a relatively short time.

"The agreement by the United States and Great Britain at the present time to Soviet territorial demands . . . would be sure to have an unfortunate effect."

The United States Should Not Assent to Soviet Territorial Demands

U.S. Department of State

One of the diplomatic challenges facing the United States during World War II was how to balance the ideals of the Atlantic Charter, in which the Allied nations officially pledged support for the principle of national self-determination, with the geopolitical objectives of the Soviet Union.

After signing a nonaggression pact with Germany in 1939, the Soviet Union occupied the Baltic states of Latvia, Lithuania, and Estonia, the Romanian province of Bessarabia, and portions of Poland and Finland—areas that had been part of the Russian Empire prior to World War I. Following Germany's June 1941 attack and subsequent drive into the Soviet Union, Soviet leader Joseph Stalin soon began asking his new wartime allies, Great Britain and the United States, for official political recognition of the Soviet Union's "former frontiers." In December 1941 British foreign Secretary Anthony Eden met with Stalin in Moscow, where the Soviet leader again asked for a formal political agreement recognizing Soviet jurisdiction over the Baltic states and other areas.

Eden had been warned by his American counterpart, Secretary of State Cordell Hull, not to enter into any "secret accords" with the Soviet Union (Roosevelt, Hull, and others believed such secret agreements marred the peace after World War I). Believing that

From U.S. Department of State, *Foreign Relations of the United States, Diplomatic Papers*, vol. 3, *Europe* (Washington, DC: GPO, 1942).

Great Britain would, nevertheless, soon agree to some Soviet demands and ask the United States for its tacit support, Hull had the State Department prepare a memorandum, which was delivered to Roosevelt on February 4, 1942. In the note, from which the following viewpoint is excerpted, Hull and his staff argue that an agreement to recognize Soviet territorial claims would violate the Atlantic Charter and undermine America's official wartime goal of self-determination for all nations.

Roosevelt decided in 1942 not to make or endorse any such political deals with the Soviet Union. However, by the end of World War II the Soviet Union had realized most of its territorial demands and exerted political control over much of Europe.

Eden left London for Moscow on the evening of December 7. Almost immediately after his arrival he had his first meeting with Stalin, which lasted four hours. During the course of this meeting he presented to Stalin a draft prepared in Great Britain of a proposed political agreement. This agreement was of a general nature. It confirmed the Atlantic Charter; it provided for collaboration of the two Governments in every possible way until the German military power had been completely broken; it provided for collaboration for restoring peace at the end of the war and in maintaining the peace; it provided for the joint carrying out of the task of the reconstruction of Europe and for the safeguarding and strengthening of "the economic and political independence of all European countries either as unitary of [or] federated states"; and so forth.

Stalin, on his part, presented to Eden drafts of two treaties proposed by the Soviet Government: namely, a "treaty of alliance and mutual military assistance" and a "treaty concerning the creation of a mutual understanding between the Soviet Union and Great Britain in regard to the solution of post-war questions, and concerning their common action to ensure security in Europe after the termination of the war with Germany". In general, the provisions of these two treaties were not objectionable to the British. What was extremely important, however, was a suggestion by Stalin which proved to be a stumbling-block to the negotiations. This suggestion was that a secret protocol be entered into relating to Soviet frontiers and to the working out of arrangements for the future frontiers of Eastern and Central Europe. His initial demand apparently was that the Soviet frontiers of June 22, 1941 be recognized by Great Britain. Such an act on the part of

Great Britain would mean the British recognition of Soviet acquisition during 1939 and 1940 of certain territory and bases in Finland, of the whole territory of the three Baltic States of Estonia, Latvia, and Lithuania, of more than one-third of Poland, and of Bessarabia and other parts of Rumania. . . .

During the course of the first meeting and during other meetings that followed, Eden informed Stalin that he could not enter into agreements concerning commitments of a territorial nature without consulting the Dominions and the United States. Eden pointed out in particular that he had promised the Government of the United States that while in Moscow he would not enter into commitments of the nature requested.

Stalin continued, however to press for certain territorial commitments on the part of the British Government. When Eden insisted that he could not give the commitments desired, Stalin demanded that in any event Great Britain immediately recognize the Baltic States as a component part of the Soviet Union. He also demanded that Great Britain recognize the Soviet position in Finland and in Rumania. With regard to the frontier with Poland he said that he hoped that Poland, Great Britain, and the Soviet Union would be able to come to an agreement. . . .

When Eden continued to resist the pressure placed upon him by Stalin, the latter displayed considerable irritation. Eden finally informed Stalin as follows: "You would not respect me if I were to go back upon my arrangement with President Roosevelt. I can get a decision upon this point before the Soviet troops occupy the Baltic States, even if they continued doing as well as they are doing now."

It appears that in the end Eden gave Stalin to understand that he would return to Great Britain with Stalin's proposals, discuss them with his own Government, with the Dominions, and with the United States and let Stalin have a reply to them at a later date. Eden went so far as to indicate that he would endeavor to obtain a favorable decision if Stalin attached so great importance to the matter. . . .

The whole matter is now being considered by the British Cabinet. It is likely that within a short time the British Government will approach this Government on the subject. This approach may be in the form of a request for a statement of the position of this Government with regard to the making by the British Government of certain territorial commitments to the Soviet Union or it may be in the form of a request that this Government approve certain commitments which the British Government may desire to make.

U.S. Policy

This Government thus far has not recognized as Soviet territory any of the areas which have been annexed to the Soviet Union since the outbreak of the World War on September 1, 1939. The attitude of this Government in that respect has been predicated on its general policy not to recognize any territorial changes which have been made in European frontiers since the outbreak of the World War and not to enter into any commitments of a territorial nature in Europe which might hamper the proceedings of the post-war Peace Conference.

Supplies, Not Boundaries, Are Key

In a February 4, 1942, letter to President Franklin D. Roosevelt, which accompanied the State Department memorandum on British-Soviet negotiations, Secretary of State Cordell Hull reiterates the position that the United States should not make any promises regarding future Soviet boundaries.

The test of our good faith with regard to the Soviet Union should not be our willingness to agree to the recognition of extended Soviet frontiers at this time, but rather the degree of determination which we show loyally to carry out our promises to aid the Soviet Government with equipment and supplies.

I am sure that you will agree with me that by our actions we should make it clear to the Soviet Government in the future to an even greater degree that we are doing our utmost to live up to our promises.

It is believed that it would be unfortunate if, at the present time, an ally of the American Government of such standing as Great Britain, which also has thus far refused to make any commitments of a territorial nature on the European continent, should begin bargaining with the Soviet Union or any other continental country with regard to frontiers. There is little doubt that if the principle is once admitted that agreements relating to frontiers may be entered into prior to the Peace Conference, the association of nations opposed to the Axis, which thus far has been based upon the common aim of defeating the enemy, may be weakened by the introduction among its members of mutual suspicion and by efforts of various members to intrigue in order to obtain commitments with regard to territory at the expense of other members.

Furthermore, it is believed that the assent at the present time to any of the territorial demands of the Soviet Union would result in only a temporary improvement of the relations between the Soviet Union and Great Britain. If the British Government, with the tacit or expressed approval of this Government, should abandon the principle of no territorial commitments prior to the Peace Conference, it would be placed in a difficult position to resist additional Soviet demands relating to frontiers, territory, or to spheres of influence which would almost certainly follow whenever the Soviet Government would find itself in a favorable bargaining position. There is no doubt that the Soviet Government has tremendous ambitions with regard to Europe and that at some time or other the United States and Great Britain will be forced to state that they cannot agree, at least in advance, to all of its demands. It would seem that it is preferable to take a firm attitude now, rather than to retreat and to be compelled to take a firm attitude later when our position had been weakened by the abandonment of the general principle referred to above.

Stalin's Aims

It is likely that Stalin will make use of all the weapons at his disposal in order to attain immediate recognition of at least some of the territorial gains which the Soviet Union has achieved since the outbreak of the war. He already has intimated that the failure to extend such recognition shows a lack of good faith and confidence. He may go further and refuse for a time at least to cooperate with Great Britain and the United States in case he is unable to gain his points. He may even insinuate that the Soviet Union will not feel itself obligated not to enter into a separate peace unless such recognition is granted. He will without doubt cause the Communist Parties in the United States and Great Britain to use all their resources and influential friends and sympathizers in order to bring as much pressure as possible from the rear upon the British and American Governments and upon officials of those Governments. If, however, these Governments succumb to pressure of the type outlined above, Stalin will be encouraged to resort to similar tactics later in order to obtain further and more far-reaching demands.

Stalin's insistence upon obtaining at least certain territorial commitments at this time may be ascribed to his desires:

1. to break down the principle thus far observed by the American and British Governments not to make any territorial commitments prior to the Peace Conference;

2. to make use of the recognition of his territorial claims as evidence of the justification of the Soviet Union in invading Poland and the Baltic States and in making war on Finland in 1939 and 1940;

3. to have promises now with regard to Soviet frontiers which might be useful to him later at the Peace Conference in case the war should end with a weakened Soviet Union not in occupation of the territories which he has demanded.

The agreement by the United States and Great Britain at the present time to Soviet territorial demands or such agreement by

Great Britain with the assent of the United States would be sure to have an unfortunate effect upon the attitude of small countries everywhere towards the United States and Great Britain and also upon that of countries which are especially opposed to the spread of Bolshevism. In case the commitments desired are made, Axis propaganda would be quick to charge that the United States, which has for years advocated high principles of international conduct, began trafficking or at least assented to such trafficking in the independence of small countries within a few weeks after it had become involved in war. Resentment would certainly be aroused, particularly in Central and Eastern Europe, among circles which have thus far been extremely friendly to Great Britain and the United States. Moreover the American Republics, always sensitive on matters touching the rights of small countries, might well consider assent on our part to Soviet territorial expansion at the expense of other countries in Eastern Europe as a change in the policy of the United States, and would note with anxiety, quite apart from the religious aspects of the matter, such a departure from the principles the United States has hitherto advocated. Likewise the Vatican, according to reports which have reached us from Rome, has noted with concern certain rumors to the effect that the United States and Great Britain might be willing to recognize Soviet rights to territories which did not belong to the Soviet Union prior to the outbreak of the war.

The Atlantic Charter

The recognition at this time of Soviet claims to the Baltic States would be certain to have an effect upon the integrity of the Atlantic Charter. Eden apparently was concerned in this regard when in the coarse of one of his conversations on the subject with Stalin he said:

> Under the Atlantic Charter, we have pledged ourselves to take into account the wishes of the inhabitants. It may be that in this case, they have been taken into account, but that is a matter we must check upon before we arrive at a decision.

This remark contained a suggestion that certain British official circles might be considering the advisability of taking the position that the Baltic States had been annexed to the Soviet Union upon the expressed wishes of the inhabitants of those States.

It must be clear to all intelligent people who take the trouble to look into the matter that the Baltic States were invaded by Soviet armed forces and that the population of these States at no time had an opportunity freely to express their desires as to whether or not they would like to remain independent. Our own statements issued at the time showed that we had no doubt with respect to what was taking place. If, therefore, the British and

American Governments should take the position that these States entered the Soviet Union in accordance with the expressed desires of the population, every Government in the world, irrespective of what might be its views with regard to opportunism in this connection, would know, at least privately, that the British and American Governments were guilty of insincerity. It would be extremely unfortunate if the manner in which the Soviet Union invaded the Baltic States and conducted the ensuing plebiscites should be accepted as a mode of ascertaining the wishes of a people with regard to their future. The establishment of such a precedent would destroy the meaning of one of the most important clauses of the Atlantic Charter and would tend to undermine the force of the whole document.

"I am willing to sponsor and support the Soviet arguments if it will save American lives in winning the war."

The United States Should Assent to Soviet Territorial Demands

John Hickerson (1898–1989)

Throughout World War II President Franklin D. Roosevelt's policy was to postpone decisions regarding territorial settlements, including those involving the Soviet Union, while the war continued. By February 1945, when Roosevelt, Stalin, and Churchill met for their final summit at Yalta, circumstances in Europe had changed much from previous years. Russian armies had succeeded in driving German troops out of the Soviet Union. In doing so, the Soviets had reabsorbed the Baltic states of Estonia, Latvia, and Lithuania, and were in the process of occupying disputed territories and establishing compliant governments in eastern European states—actions that the American government had consistently opposed on the grounds that they violated the Atlantic Charter's pledges of support of democracy and national self-determination.

The following viewpoint is excerpted from a memorandum John Hickerson wrote in preparation for the Yalta Conference. Hickerson, then deputy director of the State Department's Office of European Affairs, argues that given Soviet military advances, the United States has little choice but to recognize Soviet claims over the Baltic states and other disputed territories. He argues that rather than focusing on territorial issues, American diplo-

From U.S. Department of State, *Foreign Relations of the United States, Diplomatic Papers: The Conferences of Malta and Yalta, 1945* (Washington, DC: GPO, 1955).

macy should concentrate on enlisting Soviet cooperation in finishing the war against Germany and in joining the war against Japan. Hickerson argues that the United States should accept the reality of Soviet control over much of Europe.

At the Yalta meeting, Soviet leader Joseph Stalin promised to hold free elections in Eastern Europe, then under Soviet military control. After he broke these promises and installed Soviet-dominated regimes in Poland, Hungary, and other countries, some Americans reacted by charging that Roosevelt had "sold out" to the Soviet Union. Roosevelt's diplomacy with the Soviet Union during World War II remains an area of some controversy.

We have a pretty clear idea of the Soviet objectives in Eastern Europe. We know the terms of their settlement with Finland. We know that the three Baltic States have been re-incorporated into the Soviet Union and that nothing which we can do can alter this. It is not a question of whether we like it; I personally don't like it although I recognize that the Soviet Government has arguments on its side. The point is it has been done and nothing which it is within the power of the United States Government to do can undo it. We know that the Russians will insist on the annexation of a substantial portion of East Prussia and a boundary with Poland roughly in accordance with the Curzon line [established in 1919 at the Versailles Peace Conference]. The Soviet Union has already re-incorporated Bessarabia into its territory. The Soviet Union may insist on minor adjustments in its boundaries with Rumania.

I would favor using any bargaining power that exists in connection with the foregoing matters to induce the Russians to go along with a satisfactory United Nations organization and the proposed Provisional Security Council for Europe to deal with Poland, Greece and other trouble spots. I would favor our agreeing to accept as a fact the re-incorporation of the three Baltic States into the Soviet Union and our recognition of these areas as Soviet territory. This would involve our withdrawing recognition from the three diplomatic representatives of those countries in the United States.

I would favor our agreeing at the appropriate time to accept the transfer of that portion of East Prussia to the Soviet Union which that country insists on having. I would likewise favor our agreeing to accept as a fact at the appropriate time, the Curzon line as a frontier between Poland and the Soviet Union, and to agree to an-

President Franklin D. Roosevelt of the United States, Prime Minister Winston Churchill of Great Britain, and Premier Joseph Stalin of the Soviet Union met at the resort city of Yalta in Ukraine in February 1945. The accords they reached included agreements to extend Soviet boundaries into Poland, to recognize the Soviet-sponsored government in Poland, and to support free elections in liberated Europe. Critics later attacked the Yalta agreements after the Soviet Union created regimes under its control in Eastern Europe.

nounce publicly such acceptance.

The recognition of the return of Bessarabia to the Soviet Union should present no difficulties to us.

We Need the Soviet Union's Help

We must have the support of the Soviet Union to defeat Germany. We sorely need the Soviet Union in the war against Japan when the war in Europe is over. The importance of these two things card be reckoned in terms of American lives. We must have the cooperation of the Soviet Union to organize the peace. There are certain things in connection with the foregoing proposals which are repugnant to me personally, but I am prepared to urge their adoption to obtain the cooperation of the Soviet Union in winning the war and organizing the peace. By acting on these things, we may be able to work out a regime which will obtain the cooperation of the Soviet Union for the rest of Europe and the rest of the world. There are good arguments from the Soviet point of view in favor of all of these proposals. I am willing to sponsor and support the Soviet arguments if it will save American lives in winning the war and if it will save the rest of Europe from the diplomacy of the jungle which is almost certain to ensue otherwise.

If the proposals set forth in the foregoing paragraphs should be adopted as the policy of the United States Government, a program should be undertaken immediately to prepare public opinion for them. This would involve off-the-record discussions with Congress, with outstanding newspaper editors and writers, columnists and radio commentators.

"Use . . . of the atomic bomb has placed our nation in an indefensible moral position."

Use of the Atomic Bomb Was Not Justified

Christian Century

In 1942 the United States undertook a secret research effort—the Manhattan Project—to develop a new kind of weapon powered by the splitting of the atom. The original impetus for the Manhattan Project was the fear that Germany would first develop and use such a weapon. The scientific team successfully tested the first atomic bomb in a New Mexico desert on July 16, 1945—a little more than two months after Germany's surrender. President Harry S. Truman (who became president following Franklin D. Roosevelt's death on April 12, 1945) and his advisers decided to use the weapon against America's other wartime enemy, Japan. The United States dropped an atomic bomb on the Japanese city of Hiroshima on August 6, 1945, and a second bomb on Nagasaki three days later. The two detonations reduced most of both cities to rubble and killed tens of thousands of Japanese citizens (estimates range from eighty thousand to two hundred thousand). Japan surrendered soon after the bombings.

The joy many Americans felt over the war's end was tempered by the realization of the destructiveness of these new weapons. Some Americans were profoundly disturbed at what they saw as an immoral mass killing of civilians. Others were convinced that the bombings were a justified use of force that prevented large numbers of additional U.S. casualties. Many felt that the atomic bomb would change the future of all wars. The following viewpoint is taken from an editorial in the *Christian Century*, a Protestant journal. The editors of the magazine question both the morality of and the military necessity for deploying such a weapon, and they argue that its use has marred America's victory.

Something like a moral earthquake has followed the dropping of atomic bombs on two Japanese cities. Its continued tremors throughout the world have diverted attention even from the military victory itself. . . . It is our belief that the use made of the atomic bomb has placed our nation in an indefensible moral position.

We do not propose to debate the issue of military necessity, though the facts are clearly on one side of this issue. The atomic bomb was used at a time when Japan's navy was sunk, her airforce virtually destroyed, her homeland surrounded, her supplies cut off, and our forces poised for the final stroke. Recognition of her imminent defeat could be read between the lines of every Japanese communique. Neither do we intend to challenge Mr. Churchill's highly speculative assertion that the use of the bomb saved the lives of more than one million American and 250,000 British soldiers. We believe, however, that these lives could have been saved had our government followed a different course, more honorable and more humane. Our leaders seem not to have weighed the moral considerations involved. No sooner was the bomb ready than it was rushed to the front and dropped on two helpless cities, destroying more lives than the United States has lost in the entire war.

Perhaps it was inevitable that the bomb would ultimately be employed to bring Japan to the point of surrender. . . . But there was no military advantage in hurling the bomb upon Japan without warning. The least we might have done was to announce to our foe that we possessed the atomic bomb; that its destructive power was beyond anything known in warfare; and that its terrible effectiveness had been experimentally demonstrated in this country. We could thus have warned Japan of what was in store for her unless she surrendered immediately. If she doubted the good faith of our representations, it would have been a simple matter to select a demonstration target in the enemy's own country at a place where the loss of human life would be at a minimum.

If, despite such warning, Japan had still held out, we would have been in a far less questionable position had we then dropped the bombs on Hiroshima and Nagasaki. At least our record of deliberation and ample warning would have been clear. Instead, with brutal disregard of any principle of humanity we "demonstrated" the bomb on two great cities, utterly extinguishing them. This course has placed the United States in a bad light throughout the world. What the use of poison gas did to the reputation of Germany in World War I, the use of the atomic bomb has done for the reputation of the United States in World War II. Our future security is menaced by our own act, and our influence for justice and humanity in international affairs has been sadly crippled.

Effects on Japan

We have not heard the last of this in Japan itself. There a psychological situation is rapidly developing which will make the pacification of that land by our occupying forces—infinitely delicate and precarious at best—still more difficult and dubious. In these last days before the occupation by American forces, Japanese leaders are using their final hours of freedom of access to the radio to fix in the mind of their countrymen a psychological pattern which they hope will persist into an indefinite future. They reiterate that Japan has won a moral victory by not stooping as low as her enemies, that a lost war is regrettable but not necessarily irreparable, that the United States has been morally defeated because she has been driven to use unconscionable methods of fighting. They denounce the atomic bomb as the climax of barbarity and cite its use to prove how thin the veneer of Christian civilization is. They declare that Japan must bow to the conqueror at the emperor's command, but insist that she must devote all her available energies to scientific research. That of course can mean only one thing—research in methods of scientific destruction. Some officials have openly admonished the people to discipline themselves until the day of their revenge shall come.

Vengeance as a motive suffers from no moral or religious stigma in Japanese life. In the patriotic folklore of that land, no story is more popular than that of the Forty-Seven Ronin. It is a tale of revenge taken at the cost of their lives by the retainers of a feudal lord on an enemy who had treacherously killed their master. Every Japanese child knows that story. Until 1931, when Japan took Manchuria, the sacred obligation of retaliation was directed against the nations which had prevented Japanese expansion in that area and then had expanded their own holdings. After that it was aimed at white imperialism which was held to be the enemy of all people of color in the world, and particularly those in east Asia. In each case the justification of revenge was found in a real weakness in the moral position of the adversary. Our widespread use of the diabolic flame-thrower in combat, our scattering of millions of pounds of blazing jellied gasoline over

116

wood and paper cities, and finally our employment of the atomic bomb give Japan the only justification she will require for once more seeking what she regards as justified revenge. . . .

The Franck Committee

Many of the scientists who helped develop the atomic bomb were troubled by questions regarding its use. The Franck Committee, a group of scientists led by physicist James Franck, a German expatriate, wrote a report in June 1945 for the president and secretary of war in which they argued that use of the bomb against Japan would jeopardize any future attempts to prevent a nuclear arms race.

Nuclear bombs cannot possibly remain a "secret weapon" at the exclusive disposal of this country for more than a few years. The scientific facts on which their construction is based are well known to scientists of other countries. Unless an effective international control of nuclear explosives is instituted, a race for nuclear armaments is certain to ensure following the first revelation of our possession of nuclear weapons to the world. Within ten years other countries may have nuclear bombs, each of which, weighing less than a ton, could destroy an urban area of more than ten square miles. In the war to which such an armaments race is likely to lead, the United States, with its agglomeration of population and industry in comparatively few metropolitan districts, will be at a disadvantage compared to nations whose population and industry are scattered over large areas.

We believe that these considerations make the use of nuclear bombs for an early unannounced attack against Japan inadvisable. If the United States were to be the first to release this new means of indiscriminate destruction upon mankind, she would sacrifice public support throughout the world, precipitate the race for armaments, and prejudice the possibility of reaching an international agreement on the future control of such weapons.

Much more favorable conditions for the eventual achievement of such an agreement could be created if nuclear bombs were first revealed to the world by a demonstration in appropriately selected uninhabited area.

The Japanese leaders are now in the act of creating a new myth as the carrier of the spirit of revenge. The myth will have much plausible ground in fact to support it. But its central core will be the story of the atomic bomb, hurled by the nation most reputed for its humanitarianism. Myths are hard to deal with. They lie embedded in the subconscious mind of a people, and reappear with vigor in periods of crisis. The story of the bomb will gather to itself the whole body of remembered and resented inconsistencies and false pretensions of the conquerors. The problem of spiritual rapprochement between the West and the Japanese will thus baffle the most wide and sensitive efforts of our occupying forces to find a solution. Yet our theory of occupation leaves us with no chance ever to let go of our vanquished foe until the roots of revenge have been extirpated. The outlook for the reconciliation of Germany with world civilization is ominous enough, but the outlook for the reconciliation of Japan is far more ominous. . . .

This act which has put the United States on the moral defensive has also put the Christian church on the defensive throughout the world and especially in Japan. . . .

The Shame of the American People

The churches of America must dissociate themselves and their faith from this inhuman and reckless act of the American government. There is much that they can do, and it should be done speedily. They can give voice to the shame the American people feel concerning the barbaric methods used in their name in this war. In particular, in pulpits and conventions and other assemblies they can dissociate themselves from the government's use of the atomic bomb as an offensive weapon. They can demonstrate that the American people did not even know of the existence of such a weapon until it had been unleashed against an already beaten foe. By a groundswell of prompt protest expressing their outraged moral sense, the churches may enable the Japanese people, when the record is presented to them, to divorce the Christian community from any responsibility for America's atomic atrocity.

VIEWPOINT 8

"This deliberate, premeditated destruction was our least abhorrent choice. The destruction of Hiroshima and Nagasaki put an end to the Japanese war."

Use of the Atomic Bomb Was Justified

Henry L. Stimson (1867–1950)

Henry L. Stimson was intimately involved in one of America's controversial wartime judgments—the decision to drop two atomic bombs on Japan in August 1945. Stimson, a secretary of state under President Herbert Hoover in the 1930s, was appointed secretary of war by President Franklin D. Roosevelt in 1940. After Roosevelt's death on April 12, 1945, Stimson continued to serve as secretary of war under new president Harry S. Truman until September 1945. Stimson was the chief adviser to Roosevelt and Truman on atomic policy and was in charge of the effort to produce an atomic bomb. On May 31, 1945, he chaired a special Interim Committee of leading scientists and government and military officials. Following this and other meetings, he and the committee recommended to Truman that the atomic bomb be used against Japan.

The following viewpoint is excerpted from a February 1947 article in *Harper's Magazine*. In the article, Stimson defends the choice to use the new weapon and describes the process behind the decision.

In recent months there has been much comment about the decision to use atomic bombs in attacks on the Japanese cities of Hiroshima and Nagasaki. This decision was one of the gravest made by our government in recent years, and it is entirely proper that it should be widely discussed. I have therefore decided to record for all who may be interested my understanding of the events which led up to the attack on Hiroshima on August 6, 1945, on Nagasaki on August 9, and the Japanese decision to surrender, on August 10. No single individual can hope to know exactly what took place in the minds of all of those who had a share in these events, but what follows is an exact description of our thoughts and actions as I find them in the records and in my clear recollection.

It was in the fall of 1941 that the question of atomic energy was first brought directly to my attention. At that time President Roosevelt appointed a committee consisting of Vice President [Henry] Wallace, General [George C.] Marshall, Dr. Vannevar Bush, Dr. James B. Conant, and myself. The function of this committee was to advise the President on questions of policy relating to the study of nuclear fission which was then proceeding both in this country and in Great Britain. For nearly four years thereafter I was directly connected with all major decisions of policy on the development and use of atomic energy, and from May 1, 1943, until my resignation as Secretary of War on September 21, 1945, I was directly responsible to the President for the administration of the entire undertaking; my chief advisers in this period were General Marshall, Dr. Bush, Dr. Conant, and Major General Leslie R. Groves, the officer in charge of the project. At the same time I was the President's senior adviser on the military employment of atomic energy. . . .

In the spring of 1945 it became evident that the climax of our prolonged atomic effort was at hand. By the nature of atomic chain reactions, it was impossible to state with certainty that we had succeeded until a bomb had actually exploded in a fullscale experiment; nevertheless it was considered exceedingly probable that we should by midsummer have successfully detonated the first atomic bomb. This was to be done at the Alamogordo Reservation in New Mexico. It was thus time for detailed consideration of our future plans. What had begun as a well-founded hope was now developing into a reality. . . .

Interim Committee

The Interim Committee was charged with the function of advising the President on the various questions raised by our apparently imminent success in developing an atomic weapon. I was its chairman, but the principal labor of guiding its extended deliberations fell to George L. Harrison, who acted as chairman in my absence. It will be useful to consider the work of the committee in some detail. . . .

The discussions of the committee ranged over the whole field of atomic energy, in its political, military, and scientific aspects. That part of its work which particularly concerns us here relates to its recommendations for the use of atomic energy against Japan, but it should be borne in mind that these recommendations were not made in a vacuum. The committee's work included the drafting of the statements which were published immediately after the first bombs were dropped, the drafting of a bill for the domestic control of atomic energy, and recommendations looking toward the international control of atomic energy. The Interim Committee was assisted in its work by a Scientific Panel whose members were the following: Dr. A.H. Compton, Dr. Enrico Fermi, Dr. E.O. Lawrence, and Dr. J.R. Oppenheimer. All four were nuclear physicists of the first rank; all four had held positions of great importance in the atomic project from its inception. At a meeting with the Interim Committee and the Scientific Panel on May 31, 1945, I urged all those present to feel free to express themselves on any phase of the subject, scientific or political. Both General Marshall and I at this meeting expressed the view that atomic energy could not be considered simply in terms of military weapons but must also be considered in terms of a new relationship of man to the universe.

On June 1, after its discussions with the Scientific Panel, the Interim Committee unanimously adopted the following recommendations:

(1) The bomb should be used against Japan as soon as possible.

(2) It should be used on a dual target—that is, a military installation or war plant surrounded by or adjacent to houses and other buildings most susceptible to damage, and

(3) It should be used without prior warning [of the nature of the weapon]. One member of the committee, Mr. [Ralph A.] Bard, later changed his view and dissented from recommendation (3).

In reaching these conclusions, the Interim Committee carefully considered such alternatives as a detailed advance warning or a demonstration in some uninhabited area. Both of these suggestions were discarded as impractical. They were not regarded as likely to be effective in compelling a surrender of Japan, and both of them involved serious risks. Even the New Mexico test would not give final proof that any given bomb was certain to explode when dropped from an airplane. Quite apart from the generally unfamiliar nature of atomic explosives, there was the whole prob-

Ashley Zartengo

lem of exploding a bomb at a predetermined height in the air by a complicated mechanism which could not be tested in the static test of New Mexico. Nothing would have been more damaging to our effort to obtain surrender than a warning or a demonstration followed by a dud—and this was a real possibility. Furthermore, we had no bombs to waste. It was vital that a sufficient effect be quickly obtained with the few we had.

Views of Other Scientists

The Interim Committee and the Scientific Panel also served as a channel through which suggestions from other scientists working on the atomic project were forwarded to me and to the President. Among the suggestions thus forwarded was one memorandum which questioned using the bomb at all against the enemy. On June 16, 1945, after consideration of that memorandum, the Scientific Panel made a report, from which I quote the following paragraphs:

> The opinions of our scientific colleagues on the initial use of these weapons are not unanimous: they range from the proposal of a purely technical demonstration to that of the military application best designed to induce surrender. Those who advocate a purely technical demonstration would wish to outlaw the use of atomic weapons, and have feared that if we use the weapons now our position in future negotiations will be prejudiced. Others emphasize the opportunity of saving American lives by immediate military use, and believe that such use will improve the international prospects, in that they are more concerned with the prevention of war than with the elimination of this special weapon. We find ourselves closer to these latter views; *we can propose no technical demonstration likely to bring an end to the war; we see no acceptable alternative to direct military use.* [Italics mine]

> With regard to these general aspects of the use of atomic energy, it is clear that we, as scientific men, have no proprietary rights. It is true that we are among the few citizens who have had occasion to give thoughtful consideration to these problems during the past few years. We have, however, no claim to special competence in solving the political, social, and military problems which are presented by the advent of atomic power.

The foregoing discussion presents the reasoning of the Interim Committee and its advisers. I have discussed the work of these gentlemen at length in order to make it clear that we sought the best advice that we could find. The committee's function was, of course, entirely advisory. The ultimate responsibility for the recommendation to the President rested upon me, and I have no desire to veil it. The conclusions of the committee were similar to my own, although I reached mine independently. I felt that to extract a genuine surrender from the Emperor and his military advisers, they must be administered a tremendous shock which would carry convincing proof of our power to destroy the Empire. Such an effective shock would save many times the number of lives, both American and Japanese, that it would cost. . . .

Memorandum on Japan

I wrote a memorandum for the President, on July 2, which I believe fairly represents the thinking of the American government as it finally took shape in action. This memorandum was prepared after discussion and general agreement with Joseph C. Grew, Acting Secretary of State, and Secretary of the Navy [James] Forrestal, and when I discussed it with the President, he expressed his general approval.

Memorandum for the President, Proposed Program for Japan, July 2, 1945

1. The plans of operation up to and including the first landing have been authorized and the preparations for the operation are now actually going on. This situation was accepted by all members of your conference on Monday, June 18.

2. There is reason to believe that the operation for the occupation of Japan following the landing may be a very long, costly, and arduous struggle on our part. The terrain, much of which I have visited several times, has left the impression on my memory of being one which would be susceptible to a last ditch defense such as has been made on Iwo Jima and Okinawa and which of course is very much larger than either of those two areas. According to my recollection it will be much more unfavorable with regard to tank maneuvering than either the Philippines or Germany.

3. If we once land on one of the main islands and begin a forceful occupation of Japan, we shall probably have cast the die of last ditch resistance. The Japanese are highly patriotic and certainly susceptible to calls for fanatical resistance to repel an invasion. Once started in actual invasion, we shall in my opinion have to go through with an even more bitter finish fight than in Germany. We shall incur the losses incident to such a war and we shall have to leave the Japanese islands even more thoroughly destroyed than was the case with Germany. This would be due both to the difference in the Japanese and German personal character and the differences in the size and character of the terrain through which the operations will take place.

4. A question then comes: Is there any alternative to such a forceful occupation of Japan which will secure for us the equivalent of an unconditional surrender of her forces and a permanent destruction of her power again to strike an aggressive blow at the "peace of the Pacific"? I am inclined to think that there is enough such chance to make it well worthwhile our giving them a warning of what is to come and a definite opportunity to capitulate. As above suggested, it should be tried before the actual forceful occupation of the homeland islands is begun and furthermore the warning should be given in ample time to permit a national reaction to set in. . . .

5. It is therefore my conclusion that a carefully timed warning be given

to Japan by the chief representatives of the United States, Great Britain, China, and, if then a belligerent, Russia by calling upon Japan to surrender and permit the occupation of her country in order to insure its complete demilitarization for the sake of the future peace.

This warning should contain the following elements:

The varied and overwhelming character of the force we are about to bring to bear on the islands.

The inevitability and completeness of the destruction which the full application of this force will entail.

Bombing Nagasaki

William L. Lawrence, a reporter for the New York Times, *won a Pulitzer Prize for his reporting on the atomic bomb. In this excerpt from his account of the mission to bomb Nagasaki on August 9, 1945 (in which he flew as an observer), he writes that his own misgivings about the bomb are offset by anger at the Japanese for attacking Pearl Harbor and mistreating and killing American prisoners of war in the Bataan peninsula in the Philippines.*

The first signs of dawn came shortly after 5 o'clock. Sergeant Curry, who had been listening steadily on his earphones for radio reports, while maintaining a strict radio silence himself, greeted it by rising to his feet and gazing out the window.

"It's good to see the day," he told me. "I get a feeling of claustrophobia hemmed in in this cabin at night."

He is a typical American youth, looking even younger than his 20 years. It takes no mind-reader to read his thoughts.

"It's a long way from Hoopeston, Ill.," I find myself remarking.

"Yep," he replies, as he busies himself decoding a message from outer space.

"Think this atomic bomb will end the war?" he asks hopefully.

"There is a very good chance that this one may do the trick," I assure him, "but if not, then the next one or two surely will. Its power is such that no nation can stand up against it very long."

This was not my own view. I had heard it expressed all around a few hours earlier, before we took off. To anyone who had seen this man-made fireball in action, as I had less than a month ago in the desert of New Mexico, this view did not sound overoptimistic. . . .

Somewhere beyond these vast mountains of white clouds ahead of me there lies Japan, the land of our enemy. In about four hours from now one of its cities, making weapons of war for use against us, will be wiped off the map by the greatest weapon ever made by man. In one-tenth of a millionth of a second, a fraction of time immeasurable by any clock, a whirlwind from the skies will pulverize thousands of its buildings and tens of thousands of its inhabitants. . . .

Does one feel any pity or compassion for the poor devils about to die? Not when one thinks of Pearl Harbor and of the Death March on Bataan.

The determination of the Allies to destroy permanently all authority and influence of those who have deceived and misled the country into embarking on world conquest.

The determination of the Allies to limit Japanese sovereignty to her main islands and to render them powerless to mount and support another war.

The disavowal of any attempt to extirpate the Japanese as a race or to destroy them as a nation.

A statement of our readiness, once her economy is purged of its militaristic influence, to permit the Japanese to maintain such industries, particularly of a light consumer character, as offer no threat of aggression against their neighbors, but which can produce a sustaining economy, and provide a reasonable standard of living. The statement should indicate our willingness, for this purpose, to give Japan trade access to external raw materials, but no longer any control over the sources of supply outside her main islands. It should also indicate our willingness, in accordance with our now established foreign trade policy, in due course to enter into mutually advantageous trade relations with her.

The withdrawal from their country as soon as the above objectives of the Allies are accomplished, and as soon as there has been established a peacefully inclined government, of a character representative of the masses of the Japanese people. I personally think that if in saying this we should add that we do not exclude a constitutional monarchy under her present dynasty, it would substantially add to the chances of acceptance.

6. Success of course will depend on the potency of the warning which we give her. She has an extremely sensitive national pride and, as we are now seeing every day, when actually locked with the enemy will fight to the very death. For that reason the warning must be tendered before the actual invasion has occurred and while the impending destruction, though clear beyond peradventure, has not yet reduced her to fanatical despair. If Russia is a part of the threat, the Russian attack, if actual, must not have progressed too far. Our own bombing should be confined to military objectives as far as possible.

It is important to emphasize the double character of the suggested warning. It was designed to promise destruction if Japan resisted, and hope, if she surrendered.

It will be noted that the atomic bomb is not mentioned in this memorandum. On grounds of secrecy the bomb was never mentioned except when absolutely necessary, and furthermore, it had not yet been tested. It was of course well forward in our minds, as the memorandum was written and discussed, that the bomb would be the best possible sanction if our warning were rejected.

The Use of the Bomb

The adoption of the policy outlined in the memorandum of July 2 was a decision of high politics; once it was accepted by the President, the position of the atomic bomb in our planning became quite clear. I find that I stated in my diary, as early as June 19, that "the last chance warning . . . must be given before an actual landing of the ground forces in Japan, and fortunately the plans provide for enough time to bring in the sanctions to our warning in the shape of heavy ordinary bombing attack and an attack of S-1." S-1 was a code name for the atomic bomb.

There was much discussion in Washington about the timing of the warning to Japan. The controlling factor in the end was the date already set for the Potsdam meeting of the Big Three. It was President Truman's decision that such a warning should be solemnly issued by the U.S. and the U.K. from this meeting, with the concurrence of the head of the Chinese government, so that it would be plain that *all* of Japan's principal enemies were in entire unity. This was done, in the Potsdam ultimatum of July 26, which very closely followed the above memorandum of July 2, with the exception that it made no mention of the Japanese Emperor.

On July 28 the Premier of Japan, [Kantaro] Suzuki, rejected the Potsdam ultimatum by announcing that it was "unworthy of public notice." In the face of this rejection we could only proceed to demonstrate that the ultimatum had meant exactly what it said when it stated that if the Japanese continued the war, "the full application of our military power, backed by our resolve, will mean the inevitable and complete destruction of the Japanese armed forces and just as inevitably the utter devastation of the Japanese homeland."

A Suitable Weapon

For such a purpose the atomic bomb was an eminently suitable weapon. The New Mexico test occurred while we were at Potsdam, on July 16. It was immediately clear that the power of the bomb measured up to our highest estimates. We had developed a weapon of such a revolutionary character that its use against the enemy might well be expected to produce exactly the kind of shock on the Japanese ruling oligarchy which we desired, strengthening the position of those who wished peace, and weakening that of the military party. . . .

Hiroshima was bombed on August 6, and Nagasaki on August 9. These two cities were active working parts of the Japanese war effort. One was an army center; the other was naval and industrial. Hiroshima was the headquarters of the Japanese Army defending southern Japan and was a major military storage and assembly point. Nagasaki was a major seaport and it contained several large industrial plants of great wartime importance. We believed that our attacks had struck cities which must certainly be important to the Japanese military leaders, both Army and Navy, and we waited for a result. We waited one day.

Many accounts have been written about the Japanese surrender. After a prolonged Japanese cabinet session in which the deadlock was broken by the Emperor himself, the offer to surrender was made on August 10. It was based on the Potsdam terms, with a reservation concerning the sovereignty of the Emperor. While the Allied reply made no promises other than those already given, it implicitly recognized the Emperor's position by prescribing that his power must be subject to the orders of the Allied Supreme Commander. These terms were accepted on August 14 by the Japanese, and the instrument of surrender was formally signed on September 2 in Tokyo Bay. Our great objective was thus achieved, and all the evidence I have seen indicates that the controlling factor in the final Japanese decision to accept our terms of surrender was the atomic bomb. . . .

In the foregoing pages I have tried to give an accurate account of my own personal observations of the circumstances which led up to the use of the atomic bomb and the reasons which underlay our use of it. To me they have always seemed compelling and clear, and I cannot see how any person vested with such responsibilities as mine could have taken any other course or given any other advice to his chiefs. . . .

War and Death

As I read over what I have written, I am aware that much of it, in this year of peace, may have a harsh and unfeeling sound. It would perhaps be possible to say the same things and say them more gently. But I do not think it would be wise. As I look back over the five years of my service as Secretary of War, I see too many stern and heartrending decisions to be willing to pretend that war is anything else than what it is. The face of war is the face of death; death is an inevitable part of every order that a wartime leader gives. The decision to use the atomic bomb was a decision that brought death to over a hundred thousand Japanese. No explanation can change that fact and I do not wish to gloss it over. But this deliberate, premeditated destruction was our least abhorrent choice. The destruction of Hiroshima and Nagasaki put an end to the Japanese war. It stopped the fire raids and the strangling blockade; it ended the ghastly specter of a clash of great land armies.

In this last great action of the Second World War we were given final proof that war is death. War in the twentieth century has grown steadily more barbarous, more destructive, more debased in all its aspects. Now, with the release of atomic energy, man's ability to destroy himself is very nearly complete. The bombs dropped on Hiroshima and Nagasaki ended a war. They also made it wholly clear that we must never have another war. This is the lesson men and leaders everywhere must learn, and I believe that when they learn it they will find a way to lasting peace. There is no other choice.

CHAPTER 3

The Home Front

Chapter Preface

American society was profoundly affected by World War II as the United States sought to mobilize its resources and population for "total war." These changes, including a massive expansion of the federal government and a dramatic transformation of the role of women in the workplace, were often the focus of controversy and debate.

Americans who remained in the United States endured the rationing of gasoline and other goods, grew "victory gardens," purchased war bonds, and suffered the loss of family members and friends as American battle casualties mounted. Ironically, however, for many the overall effect of the war was a rising standard of living. Massive government spending, which rose from $9 billion in 1940 to $100 billion in 1945, effectively ended the Great Depression, which had stunted America's economy throughout the 1930s. The unemployment rate dipped below double digits in 1941 after averaging as much as 18 percent during the previous decade; by 1943 it was 1.9 percent. The incomes of farmers and the wages of many workers rose to record highs.

As the federal government grew during World War II, government policies greatly affected American consumers, businesses, workers, and farmers. On the consumer level, various government agencies created by President Franklin D. Roosevelt enacted price controls and rationing in order to control inflation and manage the economy. To encourage war production, the government rewrote tax laws, underwrote construction of factories, relaxed enforcement of antitrust laws, and recruited businessmen to serve on wartime government agencies. These government measures resulted not only in a remarkable display of industrial productivity (U.S. production of airplanes, for instance, rose from 1,800 in 1939 to 96,000 in 1944), but also in the concentration of economic power among large corporations.

Such a large industrial expansion required workers. During the war millions of Americans migrated because of military relocation and the pull of defense industry employment. Whole new "boomtowns" were created in the wake of defense industrialization, and the populations of states in the southern and western parts of the United States grew considerably. Communities new and old experienced overcrowding as demand for housing and schools outstripped supply.

A significant part of the World War II labor force consisted of women. During the war 6 million women worked outside the home—three-quarters of whom, in contrast to past labor patterns, were married. Many found employment in factories, shipyards, and other workplaces that had previously been dominated by men. The U.S. government encouraged the influx of women into the workforce in order to maximize productivity and to free men for military service. Some women found new opportunities in the military itself; during the war all the military services recruited women to serve as nurses, clerks, technicians, and in other non-combat positions. Many people assumed that the increased employment of women was a temporary wartime phenomenon. But while polls at the start of World War II showed that 95 percent of women intended to quit their jobs when the war was over, by 1945, according to some surveys, 80 percent of women workers desired to keep working outside the home. Although most women did leave the workforce after the war ended, their contributions to the wartime economy stimulated debate and left a lasting impact on social attitudes regarding women's roles in America.

The changing role of women is just one of the issues discussed in the following chapter on the home front during World War II.

"The rationing that we have undertaken flows directly from the realities of the war."

Consumer Goods Rationing Is Necessary for the War Effort

Leon Henderson (1895–1986)

During World War II, President Franklin D. Roosevelt created numerous government agencies charged with allocating industrial materials, organizing the production of wartime goods, and controlling inflation. Critics of the Roosevelt administration often focused on confusion created by these agencies and their overlapping responsibilities. Among these regulatory bodies was the Office of Price Administration and Civilian Supply (OPACS), created by executive order on April 11, 1941, "to prevent spiraling, rising costs of living, profiteering, and inflation resulting from market conditions." OPACS was later divided into the Office of Price Administration (OPA) and the Division of Civilian Supply (DCS), which became a unit of the Office of Production Management (OPM).

Over the course of the war, several consumer staples, including gasoline, tires, sugar, beef, and coffee, were rationed under a system of stamps and coupons imposed by these agencies. Many consumers and producers complained about rationing, price controls, and other OPA measures.

Leon Henderson, an economist and government official who was one of the more prominent figures of Roosevelt's administration in the 1930s, was named director of OPACS in 1941, and he continued as head of OPA when that office was established. His authority over prices and rationing was increased by the Emer-

From Leon Henderson, "More Dollars Do Not Mean More Goods," speech delivered to the Chicago Better Business Bureau, February 20, 1942.

gency Price Control Act, which was passed by Congress in January 1942. Henderson also served on several other agencies, including the War Production Board (WPB).

The following viewpoint is taken from an address Henderson delivered to the Chicago Better Business Bureau in February 1942, one of many public speeches he made explaining the policies of his agency and calling for wartime sacrifices by consumers. He argues that the production of consumer goods and commodities must be curtailed so that defense production can increase. Rationing and price controls are sometimes necessary, he asserts, to prevent inflation created by the imbalance between dollars and consumer goods. Henderson resigned as OPA administrator amid political pressure and public unpopularity in January 1943.

War does strange things to people, to ideas, and to institutions. I wonder though if you have ever found yourself bewildered as I have with the contradictions of the various jobs I undertake to perform in the war program. In the first place, as Price Administrator, I am supposed to establish fair prices on commodities, some of which are no longer manufactured because, as Director of Civilian Supply, I have established programs of curtailment because as a member of the War Production Board, I have already voted to give the commodities to the Army and Navy. To further compound the complexity, the War Production Board tells me that they have a few tires and automobiles left over, and will I please ration these fairly and equally among 130,000,000 eager buyers, and do the rationing without causing any protests, or depriving anybody of any style of living to which they have become accustomed.

Is it any wonder that I sometimes feel like that unfortunate chameleon which got on a Scotch plaid and tried to be all colors at once?

Really, though, all these jobs tie together. As a member of the War Production Board, I am familiar with the requirements for the armed forces. After those requirements have been satisfied first, it is my job, as Civilian Supply Director, to try to act for the civilian population and decide what Mr. and Mrs. John Q. Public would choose if they were sitting in my place. Because the supply is bound to be short, prices would zoom out of sight unless strong controls were provided. Thus it is natural that I have the job of keeping prices down. And since inevitably if raw materials are scarce, the finished products are bound to be scarce, it is another additional corollary that I should do the rationing.

I feel that you are entitled to an accounting of my stewardship, as you know I am not an elected officer, although I have twice been confirmed by the United States Senate. As citizens, as taxpayers, and as Americans, you are entitled to know the principles and procedures of rationing, of price control, of the drastic curtailment of civilian industry, and finally as to the small part I perform in the conduct of production for war.

I have one simple basic promise. Hitler and the Japs must be defeated. So whether we are shutting down the automobile industry, or rationing the use of tires, or fixing the price of food, we have the same test to apply.

The Arithmetic of Inflation

Do you realize how important a part is played by arithmetic and mathematics in a war? In the logistics of combat, it is a life and death matter to know the speed of a plane, the accuracy of a bombsight, or the resistance of armor plate. In the logistics of civilian economics in a war emergency, it's a matter of life and death sometimes to know that two and two still make four. Let me give you the simple arithmetic of inflation, rationing, profits, wages, and prices for 1942. We will have 9 billion dollars less of goods and services of all kinds. That means 9 billion dollars less of refrigerators, automobiles, typewriters, and copper cuspidors. We will have at least 6 billion dollars more of purchasing power with which to buy this limited amount of goods; that is, we will have 6 billion dollars made up of more farm income, more wage income and more consumer buying power of all kinds. You don't need to be an economist, with all the fancy training that goes with the profession, to know that there is a gap of 15 billion dollars between what this country of consumers can buy and the amount of goods that there will be on the shelves. I call this plain and simple arithmetic, and if you want to know the detailed mathematics, just write me a letter to Washington. It may seem incredible that this country, which is producing goods at a rate of 50 per cent higher than 1929, should be 15 billion dollars short. The answer, of course, is that we are supplying our military machine with 40 billion dollars of the merchandise of death—guns, tanks, planes and ships, and are giving our allies several billion besides in the form of food and clothing.

I hope you will keep that 15 billion dollars in mind, because it is a simple measure of your problem of inflation. There is no way to escape it, and in the years to come, it will rise to haunt you unless, as a nation, you handle it satisfactorily. It is the reason why we must tax and tax and tax until it hurts. It's the basic reason why you must save and save and save. It explains why wages must be kept under control, why farm prices must be kept under control, why profits must not be allowed to skyrocket, and why the rise in the cost of living must be fought at every cross-roads.

Out of my experience, let me tell you that as a nation we will not handle this 15 billion dollars of deficit in its entirety. It will be many months before Congress faces up squarely to the necessity for taxes that will really hurt. Labor today, quite understandably, is thinking of priorities of unemployment, and the farmer is remembering the cruel years of the locust, when parity was something that politicians talked about to get elected. And business is thinking of those unsteady years when assets were dissolved in the bankruptcy courts, and the very name "Balance Sheet" seemed a cruel mockery.

Library of Congress

People waiting in lines for scarce or rationed goods became a common American scene during World War II.

For these reasons which I have just recited, which in the days to come may seem like national weaknesses, we shall have to fix prices and we shall have to ration goods. Let me divert for just a moment. Here is another paradox. In the days before the war, I was an orthodox economist. I hated price fixing. . . . I rested my belief in the strength of the individual acting in free association and abhorred the rise in the power of the state. At first blush it may seem analogous that I should be the price fixer and the rationer. . . . To me, however, it is the symbol of democratic America, an America whose course is still guided by facts and realities.

There is one school of thought which says don't scold. There is another school which says only ACT. We shall do both if they will help in accomplishing our objectives.

We will fix prices if that will help in combatting inflation. We will ration where that will help in securing an equitable distribution of scarce goods, but always we will be guided by our one major premise of licking the Axis.

Already we have established formal ceilings over the prices of more than 100 basic commodities or manufactured articles. That work will go on. Already we are beginning the work of rationing scarce commodities. We have imposed controls when prices began to show inflationary tendencies. We have rationed when scarcities began to become acute.

Our Duties as Americans

You, as businessmen, as housewives, as Americans, have a duty to perform in both of these fields.

In the price field you have the duty of helping us battle the menace of inflation by keeping prices down. Likewise, in your roles as consumers, you have a duty not only in resisting price increases, but also in minimizing the need for rationing by refusing to hoard goods.

Thus far the rationing that we have undertaken flows directly from the realities of the war. The Japs have nearly cut off the areas from which we secure, in normal times, 98 per cent of our crude rubber. The Japs forced us into rationing tires.

Likewise, the need for expanding our production of war materials made it necessary to draw in the vast potential productive capacity of our automobile industry. The war has forced us to ration our existing stocks of automobiles and trucks.

The story behind sugar rationing is the same. We've lost a million tons of sugar—nearly a seventh of our requirements—by the Jap inroads in the Philippines. Our imports from Hawaii will probably be cut in half because of the threat to those Islands. Our supplies from the Caribbean will have to be used in part to help meet the needs of our allies, and, what's more, to make alcohol for the production of powder required by our soldiers and sailors.

I want to talk to the housewives for a moment about sugar. We will have enough in 1942 to meet all health needs, although our supplies available for home and industrial consumption will probably be about one-third less than in 1941. That reduction of one-third, however, makes it necessary to ration, so that everyone will get his or her fair share. Some of you have become frightened in recent weeks. Some of you have built up hoards of sugar, despite the commendable efforts of grocers to distribute sugar fairly. Under the sugar rationing plan, those who have built up stocks of sugar beyond their current needs will be deprived of the right to buy more until their stocks have been brought back to normal.

In anticipation of the beginning of sugar rationing, I want to urge those housewives who became frightened about the sugar

A Ration Board at Work

Rationing was handled by thousands of local boards across the country. Brendan Gill wrote of one typical ration board in a June 13, 1942, article in the New Yorker. *In the following excerpt, Gill describes a woman's appeal to the board's chairman, Chauncey Griffen, to change her assigned "A" card (which entitled her to four gallons of gasoline a week) to a more generous "B" or "X" card (given to those who could demonstrate a greater need for gasoline, such as for commuting to defense jobs).*

A woman took his place before the desk. She said, rather archly, "My dear Mr. Griffen, is this where you ration everything?"

"Everything but the ladies, Madam," Mr. Griffen said gallantly. . . .

"Well, I've an A card," she said, "but I think I deserve better. You see, my dear mother's eighty and she's had a stroke. The only real pleasure she gets out of life is a little ride every evening in the fine summer weather. And I'm afraid we won't be able to take our little rides unless you give me a B-3 card, or perhaps an X."

His air of gallantry still intact, Mr. Griffen said, "I happen to have a mother, too, who's over eighty and has had a stroke. She likes to go out riding whenever she can, too. But she'll have to make a certain number of sacrifices, just like the rest of us. She'll have to manage on an A card."

The woman stopped smiling. "But, of course, an A card isn't enough," she said. "It may be the death of my poor mother."

"All right," Mr. Griffen said, standing up as a hint that the interview was about over. "You go out and get an affidavit from your mother's physician swearing that unless she can ride a minimum of forty or fifty miles a week, every week, she'll die. Then you can come back here and get more gas.". . .

Mr. Griffen tossed me a letter. "We get a few of these every day, but not as many as you might think."

I glanced at the letter. It began:

Dear Mr. Griffen:

I am delighted to know that a man of your integrity and high standing in this community should be chairman of our ration board. It is certainly a lucky thing for all of us that a man of your calibre is willing to serve. I am writing to explain that I'm afraid our A card isn't quite suitable for us. I must take Evangeline to school each morning. . . .

Mr. Griffen made a face. Handing me another letter, he said, "And we also get a few like this." It read:

Dear Mr. Griffen:

I hope you will check up on all drivers. While our boys are fighting and dying all over the world, I can't see why anyone should knowingly waste a fraction of an inch of rubber or a single gallon of gas.

The letter was signed: "Brokenhearted."

Mr. Griffen looked apologetic as I finished reading the letter: "Sort of emotional, of course," he said. "Some soldier's mother, I suppose."

He leaned forward over his desk toward the remaining petitioners on the benches. "Next complaint," he said, a bit severely.

situation after Pearl Harbor, to divvy up with their neighbors, or sell back some of their hoards to their grocers. By doing this, you will make it possible for everyone to get his fair share.

Remember! Hoarding helps Hitler. Hoarding of any commodity forces rationing, with all the confusion and bother that it entails. No patriotic American will hoard anything in this emergency.

The Home Front

The sons, brothers, fathers of some of us are on the fighting fronts, risking their lives to defend the ideals we all hold dear. But there is another front, the home front. The rest of us should be fighting on that front. In the months ahead, as the shortages develop, as the easy routine of our accustomed way of living is shaken and distorted, remember one thing—our deprivations, our hardships, our dangers are as nothing compared to those boys who are fighting with MacArthur for their lives on Bataan Peninsula.

On the economic side of our war effort, there is but one basic and controlling fact. We must produce more and consume less. Our reward will be the security of the growing force of ships and tanks and planes with which our civilization must be defended.

The total shrinkage in consumption will be too great to be borne by any one part of our people, whether that part be rich or poor. It must be shared. Nor are those who are already contributing their efforts exempt from the contribution that takes the shape of doing without things. Both kinds of contribution are needed, from everyone who is physically able to make them.

We are going to have enough to meet our commitments to our allies, and still meet the really essential needs of the American people—if what we have is equitably distributed. But it will not be equitably distributed if powerful economic groups within our own nation engage in a struggle, each trying to escape its share of sacrifice by raising its money income as fast as the cost of living rises, or faster. That sacrifice we cannot escape because more dollars now no longer mean more goods. From now on goods are limited by the requirements of war, no matter how many dollars people have. Those who get more goods by bidding for them with new dollars are taking goods away from others whose incomes are too small to bid successfully in the markets, and who cannot increase them. These are the people who are in danger of being deprived of the real necessities of life. These are the people for whom a runaway price inflation means both injustice and tragedy.

It is the struggle for our limited supply of goods which must at all costs be avoided. Economic groups must realize the suicidal character of such a struggle and must refrain, in their own interest and that of their fellows. The government, too, has obligations. Basic necessities, where a substantial shortage exists, must be rationed, and their retail prices controlled. The Office of Price Administration is entering on this formidable task, and is attempting to protect the people on this front. But such controls will not suffice. If our people accumulate dollars far in excess of the limited supply of goods and try to spend them, they will raise the prices of more things than can be effectively controlled and rationed. The government needs those extra dollars, and it must get them, either by taxes or by subscriptions to defense stamps and bonds, or in some other way.

In the supreme emergency we now face we must all realize that ordinary economic standards no longer hold. More dollars do not mean more goods. Taxes and loans are not the source of economic privations, but only the means of apportioning them. When some of us are giving our lives, it is little enough for the rest of us to assume cheerfully our fair share of economic sacrifice.

"The war industries very properly do come first, but civilian industries must have consideration."

Government Policies on Rationing Are Harming the War Effort

Consumers' Research Bulletin

Americans who did not serve abroad during World War II were affected by shortages of consumer goods and commodities. These shortages were the result both of direct government rationing (in the case of beef, coffee, gasoline, and other items) and of government directives that allocated industrial materials and restricted the production of consumer articles in order to maximize the manufacture of war goods. Not all Americans fully supported these actions of the federal government.

The following viewpoint is taken from an editorial that appeared in *Consumers' Research Bulletin*, a monthly consumer information magazine that was produced by Consumers' Research, a private nonprofit organization founded in 1928. The editorial was one of a series of commentaries critical of rationing and other economic policies of the Roosevelt administration. The editors argue that some consumer goods production is necessary to sustain wartime morale. Economizing measures should be directed at government bureaucracies, they contend, rather than at the American consumer. Among the government officials criticized in the editorial are Leon Henderson, head of the Office of Price Administration (OPA), and Donald Nelson, chairman of the War Production Board (WPB).

"Off the Editor's Chest," *Consumer's Research Bulletin*, vol. 11, no. 3, December 1942, p. 2. Reprinted with permission.

Although there is a fairly good supply of Christmas merchandise reported to be available this year, competent observers have predicted that when this year's gifts are bought, supplies in many lines will be exhausted and will be impossible to replace. Experts forecast, some with a sort of glee that is close to sadism, that the pinch of the war-economy will really begin to hurt after the first of the year. The government releases particularly tend to give the impression that those in government jobs empowered to restrict the flow of goods to civilians are leaving no stone unturned in their efforts to dam the flow of manufactured goods for consumers, whether or not those goods use materials vital to the requirements of the armed forces.

Scare Stories

There have been so many scare stories which failed to materialize or which materialized only to a limited extent that a good many people do not believe what they hear or read and hence do not realize till too late quite what is happening. Since stocks have been available in the stores, they do not realize that the wholesalers are beginning to scrape bottom. Friends of big business, and government officials particularly, have shed many crocodile tears over the plight of the small businessman and manufacturer, who will, according to one government expert's speech after another, be pretty largely forced out of business in the period ahead. If the little businessman is to be saved, it will be only because consumers, by continuing to require his services, come to his rescue.

Manufacturers have been forced to convert to war production or forced to suspend production and close down their plants, without any certainty whatever in many cases that there was a shortage of facilities for producing whatever they might be in a position to make in the way of war goods, or whether or not a given plant could be converted economically. By skilfully directed governmental publicity, the manufacturer who might wish to continue to reserve some small part of his output for the human needs of his customers—the taxpayers—such vitally needed items as repair parts for automobiles, cooking appliances and utensils, and certain heating appliances, has been made to feel that he was giving aid and comfort to the enemy by even trying "to do business as usual."

Such ill-conceived planning as tries to stop manufacture and trade in nearly everything but munitions can bring about a widespread breakdown on the home front, the second line of the Nation's defenses, which must operate steadily and productively also, behind the armed forces. It is reasonable of course that the major wastes and a good deal of the fat of our civilian economy must be eliminated to carry on a global war effectively and on the tremendous scale required. But there is no need, and none can be shown, for tearing a delicately-interlinked and finely functioning manufacturing and distributing economy to bits at the whim or behest of any of Leon Henderson's leftish economists or Donald Nelson's "industrial experts," so called. For these men the temptation to "direct" or "reorient" what they call "capitalist production," has often proved too great to resist; the sense of power in pushing a hundred or a thousand manufacturers out of business by mere issuance in legal form of a mimeographed "directive" or ukase apparently gives such men the same sort of satisfaction as the average businessman or engineer feels in building a business enterprise, staffing it with competent mechanics and making it run and turn out useful and needed products. It is important for every citizen and taxpayer to understand clearly this characteristic of many a governmental executive, who can say quite calmly: "It's just too bad, but we don't need your product any more, so you may close down. We'll let you know if we think of anything for you and your men to do."

Consumer Goods and the Home Front

Civilian welfare, incentive, and ability to carry on are going to need in the very near future some study and attention by men of mature sense and wisdom (and a minimum of zeal for reform or remaking of society in wartime) if the war effort is to go forward effectively. We now confidently predict that after the learned experts have worked over the patients, they will discover that what is needed is not the closing of the channels of normal industry and trade but the *provision of more consumer goods* of good and lasting quality, distributed efficiently and with a minimum of red tape and disturbance of existing relationships of manufacturers, dealers, and consumers.

As far back as May, 1942, a business journal reported the paralyzing effect on certain war industries of "absenteeism," particularly on the part of skilled workers. Various causes for this playing hookey from highly paid jobs were suggested. One of them is that because earnings have risen and opportunities to spend have been restricted, some individuals prefer to take it easy as long as they are making more than enough to pay the landlord and the grocer, since they have been deprived of such incentives to hard work and long hours of labor as were once afforded by the opportunities to buy new cars, new radio sets, fur coats, electric refrigerators, new gas ranges.

Not long ago there appeared in one of the most widely read magazines in this country, the revealing anecdote of an American employer who ran a small factory in the Panama Canal Zone. The native girls announced one day quite suddenly that they had all decided to quit. The manufacturer, in attempting to find out what the difficulty was, discovered that they felt there was just nothing more to spend their money on. The stoppage of work was quickly remedied when the manager obtained a Sears-Roebuck mail-order catalog and spread its treasures before them. Back to work they went pronto, with an incentive for further working and earning.

Rationing and Common Sense

An editorial in the January 1943 issue of Consumers' Research Bulletin *questioned the fairness of coffee rationing and the government's handling of rationing in general.*

Anyone with common sense can see the basic fallacy in the asserted guiding doctrine of share and share alike. It is *no* sacrifice to be restricted to one cup a day, for the person who can take his coffee or leave it, or who is not working under stress and strain and therefore may not need the stimulus of an extra cup of coffee. The man doing hard work in a plant making war materials where a high output is required and where strain and noise or cold drafts abound, may be democratically sharing his privation with the afternoon bridge player, but the potential loss in his capacity for extra effort and long hours to help win the war is not a problem that can be dealt with by statistics or averages. . . .

As our experience with the process of rationing increases, a familiar pattern begins to take shape. The first thing that happens is that supplies begin to be tight. Under the system of price ceilings presently in favor, the price of a particular commodity is held down by governmental fiat. Thus the normal brake on consumption of scarce stocks afforded by a free market system through a rise in price is not applied, and consumption instead of being reduced gradually and with a minimum of shock, is given the sudden, painful, and morale-depressing jolt of sharply applied government shutdown and restriction orders. Then Cassandras from Washington, D.C., and "regional" offices begin to make speeches over the radio and statements to the press about the forthcoming shortage and how impossible it will be to avoid it. There is the resulting natural scramble on the part of the public for available stocks in the course of which the Johnny-Come-Latelies fail to get their share, and a tremendous cry is raised by the pressure-group claque (which has lately been demanding that *everything* must be rationed) for dividing up. The government then yields gracefully to "public demand" for rationing and a new set of forms and instructions and legal notices is set in motion at the taxpayer's expense with a prodigious expense in time and irritation, and wasted gasoline, tires, and mountainous paper-work.

The propaganda experts may try to conduct pep rallies in mining towns at taxpayers' expense to stimulate greater production, but radio speeches and rallies with alluring movie stars will not equal in effectiveness the stimulation of an efficient new refrigerator, whose purchase has been looked forward to for several years, a better stove in the kitchen, a time- and labor-saving washing machine in the laundry, or a pressure cooker to aid in canning and cooking and to save time and fuel. These appliances rank high in the list of consumer wants.

To the cry that these appliances use scarce materials, the answer is that if their manufacture on a limited scale increases the effectiveness of the war effort on the whole, then wise planners would permit them to be made. We can afford steel for refrigerators if we can afford 35,000 government propaganda experts to spread "morale," and "sell the war effort." In any event, there needs to be a little better understanding on the part of our planners of the importance of keeping the home fires burning. The war industries very properly do come first, but civilian industries must have consideration.

Next time anyone says we just can't afford to allow even scraps of waste metal to be used for making children's toys, or steel pipe to be bought for a plumbing job, ask him how a nation so poor in materials and man power can possibly afford a bill of nearly *$150,000,000 a year for travel* by steamship, train, plane and automobile of federal employees on "government business." (Two non-military departments of the government used over $16,000,000 each for travel in a recent year.) Time enough to start living on the German, Italian, or Japanese level of consumer incomes when Washington officialdom starts doing without its peace-time luxuries of propaganda, and sociologic job-making agencies like the National Youth Administration and the *Surplus* Commodities Corporation. Consumers have a right to insist that the "conversion" of our resources and methods to the lean wartime level of economy begin in the government itself. If our economy can't afford stoves and other essential heating and cooking appliances, and sewing machines, it surely cannot afford the luxury of high-salaried governmental Supervisors of Recreation and of Interpretation, Coordinators of Compliance, nor whole bevies of chiefs, directors, supervisors, consultants, and coordinators of publicity.

When it comes to lopping off unneeded activities and converting to wartime frugality and efficiency, the place to begin "converting" is at the top, in the federal bureaucracy itself. Such transfer of man power and equipment to work directly useful in the war and in the service of consumers remaining on the home front, can greatly strengthen the war effort. Changes of this sort are surely coming; the public temper plainly demands them.

VIEWPOINT 3

"The passage of a national service act . . . would in fact shorten the war and save life."

Mandatory National Service Legislation Should Be Passed

Warren H. Atherton (1891–1976)

During World War II all men ages 18 to 65 were required to register for the military draft, and approximately ten million were drafted through the Selective Service System. Some Americans suggested that all adults in America—men and women—be required to register for possible conscription into civilian defense work as well. President Franklin D. Roosevelt called for such "national service" legislation in his State of the Union address in 1944.

The following viewpoint in favor of national service is by Warren H. Atherton, national commander of the American Legion, a membership association of American war veterans. Speaking before a Senate committee on February 2, 1944, Atherton argues that the lives of American soldiers are in jeopardy because labor shortages in the United States have slowed production of needed war materials. Voluntary methods, he states, are insufficient for the task of ensuring that the necessary labor for the American war effort is fully utilized. National service legislation would also be a step toward equalizing the sacrifices being made for the war by soldiers and civilians, he argues.

Warren H. Atherton, testimony before the Senate Committee on Military Affairs, February 2, 1944, in *Congressional Digest*, April 1944.

When it is necessary to draft manpower for the armed forces, it is only right and fair that the Nation should impose a correlative obligation on the people who are left behind. Democracy implies equal obligations as well as equal rights, and it is a flouting of democracy to permit a continuance of the present double standard of duty—a standard of compulsion and risk of death for the soldier and of freedom and safety for the civilian. When we fail to adopt a single standard for all we are deviating dangerously from the very principles on which this Nation was founded. While the sacrifice of the civilian can never equal that of his military compatriot, we can certainly call upon him for a commensurate degree of effort. This can only be done through the passage of a national service act which would weld a steel bond of fellowship between our two groups of citizens by establishing a common obligation on both to serve. I know of no other way to remove the growing doubts of our soldiers and sailors as to the support they can expect when they storm the citadel of Europe and as they pursue their relentless drive toward Tokyo. We have no right to give cause for these doubts.

I have stressed the moral necessity for the enactment of a national service law because the [American] Legion is so keenly aware of the close relationship between such a step and the present and future attitude of the men overseas. The passage of a national service act could rest on this necessity alone, but it is also abundantly clear that such a law would in fact shorten the war and save life. It would be the final and most important step in getting the necessary weapons to the fields of battle on time. A few simple and uncontroverted facts demonstrate this beyond a shadow of doubt. Let me give them to you.

1. *Certain essential weapons have not reached our soldiers and sailors on time or in sufficient quantity.* Lack of aviation gasoline has grounded planes that could have given helpless soldiers the necessary air cover and pounded the industrial heart of the Axis. The Army truck program is behind schedule. Landing craft are not coming off production lines in the quantity which our troops require. We have been unable to obtain sufficient radio and radar equipment of the latest design. Our men have been short of planes—cargo planes to evacuate the wounded or to bring in supplies; long-range fighters to protect our fortresses deep over the European Continent; and heavy bombers to heap greater fire and destruction on a partly groggy enemy. We have done well, but not well enough; and not as well as we might have done if we had gone all out. The lack of specific equipment that we could have produced has unquestionably cost us, and is unquestion-

ably now costing us, many casualties.

2. *A large share of our specific failures can be directly attributed to a shortage of manpower.* Trucks have not been manufactured because of a shortage in certain types of forgings and castings—shortages that resulted from a lack of labor in many of our foundries and forge shops. We lost 90 flying fortresses last summer because of manpower difficulties at the Seattle plant of Boeing. Shortages of workers throughout the bearings industry have had their effect upon the production of many types of important mechanized equipment. A scarcity of help in the electronics industry has delayed delivery of many critical radio and radar devices. In fact, shortages of men and women in many specific plants can be concretely demonstrated to have been the limiting production factor.

3. *Far more serious manpower problems threaten war production in the days ahead.* According to War Production Board figures, the over-all war program must be increased in 1944 some 16 per cent above the level achieved in 1943. Aircraft procurement alone must go up more than 70 per cent. This increase must be effected simultaneously with the withdrawal before summer of a million additional men for the armed services, and in the face of our present inability to mobilize labor for certain of our most critical programs. Furthermore, American industry and the American labor force will have to become more flexible and more adaptable to meet the rapidly shifting military requirements of 1944. In 1944 the preliminary skirmishes will be over, and the final crucial battles will begin. We shall have to be in a position to meet, on a moment's notice, the changing needs of our soldiers as they are demonstrated by the course of the battle itself. The field of combat is the greatest laboratory for the development of new weapons, and we can be sure that in the battles to come, more than in any other previous battles, this fact will be demonstrated time and again. Are we now in a position to mobilize a thousand men for a plant which must manufacture some new item needed at once for troops faced with some new Nazi device of destruction? It is plain that we are not. We must also remember the cumulative effect of progressively increasing labor shortages in certain basic industries is likely to have a serious effect on our entire program. Stock piles on which we have previously drawn to make up our production shortages are in some cases approaching the point of exhaustion. Nor can the railroads be expected to operate indefinitely with the same degree of efficiency, with a badly depleted and still sharply declining work force. It is evident that consequent break-downs in equipment, with their resulting delays to transport, can slowly throttle our production machine. The dwindling staffs of certain essential service industries are already hard put to furnish those things upon which the civilian

war worker must depend. I know of no more striking illustration than the plight of the Los Angeles transportation system. More than one-third of its equipment lies idle in car barns and garages solely because of a lack of sufficient operators and maintenance men. What would happen to production at the vast network of aircraft, rubber, gasoline, and other war plants in this area if it should suddenly become necessary to curtail drastically the allocation of gasoline for civilian use? It is plain that the items which our soldiers are not receiving today because of manpower difficulties at home will be multiplied both in kind and in number unless positive measures are taken at once.

Roosevelt and National Service

In his annual message to Congress on January 11, 1944, President Franklin D. Roosevelt came out in favor of national service legislation.

As you know, I have for three years hesitated to recommend a national service act. Today, however, I am convinced of its necessity. Although I believe that we and our allies can win the war without such a measure, I am certain that nothing less than total mobilization of all our resources of manpower and capital will guarantee an earlier victory, and reduce the toll of suffering and sorrow and blood.

I have received a joint recommendation for this law from the heads of the War Department, the Navy Department, and the Maritime Commission. These are the men who bear responsibility for the procurement of the necessary arms and equipment, and for the successful prosecution of the war in the field. They say:

> When the very life of the Nation is in peril the responsibility for service is common to all men and women. In such a time there can be no discrimination between the men and women who are assigned by the Government to its defense at the battle front and the men and women assigned to producing the vital materials essential to successful military operations. A prompt enactment of a national service law would be merely an expression of the universality of this responsibility.

I believe the country will agree that those statements are the solemn truth.

National service is the most democratic way to wage a war. Like selective service for the armed forces, it rests on the obligation of each citizen to serve his Nation to his utmost where he is best qualified.

---

4. *Present and threatened manpower problems are of such a magnitude and such a type that they cannot be solved under present methods.* The manpower problems of today, not alone the infinitely greater ones of tomorrow, are insoluble if we continue with our current approach. The following general facts obvious to anyone who takes the trouble to examine the present manpower situation in

even a casual fashion demonstrate this plainly:

(a) The civilian labor force was 1.7 millions smaller at the end of 1943 than it was at the end of 1942. Present techniques for the handling of manpower have not prevented this reduction.

(b) The total number of women in the labor market declined from July to November by 1.4 millions. Measures currently possible cannot stop this dangerous drift of women from the labor market.

(c) Peacetime turn-over rates of from 2 to 3 per cent had increased to an average of more than 7 per cent in the first ten months of 1943, and in September reached a rate of more than 8 per cent. Most of this turn-over represented voluntary quits. Controls now at our disposal have not stopped this increase.

(d) Since the start of the war there has been only an insignificant change in the aggregate number of persons engaged in trades and services, many of which are wholly nonessential in character. We cannot expect to fight a total war and carry on our normal peacetime activities as well. None of our present methods have succeeded in loosing this vast reservoir of potential war workers.

(e) The number of critical labor market areas has increased to almost 70; that is to the point where nearly every important industrial community finds itself in need of additional workers.

(f) There is a growing tendency for persons in essential war jobs to leave for nonessential positions which seem to offer a better post-war future. This tendency will inevitably be accelerated as people increasingly attach false significance to military victories in battles which are in fact only part of the preliminary rounds. At present we have no means of preventing this dangerous outmigration from war work.

5. *Our manpower problems are easily soluble if we adopt the proper methods.* As the Under-Secretary of War has testified, this Nation with its vast human resources, could easily support an Army of 16,000,000 or more men. We have more than enough individuals to do the job required. There is no over-all manpower shortage. The shortage is in specific plants, industries, and areas. It exists because men who could do war work are doing non-essential work; because women who could do their share are staying at their bridge tables or gossiping in their clubs instead; because workers have been unwilling to move in sufficient numbers from areas of labor surplus to areas of labor shortage; because of the excessive waste of manpower that is resulting from the incredibly high rate of turnover; and because those who are in war jobs are not always putting their shoulders to the wheel. We can solve the manpower problem, but only if we are prepared to alter our approach.

6. *A national service law would solve many of our present manpower difficulties.* National service alone will not solve all our difficul-

ties, but it is the essential, presently lacking element in any solution. Under a national service law we could call upon the idle women and upon the non-essential worker to render service in those places where his services were most needed. We could likewise reduce turn-over in our war plants to a reasonable level. Men and women would be under an obligation to render service where their service would count most. It is the democratic way, and the only effective way, in which our present manpower difficulties can be met. No one has suggested any reasonable alternative that has the slightest possibility of success.

7. *Failure to enact a National Service Act will increase American casualties.* Without a national service act we cannot cure our manpower shortages and with these shortages remaining and increasing we will be unable to produce the weapons which our soldiers need. Without those weapons our soldiers are less able to defend themselves, and less capable of inflicting decisive and paralyzing blows on the enemy. This means a long war—a more costly war.

There are other broad aspects of this problem which should cause us all great concern. We are apt to think of manpower as being a problem solely of the home front and thus overlook the inseparability of the manpower problems of the home front and those of the armed forces. We are apt to think too much in terms of numbers and too little in terms of qualities.

On the early success of our arms in this great war countless lives depend. Are we fighting this war with the men best fitted to bear arms? Are we putting into battle the best Army this country can raise? Those are important questions which deserve careful thought by every citizen.

Why are we taking fathers of 37 today? Why are many men over 30 being inducted? Is it because we do not have younger men at home whom we all know would make better soldiers?

I think the answer is plain. We have not made the best use of our manpower. We have had no effective system of civilian manpower controls under which our men and women can be guided to the jobs in which they can best serve in order that men qualified to fight can be released for service.

We should have adopted a National War Service Act on Pearl Harbor Day. It is never too late, though, to admit a mistake. Let's admit that high prices, high profits, high wages, and high jinks were not the best way to win a total war.

VIEWPOINT 4

"Conscription of labor is a foreign ideology that should not be permitted to take root in America, even in wartime."

Mandatory National Service Legislation Should Not Be Passed

Chamber of Commerce of the United States

In 1944 President Franklin D. Roosevelt proposed the passage of national service legislation that would empower the government to conscript and assign American men and women to jobs deemed essential for America's war effort. Although the legislation (known as the Austin-Wadsworth bill) was supported by some Americans, it was opposed by many, including groups representing business and organized labor. Among the opponents was the Chamber of Commerce of the United States, a national federation of business and trade associations that frequently lobbied Congress. The following viewpoint is excerpted from a report prepared by the federation's committee on governmental affairs. The report contains the following arguments against national service legislation: U.S. industry is successfully creating great quantities of supplies and munitions without government-assigned labor; shortages that do exist should be blamed on conflicting and uncoordinated government policies rather than on American workers; conscripted labor would be a hardship for workers and would lower morale. The opposition to national service legislation proved sufficient to prevent its passage by Congress.

Chamber of Commerce of the United States, Department of Government Affairs, report to the Senate Committee on Military Affairs, February 1944, in *Congressional Digest*, April 1944.

Legislation for compulsory labor service again has the spotlight. It now has received the President's qualified endorsement, in addition to the unqualified approval of the War and Navy Departments and the Maritime Commission. Organized labor, on the other hand, is as vigorously opposed as ever to a labor draft.

This issue does not concern the armed forces and organized labor alone. Every American, and every member of every allied nation as well, has a critical stake in its proper solution.

The United States is the only major nation that still relies on voluntary labor. However, with this system its production record has astonished the world. Its 135,000,000 people make up only one-eighth of those engaged on the allied side. Yet they will supply one of the United Nations' greatest military forces. In addition, they will continue to outbuild the rest of the world in ships and airplanes while producing tremendous quantities of food, tanks, guns, ammunition and other implements of war. There is no reason to believe that our voluntary labor will not continue to excel the draft labor of other nations in production per man-hour.

Any radical changes in a system which has done so much, and upon which so much still depends, should be approached with caution. There should be a most convincing showing of need. Moreover, if serious defects are shown to exist, it should be clearly demonstrated that a labor draft is the best way to solve them. Ill-suited remedies are worse than none at all.

A Bad Idea

A foreign ideology. Conscription of labor is a foreign ideology that should not be permitted to take root in America, even in wartime. Such legislation is nothing but a grant of brute power over the manpower of America.

Imposes involuntary servitude. This bill savors of the involuntary servitude which is prohibited by the Thirteenth Amendment to the Constitution. Men and women are to be conscripted to work in factories and on farms owned by other individuals, necessarily for the profit of the latter.

There is a vast difference between conscription for the armed forces and compulsion to work for a private profit-making employer, even though the employer may be manufacturing essential war needs. Soldiers are conscripted for the direct service of their country, and the Government is responsible for their welfare. The lot of conscripted workers is quite different.

The bill is based on false assumptions. It assumes that we have a unified and balanced war-production program. It also assumes that our current difficulties are due to the unwillingness of substantial numbers of people to enter into such a program.

This ignores the delays that have been brought about by conflicting governmental policies. It ignores the lack of coordination between the War Manpower Commission, the War Production Board, the Army, the Navy and the Maritime Commission. It overlooks the fact that procurement agencies have allocated contracts to areas in which there were not enough people to do the job. It ignores the fact that existing convertible facilities with ready supplies of labor have been by-passed while new factories have been planned and built in areas into which manpower would have to be drawn.

Involuntary Servitude

C.W. Brooks, Republican senator from Illinois, spoke against a national service bill in a March 22, 1944, speech in the Senate.

We still live in a free country under a Constitution guaranteeing a representative republican form of government. Under our system, both labor and private enterprise are producing the greatest supply of war materials ever known in the history of the world. They have brought about the production miracle of the ages—one which has astounded not only our enemies, but our allies as well. Now, to say that any individual shall be conscripted under Government direction to work for any private employer smacks of that involuntary servitude to rid ourselves of which our Nation once engaged in a bitter Civil War.

While 10,000,000 men are away from home in the armed services fighting for American freedom, we, above all others, should defend their wives, sisters, daughters, and families from involuntary servitude and serfdom. Conscription of labor in America would destroy rather than implement our miracle of production, and might well destroy our free country.

All must admit that in order to achieve maximum production the first indispensable is a coordinated and consistent war program administered in a coordinated and consistent manner.

The bill, with its emphasis upon a labor draft, merely diverts attention from the real problems. Its enactment would give a sense of false security. It would complicate, rather than lessen, war problems.

Draft labor less efficient. Compulsory labor service would impair morale. It would take from millions of workers the very essence and meaning of the war and would destroy the enthusiastic zeal and spirit that now mark their efforts.

Workers transferred to a lower wage scale would be inclined to resent it, and would not be the most effective workers there. You can lead a horse to water but you can't make him drink.

If men can be moved around like pawns on a chessboard with good results, why didn't slavery work better?

Industrial Conscription

Would lead to industrial conscription. Not only would labor's zeal be impaired, but a labor draft law would lead inevitably to conscription of capital as well, with damaging effect on initiative and production.

When a worker is drafted and is put in a certain job and told to stay and work there in the service of a private employer who is making a profit, the next step is elimination of the profit-taking private employer. This is inevitable.

Conscripting industry no remedy. Management of industry by Government agencies would interfere dangerously with production. Some corporate boards of directors may seem slow in dealing with management problems. But they are race horses compared with Washington agencies.

Taking over all the war industries of this country in order to enhance production of war materials, with the idea of winning the war, would be one of the most dangerous things that the Government could do.

Discrimination and Favoritism

Would discriminate between assigned workers. The Austin-Wadsworth Bill would perpetuate those inequalities in wages and working conditions which have led workers to leave one industry for another. Employees in the lower-wage positions would be frozen to their jobs as effectively as those in the higher. Moreover, many workers would be transferred from the higher-wage fields and industries to the lower. The former farm hand, now in the shipbuilding or airplane industry, would be returned to the longer hours and lower wages of the farm; the logger to the woods; and the miner to the mines.

Under such a measure, two workers could be taken from the same community and one be sent to a low-wage field or industry and the other to a high-wage field or industry.

There is too much chance for favoritism in such a measure.

All of the advantages of social-security legislation and of the 40-hour week, with its attendant time-and-a-half for overtime, would be guaranteed to those workers assigned to the industries covered by such laws. But no such benefits would be provided for workers assigned to other industries.

There also would be inequalities in the payment of workmen's compensation, depending upon the state to which the worker was sent, in hospitalization for workers (particularly for minority groups), and in unemployment compensation.

Army service involves no such inequalities among selectees.

Other Problems

Could cause loss of voting rights. Transfer of workers could cause many of them to lose their right to vote, since about one-fourth of the states do not permit absentee voting and no provision is made for workers to return to their homes on election day.

Could send workers out of country. The Austin-Wadsworth Bill is not limited to the United States or the continental limits of the United States. Drafted men and women could be sent to any quarter of the globe to work for private employers.

Would destroy labor's rights. Compulsory service legislation would be used as an opening wedge to destroy labor unions, labor's collective bargaining rights, and its seniority rules. The arguments which have been advanced by the bill's proponents on the subject of closed-shop agreements, maintenance-of-membership, and collective bargaining agreements are eloquent on this. Labor's social gains could be destroyed. . . .

The Volunteer System

Our production leads the world. The volunteer system certainly has not failed in the United States. The simple fact is that American war production has been better than that of any other nation, allied or enemy. Not only in agriculture but in industrial products as well, we produce, in general, a greater output per man-hour than any other country.

Magnificent job done. Management and labor have performed a modern miracle in production. Striking reductions have been made in man-hours per cargo ship constructed, as management and labor have hit their stride. Construction time has been reduced from over 1,000,000 man-hours per ship to less than 500,000.

America's production achievements in this and other fields are all the more striking when one considers the short time taken for the changeover from a purely peacetime basis. Labor has clearly demonstrated its patriotism.

VIEWPOINT 5

"If we are to have total war—and that is what we are experiencing at the present time—there is a very definite place for women in it."

Women Should Be Recruited for the Armed Forces

Edith N. Rogers (1881–1960)

During World War I, thirteen thousand women worked in the navy and marines (primarily as clerical workers), and women had been serving alongside military units in the Army Nurse Corps since 1901. During World War II, women were actively recruited for all of the nation's armed forces (albeit for noncombat jobs) for the first time. This development was the focus of several debates.

In May 1941, Edith N. Rogers, a Republican member of Congress representing Massachusetts, introduced a bill establishing the Women's Army Auxiliary Corps (WAAC). After a delay of several months, hearings on the bill were finally held in 1942, a few months after the United States had been attacked in Pearl Harbor and had officially entered the war. In the following viewpoint, excerpted from the *Congressional Record* of March 17, 1942, Rogers argues for her proposed legislation. She asserts that the United States must follow the lead of Great Britain in the wartime utilization of women. She cites letters from women constituents as well as from George C. Marshall, chief of staff of the U.S. Army, supporting the concept of women in the military. She argues that while women volunteers have performed a great service in such areas as spotting enemy aircraft, the U.S. military

Edith N. Rogers, *Congressional Record*, 77th Cong., 2nd sess., March 17, 1942, pp. 2582–84.

needs a more structured and formal program in order to make use of the women who are willing to serve.

Rogers's bill creating the WAAC passed Congress and was signed into law by President Franklin D. Roosevelt on May 15, 1942. In July 1943 the WAAC became the WAC, or Women's Army Corps, after its auxiliary status was removed. A total of 100,000 women served as officers and enlisted personnel in the WAC during World War II, and a greater number served in other branches of the U.S. armed forces.

Almost a year ago I introduced this bill in Congress, on May 28, 1941, but the proposal for an organization of women to serve as noncombatants with the Army of the United States has long been in my mind. So far back as the first World War, when I was in England and France, I saw the need for such an adjunct to our military forces. Great Britain had a well-organized, smoothly operated women's auxiliary during the last war. I was thrown in close contact with them, worked with them myself, and came to appreciate and realize how extremely valuable the auxiliaries are in their performance of tasks for which women are suited or which they can do with equal facility as men. Even then I felt that our military forces should have an auxiliary force—one recognized as official, and one authorized by law to serve with the Army and to be subject to military control. In our first World War we did have women who served and who gave fine service. There were dieticians, physiotherapists, telephone operators—in fact, a number of categories—but their status was vague. Of course, nurses served as a part of our military services. They were not under military control in the strictest sense of the word. They received no compensation of any kind in the event they were sick or injured—and many were. It was a most unsatisfactory arrangement and has been the cause of much dissatisfaction ever since the Armistice. Many Members of Congress have felt as I do, that these women who gave of their service, unselfishly, patriotically, and under conditions comparable to that of men, should have received pay privileges for that service. The knowledge of these heart-breaking cases, the bitterness which some of these loyal, patriotic women felt, was one of the prime factors in my plan for a Women's Army Auxiliary Corps.

In planning the measure I conferred with many persons who had first-hand knowledge of the splendid women's corps in Great Britain. They were most helpful and their suggestions will in great measure enable us to avoid some of the errors and difficulties encountered in bringing the services up to their present state of perfection.

Last May I introduced my bill, H.R. 4906, calling for the establishment of a Women's Army Auxiliary Corps for service with the Army of the United States. It was referred to the Committee on Military Affairs of the House, and the Secretary of War was requested to make a report and submit his recommendations to the chairman of the committee.

The officials of the General Staff at the War Department studied the proposal very carefully, and the Secretary of War did not make public his recommendations until December 24, 1941, when he suggested a few minor changes in the bill and strongly advocated its enactment by Congress. The Chief of Staff, General Marshall, submitted a similar letter, in which he gave his opinion that—

> The Corps would provide a sound and practicable method of meeting military requirements with respect to the employment of women. . . . There are innumerable duties now being performed by soldiers that actually can be done better by women. . . . The efficient use of women for noncombatant service with the Army requires systematic organization and training of this personnel under military supervision and control.

The hearings held before the Military Affairs Committee of the House brought out that the General Staff wants the Corps and needs it at once. It was emphasized that the proposal is a military proposition pure and simple and has nothing whatever to do with civilian defense as that term is commonly used.

In simple language, the bill provides for the voluntary enrollment of women of excellent character, in good physical health, between the ages of 21 and 45 years, and who are citizens of the United States, in the Women's Army Auxiliary Corps for service with the Army of the United States. The term of service is defined in the bill as being for 1 year with the customary proviso that in time of war, or of national emergency the Secretary of War may, by order, extend the term of service to include the period of the war or national emergency, plus not to exceed 6 months. . . .

The auxiliaries, who are comparable to privates in the Army, receive the same pay as an enlisted man, $21 per month for the first 4 months of service and $30 a month thereafter. They are permitted to qualify as specialists and those of the first class would receive $15 per month in addition to their base pay, specialists of the second class, $10 per month additional, and specialists third class, $5 per month additional.

Quarters would be provided for the members of the Corps either on established Army posts, camps, or stations, or when such is not available pay allowances in lieu of these are provided at the rate of $1.15 per day. Similarly, subsistence is furnished, or provided for by allowances when such is not supplied.

The Corps will be a uniformed organization and the Secretary of War is authorized to furnish such uniforms, insignia, and so forth, under the regulations now being used for our Army.

Medical and dental services, hospitalization, and burial allowances in case of death are provided.

A Glorious War Record

This passage from a 1944 book published by the Women's Army Corps (WAC) describes in glowing terms the achievements of military women in World War II.

The Army in warfare today is a vast organization of "specialists" . . .
Pilots and bombardiers and engineers . . . obviously, these are jobs for men.

Stenographers and typists and map makers and telephone operators . . .

Just as obviously, these are jobs for women as well as men.

So the Army takes both men and women specialists and places them where their own particular skills will do the most good. . . .

Clear-headed Wacs handle the high-pressure routine of an overseas headquarters as calmly as if they were in an office back home. Turn out an incredible volume of secret orders, reports, dispatches in record-breaking time, thereby keeping our infantry moving forward.

Wacs serve in Army hospitals, helping wounded men to overcome handicaps and battle shock. Wacs check troop sailing lists, handle V-Mail at the ports of embarkation. Wacs make strategy maps for invading enemy territory.

Wacs decode, file, tabulate, take blood counts, repair cameras and radios, issue supplies to men bound for overseas. Wacs do 239 Army jobs.

And above all, Wacs do every job—little or big—with a thrilling competence that awakens respect in the eyes of even the ablest G.I.

For wherever they serve—around the world and back—Wacs are doing a job. A gallant, soldier's job. Making a glorious war record!

In the event of injury in line of duty, or of illness, members of the Corps would be entitled to the same benefits prescribed by law for civilian employees of the United States Government, such jurisdiction to rest in the United States Employees' Compensation Commission.

The measure provides also for the establishment and maintenance of schools for the training of candidates for officers of the Corps. While attending such schools, candidates will receive pay at the rate of $50 per month, and will be furnished living quarters, uniforms, medical and dental services, medicines, medical and hospital supplies, hospitalization, subsistence, and necessary school supplies.

It is expressly provided that the corps shall not be a part of the Army, but it shall be the only women's organization authorized to serve with the Army, exclusive of the Army Nurse Corps. In order to protect the Army Nurse Corps a clause is inserted in the bill providing that nurses shall not be enrolled in the Women's Army Auxiliary Corps, and nothing in this act shall be constructed to affect or change the Army Nurse Corps as now established by law.

Authorization is given to the Secretary of War to prepare and issue regulations, rules, and orders and to employ any and all the facilities of the War Department and of the Army of the United States to carry out the provisions of the act.

Members of the corps are not subject to court martial, but shall be subject to disciplinary regulations which the Secretary of War may prescribe. The officers of the General Staff feel that discipline can be maintained under such regulations, with the worst punishment being a bad conduct discharge, a discharge without honor.

Public Reaction

There has been a tremendous, spontaneous, widespread approval of this proposal. I have received thousands of letters from women in every State of the Union—women who are anxious and eager to serve, who want to enroll at once. Significantly, almost all of these letters are from women who are not seeking the higher positions in the corps, but who wish to enroll as auxiliaries and prove their worth and ability through their service.

Two of these letters follow:

SANTA FE, N. MEX.

DEAR MRS. ROGERS: I see by the papers that you are urging the House to give us a chance to work for America, too. By us, I mean the young women of America who want so much to do war work but are unable to do much, as we have to make our own living, We are young, strong, and anxious to do what we can. I sincerely hope you can make the men see it our way. As you say, the women of England are doing a tremendous job. And so can we.

Sincerely,

———— ————.

————

WASHINGTON, D.C., *March 16, 1942.*

HON. EDITH NOURSE ROGERS,
   United States House of Representatives, Washington, D. C.

DEAR EDITH: You have long known of my interest in and enthusiasm for your projected Women's Auxiliary Corps for the

Army; but, as the bill goes up for final vote, I want to tell you that because of what I saw on my recent trip through the West and South, I have come to realize an added importance to your idea—

And this is it:

The women of this country are being thwarted in their great eagerness to help and share in the national war effort, because no national plan for women's activities has been produced. Consequently this tremendous reservoir of ability and usefulness has, to a great extent, remained untapped and undirected. The force is so great, however—the desire to serve and be of use so irresistible that it has broken through the dam of national indifference and rushed into whatever channels of activity seemed to offer opportunities of service. The result is that in almost every locality I visited I found duplication of effort, misdirected energy and—most regrettable of all—mounting jealousy and ill feeling between the different groups. Furthermore, while certain activities were beings greatly overdone, others—and these the most important in our war effort, such as salvage, conservation, planting, and so forth—were, in default of a national program and direction, being almost totally neglected.

Everywhere I found confusion, bewilderment, and dismay on the part of women that their energy and ability to help in the war effort were not being recognized and focused in a national program. You know so well how shattering this state of mind is to morale.

Therefore I see in your project a value beyond the assistance the corps will undoubtedly bring to the Army; I see it providing an urgently needed support to the morale of the Nation. It creates the first chance which has been given to American women in this war to share directly in the war effort on a national plan under the direction and discipline of a Government agency.

In this time of great stress, your plan will prove, as England has proved, that the strongest shock-absorber against the strain and worries of war is the steadying force of needed service efficiently performed.

I shall count it a privilege to be helpful in any way in the development and carrying out of your splendid idea.

> Yours ever,
>
> HELEN WOODS.
> (Mrs. Arthur Woods.)

It is remarkable that little or no opposition has been made to the measure itself. The only protests of a material nature I have received have been from women who are either too young or too old to qualify under the age limitations set forth in the bill. These age limits—21 to 45 years—were set by the War Department officials as being most satisfactory for the needs of the service. There is no age limit prescribed for officers, but undoubtedly the Secretary of War will fix these by regulation.

Limitations of Volunteers

No limitation is placed upon the size of the corps. In my first bill, H.R. 4906, I had a limitation of 25,000 members. However, the Secretary of War requested in his letter to the chairman of the Military Affairs Committee that size limitations be omitted, as the size of the organization would depend upon military requirements and cannot be determined at the present time. When I placed a limitation of 25,000 in the first bill, we were not at war, and I felt that if a corps of this size were authorized it would provide a basis for expansion and development. In the present bill the strength is left to the discretion of the President. In the testimony before the Military Affairs Committee the General Staff officers pointed out that 12,500 auxiliaries were needed at once, 9,700 of these to be used in the aircraft-warning service. At the present time the Interceptor Command of the United States Army is using about 6,000 women in the information or filter centers of that service. These women are volunteers, giving their services patriotically and unselfishly. They have done a fine job, and the War Department and the country at large are exceedingly grateful to them. It is pointed out, however, that it is vital to efficiency and to safety that the Army have military control over such employees. To illustrate the point, at the present time if Mrs. Smith, who is a plotter in one of the stations, found that she could not be on duty tomorrow afternoon because of some family duty requiring her presence at home, she could call the station and say that she could not be there, and the Army authorities could do nothing about it. In the case of the Women's Army Auxiliary Corps its members would be on duty, under the discipline and control of the Army authorities just as a soldier would be at any time, day or night. The War Department feels that the aircraft-warning service is much too important to leave to voluntary service without strict military control. In believing this it does not in any way cast discredit upon or minimize the fine work of the volunteers who have served so faithfully and so well. It is a matter of organization, discipline, training, and military control, and the big item is control. If women are to be used on a military basis, you have got to have military control. The information and filter centers are highly organized installations, and a large part of the work done there can be done better, according to experts, by women than by men. It is a service in which speed is the prime essential—where a matter of a few seconds may mean the difference between life and death. In Great Britain it has been demonstrated time and again that women are faster, more alert, in this work than is the case with their brothers. Thus it is extremely essential that irregular attendance and excessive turn-over in personnel be eliminated in time of war in order to have a perfectly functioning, smooth organization under strict military control.

In addition to the needs of the Aircraft Warning Service, the members of the Women's Army Auxiliary Corps could be assigned as clerks, machine operators, telephone, telegraph, teletype, and switchboard operators, pharmacists, dieticians, hostesses, librarians, theater employees, welfare workers, post exchange employees, cooks, stewardesses, laundry workers, and messengers, or in any capacity which is noncombatant. . . .

I wish with all my heart I could read to you many of the letters I have received. They are so sincere, so patriotic, so eager. One of them is typical, and I will read a part of it here:

> MY DEAR MRS. ROGERS: I have read and watched with a great deal of interest the comments and discussions concerning your bill for a Women's Army Auxiliary Corps, in fact I wrote to the War Department trying to obtain information about it, and offering my services. The Army wants about 12,000 women for certain work. They are more adaptable to these jobs than men, so why do we have to have so much fuss and argument over this bill? I suppose the men think all we want is to get into a uniform. Perhaps they don't know that we realize the seriousness of the situation. They don't need to worry. I have a son, 16 years old in December, and all he talks of is getting in the Navy. I have a nephew on the Burma Road. I have two very dear cousins—handsome boys, over 6 feet tall—also two other people I love very much, who are in the Army in Florida. So I guess we women realize the situation and only want to help, and we can if we are allowed. During the World War I took a man's place as a telegraph operator. After the depression I took up telephone operating, which I am now doing. I feel equal to instructing in either type of work. Your bill is right; fight for it, and let us hope it passes. . . . I married a Twenty-sixth Division man. I saw him die for over 7 months. I hate this war and if we women can release men to fight why should we be held back? I wish you success. This is a poor effort to express what I feel, but I am sure there are plenty more who feel the same way.

If we are to have total war—and that is what we are experiencing at the present time—there is a very definite place for women in it. Modern war recognizes no limitations of battlefields, no gender of its participants. To win a total war every resource, every service must be utilized.

"War is a hard, cruel, killing business and until necessity demands, I cannot bring myself to believe that the efficiency of the fighting men will be improved by women in the fighting force."

Women Should Not Be Recruited for the Armed Forces

Clare Hoffman (1875–1967)

Clare Hoffman, a Republican congressman from Michigan, was one of the few vocal opponents of legislation to create the Women's Army Auxiliary Corps (WAAC) in 1942. The following viewpoint is excerpted from his contribution to the debate over the bill in Congress on March 17, 1942, and it includes an exchange between Hoffman and the bill's sponsor, Congresswoman Edith N. Rogers of Massachusetts. Hoffman argues that women can and should make contributions to America's war effort without necessarily joining the military, and he asserts that Rogers's legislation will impair America's armed forces.

Despite the opposition of Hoffman and others, the WAAC (later WAC, or Women's Army Corps) was passed by Congress. The nation's other armed forces followed suit in recruiting women; a total of approximately 240,000 women served in the WAC, the WAVES (Women Accepted for Volunteer Emergency Service in the Navy), and in other military branches, working as clerks, technicians, jeep drivers, and other noncombat positions. Unlike men, however, women during World War II were not subject to the military draft.

Clare Hoffman, *Congressional Record*, 77th Cong., 2nd sess., March 17, 1942, pp. 2593–94.

From the time of the Molly Pitcher episode of the Revolutionary War up to the present moment no one has ever questioned either the courage or the loyalty or the willingness to sacrifice of any of our women. On that day when her husband fell, Molly stepped forward and served in his place in the battle line. What are we doing now? People throughout the country are aware of the fact that we are in a war, but being here day after day I sometimes doubt whether or not the Members of Congress are aware of that fact. I sometimes doubt whether we want to take the shortest, straightest, the hard road to ultimate victory whether or not we are not inclined at times to follow a roundabout way, and if this is not one of those roundabout ways.

A Diversion

To me this bill is not a straightforward, plain, unvarnished, undecorated war measure which, put into effect, will increase the effective fighting force of our Army. To me it is a diversion, a detour from the straight and narrow road. Soldiers, whether we like it or not are killers, that is their profession, that is their business.

Women, thank God, are not killers. It is the soldier's business to go forward, even though his comrade falls wounded by his side. Heartlessly because he must, he leaves that comrade, even though he be his own brother or boyhood friend and goes on. His brother may drop and, because of his wound being unattended, die. The soldier may know this, nevertheless he presses forward. But let an arm or a leg be shot from one of these women, serving with the armed force, and who is there in the Army that will leave that woman to die because of a lack of a few moments first-aid attention? Where is the man fighting in a foreign land with these women in the camps or behind the battle line who will not shudder and hesitate if the tide turns against him and he knows that the women in the armed force are to become the prisoners, the slaves, or worse of the Nazis or the Japs or their island allies?

War is a hard, cruel, killing business and until necessity demands, I cannot bring myself to believe that the efficiency of the fighting men will be improved by women in the fighting force. Moreover this bill will add a cost to the maintenance of the fighting force out of all proportion to the service rendered. There must be separate and distinct uniforms, there must be separate barracks and certainly the merciless disciplining of the Army must be tempered to the punishment of the few women who will violate army regulations.

Again, is there anyone here, with experience, who believes for one moment that a woman officer, and there will be many of them, will obtain that same unquestioning obedience to her orders from other women in the service which men yield to their superiors?

Women as a class have not been trained to yield unquestioning obedience to what may seem unnecessary or foolish orders. They, and rightly, have come to expect from all men consideration, respect for their feelings, a yielding to their wishes and desires, consideration not given by men to other men. The habits the beliefs, the standards, which have grown out of years of association and experience, cannot, however willing the spirit or great the desire, be put aside or obliterated by the act of volunteering or by induction into the Army.

Women Needed at Home

Before this war is over there will [be] a thousand jobs that women desiring to serve their country can fill as well as or better than men. Before we are through, if we are to wage war in the uttermost corners of the earth, we will need our men, and all our men, in the fighting force. Here at home women will be called upon to take over the jobs and perform the tasks which men must leave when they step into armed service.

Just as vital to our success as are fighting men are those behind the fighting lines. There must be food to eat, clothing to wear, guns and ammunition, and all the tools of war. With the task that confronts us, keeping in mind the losses which we have sustained, it must be evident to everyone that the fighting men must be supported and that to do that adequately our manpower alone is not sufficient. Present events indicate that there will be urgent need for women to take the places of men on the farms, in industry, when those men are called to the battle line.

I realize that the women who are to be called to service under this bill are limited in number, but it is the opening wedge, and past experience tells us that a matter of this kind once entered into there is no turning back. Take the women into the armed service, in any appreciable number, who then will maintain the home fires; who will do the cooking, the washing, the mending, the humble homey tasks to which every woman has devoted herself; who will rear and nurture the children; who will teach them patriotism and loyalty; who will make men of them, so that, when their day comes, they too, may march away to war?

To me this bill seems to strike at and destroy the very foundation—the base—which supports and maintains our fighting men. This war, as all outside of Washington now realize, is not a social event; in it teas, dances, card parties, amusements generally play little, if any part. This war is a dirty, a bloody, a cruel, a horrifying business, and the spirit of our fighting men should not be weakened by placing at their side women they would un-consciously irresistibly protect and defend at the expense of the military objective.

Women and War

A May 27, 1942, editorial in the magazine Commonweal *raises questions about the implications of recruiting women soldiers.*

Current projects and actions revolving about the relation of the country's women to the country's war invite us to clear our minds in regard to the general truths involved. . . . Representative Edith Nourse Rogers's bill creating a Women's Army Auxiliary Corps of 150,000, to perform duties behind the lines and thereby release men for combat, has passed the House by the very respectable majority of 249 to 86. There can be no objection to these or any similar projects in such an abnormal period of national need as the present, if they are furthered in a way which does not obscure the true reality. This reality is simply that women, in the mass, have duties and functions which are at the opposite pole from those of a military body, and even more important to civilization. That women have the will and the aptitude to do, or learn to do, anything that needs to be done to keep the country afloat in wartime, needs no proving. The periphery, so to speak, of the feminine group does represent a potential reserve which the nation can and should call upon in the struggle that is beginning to touch all our lives. But the core of the feminine group is and must remain the women on the home front; and this truth moreover must be respected and reflected in all the wartime thinking of the nation. If the enthusiasm for uniforms and the whole paraphernalia of military service, natural enough perhaps in the limited groups of women involved, were allowed to infect our general thinking about women, to the obscuring of their less picturesque but absolutely vital activity in the home, it would be a disaster indeed. Women as a group bear one vital, irremovable hazard; it is not wise for society to disturb the balance by giving them another. What the general, deep instinct about this is could be ascertained by polling the men in service, for instance, on the subject of women soldiers.

Is there any service which a woman could render under this bill which she cannot render today without joining the Army?

Mrs. Rogers of Massachusetts: Will the gentleman yield?

Mr. Hoffman: I yield to the gentlewoman.

Mrs. Rogers of Massachusetts: The Army has stated repeatedly that it is vital to have women at the filter stations and our air-raid stations.

Mr. Hoffman: Well, bless your dear heart, there is no reason why they cannot serve in the filter and air-raid stations now. If the men in the Army need anything, they need the loyal support of the women at home. You take a poll of the honest-to-goodness women at home, the women who have families, the women who sew on the buttons, do the cooking, mend the clothing, do the washing, and you will find there is where they want to stay—in the homes. There and when the time comes in the fields and factories, where many are serving today; there and in the hospitals and on the lines of supply and communication—in a hundred places where they can be of more real service than with the fighting men.

Mrs. Rogers of Massachusetts: Will the gentleman yield?

Mr. Hoffman: No; I cannot yield. I know the spirit that moves this body today. You ask, am I going to vote for this bill. What else can I do? If I vote against any bill that is requested by the administration, the War Department, the Navy Department, or the Air Corps, I will be classified as one who opposes the war effort. But I venture to suggest that if we could get a secret expression or vote on this bill the Members of the House would turn the bill down today or at any other time it came up, because from what I have heard as Members expressed themselves privately, they do not believe it will actually aid in the war effort. More than one Member has said in substance that he would vote for the bill, but he hoped the Creator would forgive him. Believing as I do that the passage of the bill will hinder, not help—realizing the political retribution and the personal abuse that will follow—putting the welfare of my country first, I must vote against the bill.

VIEWPOINT 7

"This country is sending out a nation-wide appeal for woman power. . . . Folding bandages, selling war bonds, collecting books for the soldiers is not enough."

Women Are Not Contributing Their Share to the War Effort

Patricia Davidson Guinan (dates unknown)

During World War II a concerted public campaign was launched to encourage women to contribute to the war effort by entering the workforce. Over the course of the war 6 million women did so, raising the total number of women workers to 19 million. Not only did the proportion of women in the labor force grow from one-fourth of the total number of American workers in 1940 to one-third in 1945, but large numbers of women entered jobs previously dominated by men. Despite this trend, however, some people questioned whether American women were doing enough for the war effort.

The following viewpoint is taken from a September 1943 article in *House Beautiful* by Patricia Davidson Guinan, one of the magazine's editors. Introduced by the magazine as a "working wife and mother" who "speaks plainly on the subject of women's contribution to the winning of the war," Guinan argues that many women are not delivering their share, and that they represent an untapped source of labor that could conceivably shorten the war.

Women are often wonderful, always unpredictable, and sometimes disappointing.

In peacetime we are the backbone of the nation. We are the ones whom men come home to for comfort and hot meals and chatter about the children. And that's what peace is.

But war is something else again. It is men in uniform away from home, being lonesome and whistling in the dark, being scared and sticking to their guns. It is also building planes and tanks and engines and all kinds of things with desperate speed, with manpower that is not enough. It is a nation baring its teeth. It is a time when amenities and comfort don't come first. And war is today. This very minute.

A Cause for Shame

Not so long ago we women could be proud of the job we were doing of raising children, of keeping house, of entertaining gracefully, of taking part in civic activities. But now we are needed for a bigger job, gigantic in scope, ruthless in its demands. Yet our overall response to our 1943–44 role in history has been a cause for deep and bitter shame.

Why, I wonder, haven't we faced, realistically the terrifying fact of global war, with the same calm courage with which the women in Russia, England, China have answered their country's call for help? The easy answer is a geographical one. We're far from the front. No drone of enemy planes interrupts our peaceful nights and we've never known what it's like to be without the four freedoms we're fighting for.

But the real answer goes deeper than that. We're soft from resting too long on our laurels. As Americans we are known as the best-dressed women in the world, our children the most privileged, our husbands the most generous providers. We take for granted our right to sleep safely in our beds, to sit down to well-balanced meals, to go to church on Sunday, and to send letters to our Congressmen. Since our ways are so easy, it is the harder to change them. Because we cry at a war movie, tingle at a parade, throw back our shoulders as we stand for the Star Spangled Banner, we think we're a nation of Molly Pitchers incarnate. But we're not.

And please God, let us realize that we're not—before it's too late.

This country is sending out a nation-wide appeal for woman power. There are 13 million of us, without children to care for, who could take jobs. And there are 8 million of us, without children sufficiently grown to permit us to work. But we are so accustomed to hearing figures in the millions talked about in the press and over dinner tables that our minds have become numb to their implication. It's hard to reduce such magnitude to personal dimensions. But if you really want to realize the urgency of the need for women like you and me to fill full-time war jobs, think of your own efforts to find a cleaning woman or a maid. Think of the many times you have thought that if you didn't get someone, anyone, to help you take care of the children, cook, clean, wash, and iron, you simply couldn't go on. Multiply that desperation a thousandfold and you will understand why it is no longer a question of giving a few hours a week to volunteer work. Folding bandages, selling war bonds, collecting books for the soldiers is not enough. If you sat down and budgeted your time as conscientiously as you budget your housekeeping money or your ration points, could you honestly say that you're doing a job commensurate with the life given by the boy down the street who was reported killed in action?

The Duty of Women

In these passages excerpted from a November 1943 article in Woman's Home Companion, *noted author and political figure Clare Booth Luce describes what she believes to be the duties of American women both during and after the war.*

American women are justifiably proud of their sisters and they like to be told, which is no more than the truth, that if they had not stepped into these fields, victory would be, if not impossible, many long and bloody years in coming.

But American women do not like nearly so much to be told that although millions of women have done a superb job, hundreds of thousands are still holding back in the war effort. They do not like to be told that today every able-bodied woman without small children or helpless dependents who is not doing an essential job in the nation's economy, is just as much of a slacker as any able-bodied man in the community without children who avoids an essential war job or wearing the uniform of his country. This, however, is the fact. For every hour that some woman idles, by that very hour is the day of victory postponed for America. . . .

And when victory comes, what then shall become of the women who helped so overwhelmingly to win it? What shall the women in war work do then, when the men are coming home from the battlefields and looking for their old jobs or for new jobs in civilian economy? The answer is simple: All patriotic women who are now holding down soldiers' jobs in factory or field office, who do not need their wages for self-support or the support of dependents, will return to their most essential peacetime job: the resolidifying, expansion and strengthening of their war-disrupted families.

There is today an appallingly large group that represents an untapped source of woman power. Since this country has, as yet, no female conscription laws to guide us in deciding who *should* be working, we must be extra careful that we don't hide behind excuses and good intentions. We must be our own sternest critics. To do this, ask yourself such questions as these: Do you start your day hours after the happier and wiser band of women arrive behind their desks or machines? Do you smugly assert that you would not work for pay because you don't need the money? Do you claim that your children need your full time and then spend the afternoon gossiping over a bridge table? Do you refuse to get a defense job because you think ladies aren't supposed to know anything about machines?

Dear ladies, up in your ivory towers, do you have to be bombed to wake up? You who are unmarried and sound of mind and body: what excuse will you give to your future husband when he returns to tell you of the tools of war he needed that didn't come? And you who have half-grown or adolescent children: what will they think of you when they grasp the meaning of the world mess we have got ourselves into? Will the fact that you brought your children into this world be enough in their eyes?

It's not easy to give up a pleasant way of life, voluntarily, for a way that is hard and demanding and glory-free. It's not easy, that is, *unless* you can face the realities of the world you are living in. If you do face these truths then it *is* easy. For you get what you pay for. And if you work at winning this war, if you turn a deaf ear to all the inconsequential reasons why you can't take a real job, then you'll find, after it's all over, your peacetime role will have become sweeter for the waiting—even than it is now.

Necessary Jobs

Here is a list of some necessary civilian jobs for women. All the jobs mentioned are those which the War Manpower Commission considers vital and in which women already have begun to serve. They also represent work for which women are now needed and will be needed increasingly in the next few months.

In Agriculture: Canning plant worker, bottler, washer, laboratory worker on dairy farm, fruit picker, helper on poultry or truck farm, lumber worker, meat packing plant worker. In Communications: Radio technician, telegraph messenger, telegraph, telephone and teletype operators. In Education: Child psychologist, librarian, nursery school attendant, playground supervisor, school clerk or stenographer, social worker, teacher. In Medical Care: Clinic attendant, dietitian, dental hygienist, hospital attendant, laboratory technician, medical social worker, public health, hospital, and industrial nurses, physiotherapist, receptionist, assistant in doctors' or dentists' offices. In Publishing: Journalist (editor or reporter), linotype operator, news photographer, proofreader. In Restaurants, etc: Dietitian, elevator operator, floor supervisor, food buyer, hotel housekeeper, room clerk, switch board operator. In Retail Trade: Baker, butcher, department store clerk, drug store clerk, grocery store women (clerk, cashier or delivery), stock clerk, wrapper. In Service Trades: Clothes repair service, electrician, seamstress, tailor. In Technical Work: Chemist, engineer, industrial nutritionist, map maker. In Transportation: Baggage clerk, bus driver, commercial airlines worker, railroad conductor, filling station attendant, garage mechanic, information clerk, milk truck driver, motorman on trolley, taxi driver, ticket taker at railroad station. In "White Collar" Work: Bank clerk and teller, bookkeeper, cashier, file clerk, stenographer, typist.

VIEWPOINT 8

"I solemnly charge that the war is being slowed down here in America by the failure of the government and private enterprise alike to use women's brains and training."

Government and Industry are Underutilizing Women

Minnie L. Maffett (1882–1964)

Many American women found their roles and responsibilities changed by World War II. Because of patriotism, high wartime wages, or both, millions of women entered the workforce, often in previously male-dominated areas such as shipyards and factories. Some Americans, however, argued that women could and should do even more to contribute to the war effort.

The following viewpoint is taken from an address by Minnie L. Maffett, then president of the National Federation of Business and Professional Women's Clubs, given at the organization's annual conference meeting on July 8, 1943. In her speech, reprinted in the August 1943 issue of the federation's magazine *Independent Woman*, Maffett refutes the charge that women are not doing enough for the war. She contends that women have instead been held back by government policies and by the reluctance of some employers to hire women. She calls for an end to discriminatory practices and sexist prejudices that, she asserts, are preventing American women from being fully utilized.

Minnie L. Maffett, "Under-use of Womanpower Slows War Effort," *Independent Woman*, August 1943.

The bursting of bombs over Pearl Harbor on that tragic Sunday of December 7 altered the lives and futures of the people of America as has no other event in our national history. Enormous as these changes have been to date, it is apparent that they are the prelude only to ones of greater magnitude with which we must be prepared to cope.

If we compare this day in July, 1943, with December 7, 1941, we can find much to be proud of, much to be thankful for—and possibly much more to be desired. Will we be able, when our men return, to meet them as equals in this fight for freedom, and to look the wounded and the disabled squarely in the eye? Can we say to them on that day, which we hope will not be too distant, *"You have done your utmost, and we have given to the extreme of our capacities, too!"* Can the women of this country—and of this Federation—say that? Unquestionably, so far as we have been permitted to participate in the war effort, we can, for the most part, answer "Yes."

Always before in the history of this country, womanpower has been called upon to help win its wars. During the Civil War, women were called upon to help care for the wounded. During the first World War women rendered valiant and patriotic service. Great as was their contribution at that time, it seems slight now compared to that of the fifteen million women who are today working with hand and head—often at jobs previously undreamed of.

Many more will be at their sides before victory comes to us. Never before in the history of this country have women been called upon to help in a war in such stupendous numbers—especially in the field of production. In 1943, of the 52,000,000 adult women in the country, 18,000,000 will be needed in jobs for victory and in war production, and two-thirds of them will be needed, and are being urged, to take up necessary civilian occupations.

Every day more women are enlisting in the WAC [Women's Army Corps], the WAVES [Women Accepted for Volunteer Emergency Service in the Navy], the Marines, the SPARS [Coast Guard], the WAFS [Women's Air Ferrying Squadron]; in civilian defense, in even greater numbers.

In industry, women are replacing men in many new types of jobs in factory and plant. In government offices and war emergency departments, they are steadily increasing in numbers. On April 30, 1943, more than 891,000 women were employed in the executive branch of the government alone, some of them holding important professional jobs.

Yet many persons, in the very breath with which they declare this to be a people's war in which every man, woman and child is essential to victory, betray a sex antagonism that is as old as time, and that, at this time, should be as dead as yesterday.

Utilizing Womanpower

Our nation has failed signally in regard to the utilization of its womanpower. It has failed in that women are not yet permitted in any way to help direct the policies of government. The higher powers—whoever they may be and however they got that way—evidently think the women of this nation are not yet ripe for such recognition, and that they are still unqualified mentally, emotionally, and by lack of experience to take part in the national counsels.

Facts—if they are considered—prove otherwise. Convincing evidence during the past year and a half especially shows that women can do their part side by side with men—and with no favors asked.

Despite the good showing women have made, and despite much other convincing evidence as to their ability, loyalty and efficiency, they have not been trained by experience to help administer public affairs to any appreciable extent. This may come yet, but if it does, it will not be through wishful hoping, but by more aggressive action than we have shown to date.

We have elected few women to important public posts, only a handful to Congress, and just one to our august Senate. None has ever been on the Supreme Court Bench; no large city system of schools has a woman superintendent and, I think I am entirely correct in saying, no state university, though supported by public funds, has ever had a woman president.

Last year at the Denver Board meeting I was obliged to report to you an almost complete absence of women in policy-making posts in our national government. Again, I will refer to the roster taken from the latest pamphlet issued by the government as evidence that women have made only the slightest advance during the past year in securing a voice in shaping the affairs of this nation—either in the capital or elsewhere in the country. In the various war emergency agencies, the places of importance held by women at this time are far from impressive.

We must point with pride, however, to the fact that there is a Woman's Advisory Committee to the War Manpower Commission, under the direction of our own first vice-president, Margaret A. Hickey. True—she has the honor of sitting on the National Management-Labor Policy Committee of the War Manpower Commission. *But she has no vote.* She has a fine group of women on her committee, and it is to be hoped that they make their presence felt. Regionally, the War Manpower Commission has appointed at least one woman as Regional Director. In some areas, too, I understand, women advisory committees have been appointed. Seven women serve as Area Directors of the War Manpower Commission.

Gains Since 1942

Women have made a slight gain over the figures quoted last year. But the gain is very slight indeed when you consider the greater number of offices and the increased number of officials now helping in the war emergency. We want women on these committees and commissions to have voices as well as ears. I challenge you in your states, in your communities, to push to the front women who have good records in management and in labor, and urge their appointment to places with *votes* such as the Area Management-Labor Committees of the War Manpower Commission. It is up to you to help improve this situation, and I urge you to sound the alert *now*.

This Ding Darling cartoon, "Letting the Genie Out of the Bottle," examines how World War II affected traditional gender roles.

As to the place of women in professional posts, the picture is a little brighter. Women are filling many important professional assignments. They are not only being sought, but also being urged

176

to take training for various professional grades.

The list of professional women who are employed, both in Washington and throughout the country, is impressive. We have been able to send more than 450 women of professional grade into various departments where they are earning from $4,500 to $10,000 a year. Here we have made progress. Women are taking up many more unusual professions, especially in the fields of science, and are making good in them. The tremendous variety of the professional skills held by women and the great demand for women having specialized training is most impressive. Indeed, there are not nearly enough women to meet the demand that exists now, and which will certainly become greater as the war goes on.

After the War

But what of the demand for women's services *after* the war? An organization like ours must see that opportunities for a woman to use her talents are never again closed. Moreover, every woman in a high position must be made to feel that she owes it to all women who are coming after her to hold the door open. In our clubs we must take our places with organizations that are concerned with postwar economic planning, to make certain that in that planning, provision is made for jobs for both men and women. Broad expansion in industry and better systems of distribution must be developed if we are to be honest and fair to the old employees, the millions of new recruits, and the ten million returning soldiers after the war is ended.

The magazine, *Fortune,* has made recently an exhaustive survey of the womanpower of the nation. It tells us that more than 3,000,000 women must be recruited this year in fewer than 200 cities, and that if the women do not volunteer they may be drafted.

It is evident that this army of 3,000,000 new workers must be recruited, to a large extent, from the housewives of the nation, and largely from those living in cities and without dependent children. After eliminating mothers with children under sixteen, there is still left twelve million women.

Through its War Workers Recruiting Service Project, the Federation this year has endeavored to make voluntary recruitment a success. But in their work in communities, clubs have found it necessary to break down the employer's reluctance to employ women at all, or, more particularly, older women.

Equal pay for comparable work, is one of the goals we, in this Federation, have long sought to reach. In the industrial world this equality is fast becoming a standard practice in line with the ruling of the National War Manpower Board. Adjustments to equalize the rate of pay between men and women for comparable work may still be made under the hold-the-line executive order of April 8, 1943, since it would, in no sense, raise wages for a specific group, but would only establish the principle of equal pay for the job done regardless of sex.

I solemnly charge that the war is being slowed down here in America by the failure of the government and private enterprise alike to use women's brains and training in their specialized fields. Women must be used now, too, in planning for postwar economic, social, and political development at home and abroad.

This is a big order, but a strong, unselfish, and unified Federation can do much to crystallize public opinion in favor of this policy. Your potential is unlimited. Your responsibility is correspondingly great. It is up to you what you will do with it.

CHAPTER 4

Minorities and World War II

Chapter Preface

World War II brought about tremendous changes, both positive and negative, for many members of America's minority groups. The viewpoints in this chapter focus on two such peoples: blacks and Japanese Americans.

About one in ten Americans in 1940 were black and as such were treated in most parts of the United States as second-class citizens or worse. "Our war," concluded one black newspaper, "is not against Hitler in Europe but against the Hitlers in America." While many African Americans might have agreed with this sentiment to some extent, most did not conclude that the conflict was only a "white man's war." Many black organizations and individuals instead adopted the "Double V" slogan for victory over both fascism abroad and racism at home. African American leaders argued that America's total war mobilization could not afford to mistreat or underutilize this group of Americans.

During the war approximately 1 million African Americans were in the U.S. military, half of whom served overseas. In addition, numerous blacks found new jobs in defense industries. During the 1940s about 1 million blacks left the South (many from isolated and impoverished situations) to seek employment in other parts of the country.

Some progress was made during World War II against racial segregation and discrimination within both industry and the American military—usually in direct response to black political activism. When labor organizer A. Philip Randolph threatened to lead a mass demonstration of blacks in Washington, D.C., in 1941, President Franklin D. Roosevelt signed an executive order forbidding racial discrimination in defense industries and established the Fair Employment Practices Commission. Similar political pressure caused branches of the U.S. military to relax some of their racially discriminatory policies; blacks were allowed to serve in the navy in capacities other than that of messman, for instance, and bans on the enlistment of blacks in the army air corps and the marines were lifted. However, the military experience of many blacks was marred by mistreatment and racial tension on American military bases and by the continuing official policy of racially segregating all military units.

Of all minority groups, Japanese Americans were affected the most by World War II. At the start of the war, about 127,000 people of Japanese descent lived in the United States; most resided in California, Oregon, and Washington. An additional 150,000 lived in Hawaii, then a U.S. territory. After Japan's attack on Pearl Harbor, many people in the three western states and in Hawaii expressed fears that Japanese residents would conduct espionage and sabotage against the United States. Widespread rumors of sabotage and spying in Pearl Harbor by residents of Japanese descent were not confirmed by a presidential commission appointed to investigate the incidents. (The Roberts Report, named for Supreme Court justice Owen J. Roberts, who headed the commission, instead charged top military officers with "dereliction of duty" in defense preparations.) Nevertheless, fear and suspicion of Japanese Americans continued to grow.

Under authority of an executive order issued by President Roosevelt, in 1942 about 110,000 Japanese Americans on the West Coast, two-thirds of them American citizens, were forced to evacuate their homes and move to inland detention centers, where they were confined under armed guard. Military and political leaders (including the Supreme Court in several court cases) defended this internment as a necessary wartime measure to prevent spying and sabotage. However, similar mass internment measures were not taken against alien immigrants from Germany and Italy, and they did not take place at all in Hawaii, where Japanese Americans made up one-third of the territory's population. Critics of the internment argued that racial prejudice against Japanese Americans (which far predated Pearl Harbor) and political pressure were the main factors behind the internment program. Controversy over the treatment of Japanese Americans has continued in the years since the war.

Secretary of State Cordell Hull, in a 1942 speech, called World War II "a life-and-death struggle for the preservation of our freedom." For Japanese Americans interned in detention camps and blacks denied many basic civil rights, the struggle for freedom often focused on the United States rather than the battlefronts in Europe and Asia. The viewpoints in this chapter examine some aspects of the debates surrounding America's minorities during World War II.

VIEWPOINT 1

"This is a war to keep men free. The struggle to broaden and lengthen the road of freedom—our own private and important war to enlarge freedom here in America—will come later."

African Americans Should Support the American War Effort

J. Saunders Redding (1906–1988)

As the United States mobilized for war in 1942, some Americans wondered whether African Americans, then often treated as second-class citizens or worse in American society, would fully support their country. Some German and Japanese propaganda attempted to exploit America's racial divisions. "Democracy, as preached by the Anglo-Americans, may be an ideal and a noble system of life," went one 1942 Japanese radio broadcast directed at blacks, "but democracy as practiced by Anglo-Americans is stained with the bloody guilt of racial persecution and exploitation."

The following viewpoint is excerpted from a November 1942 *American Mercury* article by J. Saunders Redding. Redding, a writer and college professor, speaks of his sometimes bitter experiences growing up as an African American during and after World War I, when that war "to make the world safe for democracy" resulted in little progress for blacks in the United States. He concludes, however, that he (and other African Americans) should fully support their country in order to preserve the freedoms they have against the threats posed by Germany and Japan.

J. Saunders Redding, "A Negro Looks at This War," *American Mercury*, November 1942.

I was listening sleeplessly to an all-night program of music interspersed with war news, bad news. The bad news of the war had not seemed bad news to me. Indeed, on this night, it was again giving me a kind of grim, perverted satisfaction. Some non-white men were killing some white men and it might be that the non-whites would win. This gratified me in a way difficult to explain. Perhaps, in a world conquered and ruled by yellow men, there would be no onus attached to being black and I, a Negro. . . . Then a peculiar thing happened. Something seemed to burst and I knew suddenly that I believed in this war we Americans are fighting. I think I said aloud, and with a kind of wonder: "I, a Negro, believe in this war we Americans are fighting." The thought or revelation gave rise to an emotion—keen, purging, astringent.

The thought and the conviction amazed me, for I had thought that I could never believe in war again, or that any war in which I might believe would be truly a race war; and then, naturally, I would believe as I had been taught by innumerable circumstances to believe. I would believe in the side of the darker peoples. But I could envision no such war even in the remote future, for I had been trained in the principles called Christian. I had been trained to believe in the brotherhood of man and that we were approaching that glorious state—slowly, but before complete catastrophe could overtake us.

War had no heroic traditions for me. Wars were white folks'. All wars in historical memory. The last war, and the Spanish-American War before that, and the Civil War. I had been brought up in a way that admitted of no heroics. I think my parents were right. Life for them was a fierce, bitter, soul-searing war of spiritual and economic attrition; they fought it without heroics, but with stubborn heroism. Their heroism was screwed up to a pitch of idealism so intense that it found a safety valve in cynicism about the heroics of white folks' war. This cynicism went back at least as far as my paternal grandmother, whose fierce eyes used to lash the faces of her five grandchildren as she said, "An' he done som'pin big an' brave away down dere to Chickymorgy an' dey made a iron image of him 'cause he got his head browed off an' his stomick blowed out fightin' to keep his slaves." I cannot convey the scorn and the cynicism she put into her picture of that hero-son of her slave-master, but I have never forgotten.

World War I

I was nearly ten when we entered the last war in 1917. The European fighting, and the sinking of the *Lusitania*, had seemed as remote, as distantly meaningless to us, as the Battle of Hastings.

Then we went in and suddenly the city was flag-draped, slogan-plastered, and as riotously gay as on circus half-holidays. I remember one fine Sunday we came upon an immense new billboard with a new slogan: GIVE! TO MAKE THE WORLD SAFE FOR DEMOCRACY. My brother, who was the oldest of us, asked what making the world safe for democracy meant. My father frowned, but before he could answer, my mother broke in.

"It's just something to say, like . . ."—and then she was stuck until she hit upon one of the family's old jokes—"like 'Let's make a million dollars.'" We all laughed, but the bitter core of her meaning lay revealed, even for the youngest of us, like the stone in a halved peach. . . .

I remember that first, false, mad Armistice. Everyone seemed crazy drunk and everywhere there was a spontaneous and unabashed breakdown of lines. Banker and butcher, coal-heaver and clerk, black and white, men and women went worming and screaming joyously through the streets. I also remember the real Armistice, and that there was a block party which Negroes could not attend, and that the police would not give them a permit to hold one of their own in the narrow, factory-flanked streets where most of them lived. When the lynchings and the riots started again—in East St. Louis, Chicago, Chester, even in Washington—we knew that, so far as the Negro was concerned, the war had been a failure, and "making the world safe for democracy" a good phrase bandied about by weak or blind or unprincipled men.

And so, since I have reached maturity and thought a man's thoughts and had a man's—a Negro man's—experiences, I have thought that I could never believe in war again. Yet I believe in this one.

Freedom Is the Issue

There are many things about this war that I do not like, just as there are many things about "practical" Christianity that I do not like. But I believe in Christianity, and if I accept the shoddy and unfulfilling in the conduct of this war, I do it as voluntarily and as purposefully as I accept the trash in the workings of "practical" Christianity. I do not like the odor of political pandering that arises from some groups. I do not like these "race incidents" in the camps. I do not like the world's not knowing officially that there were Negro soldiers on Bataan with General Wainwright. I do not like the constant references to the Japs as "yellow bastards," "yellow bellies," and "yellow monkeys," as if color had something to do with treachery, as if color were the issue and the thing we are fighting rather than oppression, slavery, and a way of life hateful and nauseating. These and other things I do not like, yet I believe in the war.

The issue is plain. The issue, simply, is freedom. Freedom is a precious thing. Proof of its preciousness is that so many men wait

Why We Fight

In a speech given on the first anniversary of the December 7, 1941, attack on Pearl Harbor, Hawaii, Nick Aaron Ford, professor of English at Langston University in Ohio, attempts to answer the question of what African Americans are fighting for in World War II.

There comes a challenging question that is hurled at us from a hundred different quarters: What are Negroes fighting for? It is a question we cannot ignore, for it has been sarcastically asked by Hitler himself. . . .

We can visualize this crafty hypocrite issuing orders from one corner of his mouth for the subjugation or total destruction of all non-Nordic races, and from the other corner asking, "What are you Negroes fighting for?"

"Aren't you segregated and discriminated against in America? Aren't you denied the right to work in defense industries and the right to fight on equal terms with your white countrymen? Aren't you insulted, and cheated, and oppressed by the very country for whom you are fighting? Aren't you lynched and burned at the stake and your bleeding or charred bodies left swinging in the breeze, as your tormentors march away singing, 'My country 'tis of Thee?'

"What are you Negroes fighting for?"

Yes, Mr. Hitler, we admit the question is a challenging one. . . .

We are the first to admit that conditions are not ideal for Negroes in this country, not even during this all-out effort for national defense, but we cannot deny that powerful voices high in governmental circles are being raised in every section of the nation in behalf of equality and a full degree of democracy for our people. Where can you find in any Axis country a single voice of protest raised by a governmental official in behalf of mal-treated minorities?

America is the only country in the world whose written Constitution guarantees equal freedom and equal opportunity for all races, creeds, and religions. Certainly, there are injustices, but our *government* is committed to equal justice for all. Certainly, there are inequalities here, but our *government* is committed to the recognition of the essential equality of all men. As long as the ideal is before us, we can always have reason to hope that each new day will bring us nearer to that ideal. But if, like the Axis countries, the government acknowledges no responsibility for equality or justice, there can be no hope that they may ever be achieved. . . .

It is true that injustices and mistreatment at home can never be excused by pointing to larger and graver injustices abroad. But the odious comparison can serve notice upon us that the Negro's only hope lies in victory for the United Nations and the complete destruction of totalitarian ideals.

patiently for its fulfillment, accept defilement and insult in the hope of it, die in the attainment of it. It used to seem shamefully silly to me to hear Negroes talk about freedom. But now I know that we Negroes here in America know a lot about freedom and love it more than a great many people who have long had it. It is because we have so little of it, really, that it used to seem silly to me to hear talk about preserving it. Giving me a penny, my father would remark in a satirical way, "That's not enough money, son, to do you any good. You might as well throw it away." I did not see that there was enough freedom to do me much good. It's a stage most public-schooled Negroes go through.

We go through a stage of blind, willful delusion. Later, we come to see that in the logic of a system based on freedom and the dignity of man we have a chance. We see that now and again there are advances. And this new seeing kindles the hope that Americans are really not proud of their silly prejudices, their thick-skinned discriminations, their expensive segregations. And now, I think, we know that whatever the mad logic of the New Order, there is no hope for us under it. The ethnic theories of the Hitler "master folk" admit of no chance of freedom, but rather glory in its expungement.

This is a war to keep men free. The struggle to broaden and lengthen the road of freedom—our own private and important war to enlarge freedom here in America—will come later. That this private, intra-American war will be carried on and won is the only real reason we Negroes have to fight. We must keep the road open. Did we not believe in a victory in that intra-American war, we could not believe in nor stomach the compulsion of this. If we could not believe in the realization of democratic freedom for ourselves, certainly no one could ask us to die for the preservation of that ideal for others. But to broaden and lengthen the road of freedom is different from preserving it. And our first duty is to keep the road of freedom open. It must be done continuously. It is the duty of the whole people to do this. Our next duty (and this, too, is the whole people's) is to broaden that road so that more people can travel it without snarling traffic. To die in these duties is to die for something.

There are men who do not like the road of freedom, men who would block it, who would destroy it, and that is what the war is about. What we on our side fight for now has nothing to do with color, nor political forms. It has everything to do with the estimation in which we hold ourselves and in which, therefore, others hold us. There are these men, these "master folk," who hold that all other peoples are of less worth than they. It is an article of faith with them: not a thing of intellection, but an emotional thing, and it is hard to be rid of. Where these men find human dignity and aspiration, they set about to degrade and quench it. This is an insult and an injury that has at last to be avenged in blood. Nine-tenths of the world's people have been insulted. And certainly, since this insult is so patently the issue, once we Negroes have fought to avenge it to other men (and ourselves, also) our brothers in blood-revenge will not return that insult to us again, as, I say it softly, they have so long done. Certainly now, over the stink of blood, the holocaust, they will know that this war for their freedom will be a dead end, unless the road of freedom is made a broad, through highway for all peoples forever.

Hope and Belief

This, of course, is hope. But you cannot fight wars without hope. This is also belief. And you cannot fight a victorious war without a belief in the thing you fight for. Here in America we believe, however falteringly, in the individual worth and dignity of man. Human dignity counts here. . . .

I believe in this war because I believe in America. I believe in what America professes to stand for. Nor is this, I think, whistling in the dark. There are a great many things wrong here. There are only a few men of good will. I do not lose sight of that. I know the inequalities, the outraged hopes and faith, the inbred hate; and I know that there are people who wish merely to lay these by in the closet of the national mind until the crisis is over. But it would be equally foolish for me to lose sight of the advances that are made, the barriers that are leveled, the privileges that grow. Foolish, too, to remain blind to the distinction that exists between simple race prejudice, already growing moribund under the impact of this war, and theories of racial superiority as a basic tenet of a societal system—theories that at bottom are the avowed justification for suppression, defilement and murder.

I will take this that I have here. I will take the democratic theory. The bit of road of freedom that stretches through America is worth fighting to preserve. The very fact that I, a Negro in America, can fight against the evils in America is worth fighting for. This open fighting against the wrongs one hates is the mark and the hope of democratic freedom. I do not underestimate the struggle. I know the learning that must take place, the evils that must be broken, the depths that must be climbed. But I am free to help in doing these things. I count. I am free (though only a little as yet) to pound blows at the huge body of my American world until, like a chastened mother, she gives me nurture with the rest.

"The fact is, there still is considerable doubt and apathy in the minds of the Negro civilian and military populations, which seriously hampers the war effort."

Black Support for the War Is Impeded by America's Racism

Roi Ottley (1906–1960)

Roi Ottley was a reporter and writer who worked as a war correspondent for the Pittsburgh *Courier* and other black newspapers. His 1943 book *New World A-Coming: Inside Black America* was a best-seller and formed the basis for a series of radio programs. The following viewpoint, excerpted from that book, focuses on the complex attitudes held by many African Americans about the war and America's part in it. Ottley argues that while many blacks want to support the war effort, their loyalty and patriotism is constantly being obstructed and undermined by instances of racial prejudice and discrimination against black soldiers and civilians. For example, he cites an incident in which local officials stood by as a white mob prevented black families from moving into a new public housing project in Detroit, Michigan, in February 1942. That and other events, Ottley concludes, have caused many blacks to question their support of America's war effort.

Listen to the way Negroes are talking these days!

Gone are the Negroes of the old banjo and singin' roun' the cabin doors. Old Man Mose is dead! Instead, black men have become noisy, aggressive, and sometimes defiant. Actually, this attitude is a reflection of a cold enthusiasm toward the war brought on by what the Pittsburgh *Courier* calls 'The War Against Negroes.' The fact is, there still is considerable doubt and apathy in the minds of the Negro civilian and military populations, which seriously hampers the war effort, particularly among those who are unable to lift their eyes to the hills. This is not the idle speculation of irresponsible observers, but an implacable fact that is revealed by the casual remarks dropped daily by the Negro man-in-the-street, and by his overt acts as well.

Recently a Harlem physician was summoned to court for driving about with a large sign tied to the rear of his automobile. It read:

IS THERE A DIFFERENCE?

JAPS BRUTALLY BEAT
AMERICAN REPORTER

GERMANS BRUTALLY BEAT
SEVERAL JEWS

AMERICAN CRACKERS
BRUTALLY BEAT
ROLAND HAYES & NEGRO SOLDIERS

JOIN THE AUTO CLUB PLACARD BRIGADE

A picture of this inflammatory display was reproduced on the entire front page of Harlem's *People's Voice*, with a story applauding the doctor's daring and denouncing his arrest by the police. Such attitudes are by no means sectional. During a quarrel with her white employer in Raleigh, North Carolina, an unnamed Negro woman retorted, 'I hope Hitler does come, because if he does he will get you first!' She was sent to prison for three years. Charles Steptoe, a Negro, twenty-four years of age, was sentenced to ten days in the workhouse because he refused to stand while 'The Star-Spangled Banner' was played in a Harlem theater. When, in another instance, a young Georgia-born Negro, Samuel Bayfield, came before the federal court for sentencing on an admitted attempt to evade the draft, he was asked where he was born. Bayfield told the court, 'I was born in this country against my will!' A Philadelphia Negro truck driver, Harry Carpenter, was held on charges of treason. He was accused of having told a Negro soldier: 'You're a crazy nigger wearing that uniform—you're only out fighting for white trash. This is a white man's government and war and it's no damned good.'. . .

A fairly typical attitude is that of the Negro soldier who said, 'Sometimes I feel very proud of being a member of this big, huge army, until I pick up a paper and see where a Negro soldier was lynched and it makes me feel like, "What am I doin' here!"' Other soldiers are disappointed with their own treatment by the Army. One stationed at a camp deep in the South complained in a letter to a Harlem friend that the post restaurant—where he was stationed—was divided with one side marked 'Colored' and the other 'White.' According to his report, two Negro soldiers went into the 'Colored' section and, finding it crowded, went across into the 'White' one. A white officer was called and ordered them to leave, and when they refused, he had them arrested. 'This,' the letter concluded, 'is just one of the milder insults that we go through down here. It will not be long before the [Negro] boys here will resent these un-American practices. . . .'

This sort of attitude is heard in other quarters. A group of rural Negroes living outside Richmond, Virginia, were having a heated argument over what difference there was between the *old* and *new* Negro. 'Well, as I sees it,' drawled an octogenarian finally, 'when the old Negro was insulted he shed a tear; today, when these young ones is insulted they sheds blood.'

Disturbing Reports

This extravagant talk is perhaps wishful thinking on the old man's part. What is a fact, though, is that events since Pearl Harbor have stirred a sorely driven people. While Nazi spies and saboteurs went to trial one after another in an atmosphere of judicial fairness and public calm—six Negroes were lynched! One of these, Cleo Wright, was burned, his body mutilated and tied to an automobile, and dragged through the streets of Sikeston, Missouri. Right on the heels of this, a Negro sharecropper, Odell Waller, was executed in Pittsylvania County, Virginia, for the killing of his white landlord, though the liberal opinion of the country, acknowledging extenuating circumstances, clamored for clemency. Yet a week or so later a white man, Eugene Ekland, who vowed to exterminate the Negro race and in the process murdered five Negroes in the nation's capital, was sentenced only to fifteen years in prison! A sort of melancholy footnote was the discovery of two fourteen-year-old Negro boys hanging from a bridge in the town of Meridian, Mississippi. They had been taken from a jail, where they had been confined for reportedly confessing to an attempted rape.

When Southern gentlemen take the law in their own hands, Negro women too are victims. An Army nurse, Lieutenant Nora Green, stationed at the Tuskegee Army Air Corps School, received orders to prepare for overseas service. Before sailing, she went on a shopping tour in Montgomery, Alabama. On her return trip to Tuskegee she boarded a bus, and the white driver pummeled her into unconsciousness following a dispute over the denial of a seat she had reserved in advance. Afterward a Negro editor was heard to say, 'Something like that makes you wonder if Montgomery isn't still the capital of the Confederacy.'

Even before the United States entered the war, disturbing reports were tumbling out of the Army camps. There were race riots at Fort Oswego. Fighting between races at Camp Davis. Discrimination against Negroes at Fort Devens. Jim Crow conditions were prevalent at Camps Blanding and Lee. Stabbings occurred at Fort Huachuca, killings at Fort Bragg, and the edict 'not to shake a nigger's hand' at Camp Upton. Nearly every day reports were heard of Negroes going A.W.O.L. [absent without leave]. So moved was Harlem's *Amsterdam-Star News* that it described the situation with this headline:

TERROR REIGN SWEEPS
NATION'S ARMY CAMPS
NEGROES GO A.W.O.L.

One morning in the summer of 1941, the New York *Times* calmly reported that following friction with the white population near Little Rock, Arkansas, forty-three Negroes of the Ninety-Fourth Engineers (labor) battalion, stationed at Camp Custer, had departed from the maneuver area. Actually, they had run off to seek safety from violence of the white citizens and state police. 'As we were walking along the highway,' one of the soldiers said afterward, 'we saw a gang of white men with guns and sticks, and white state troopers were with them. They told us to get the hell off the road and walk in the mud at the side of the highway. One of our white lieutenants walked up to a state trooper and said something. I don't know what. Anyway, the trooper told him to get them blacks off the highway "before I leave 'em laying there." Then out of a clear blue sky the state trooper slapped the white lieutenant. . . . Some of our men began to talk about returning to Camp Custer for protection. That night they left by bus, train, and walking. Three of us hopped freight trains after walking forty-two miles to avoid white people, who we felt would attack us because of our uniforms.'

A Negro who has lived in the freer atmosphere of the North and has become aware of his rights will not relinquish them or put up with abuse because he happens to be in the South. That he wears the uniform of the United States Army increases his self-respect. To some Southerners such a man is a dangerous 'nigger' who must be made to 'know his place'— with violence and terror, if necessary. The prejudiced Southerner refuses to accord even the ordinary decencies to the Negro and is not impressed by the statements of the federal government about this being a war for democracy. In his view, democracy is not a way of life for all, but a luxury for better-class white people only.

'Make way for that *white* Lord God Jehovah!'

AP/Wide World Photos

Some of America's worst race riots took place during World War II, including one in Detroit, Michigan, in June 1943.

Senator John D. Bankhead of Alabama expressed the Southern viewpoint in a letter to General George C. Marshall, Army Chief of Staff. He suggested that Northern Negroes be quartered in Northern states only. 'Our people feel,' he said, 'that the government is doing a disservice to the war effort by locating Negro troops in the South in immediate contact with white troops at a time when race feeling among the Negroes has been aroused and when all the energies of both the whites and blacks should be devoted to the war effort.' If Negro soldiers must be trained in the South, he said finally, 'as a result of social and political pressure, can't you place Southern Negro soldiers there and place the Northern Negro soldiers in the North, where their presence is not likely to lead to race wars?'

The South proposes to be unbending in extending even the

simple dignities to an Army uniform—if a Negro wears one. Negroes are equally insistent that, if they must die as equals, then they must be treated as equals. These sharply differing views met head-on in a flare-up at Fort Bragg, North Carolina, the result of an affray in which a Negro soldier and a white military policeman were killed. In this instance, however, the killing of the white man was the act of a Southern Negro whose resentments against injustice mounted to a desperate thrust for human dignity. The soldier, Ned Turman, had voiced objections to an attack on a fellow Negro soldier and, for his pains, was clubbed over the head by two white M.P.'s [military police]. In wrestling to protect himself, the Negro managed to snatch the gun of one of his assailants. Brandishing it, he stepped back and cried, 'I'm gonna break up you M.P.'s beating us colored soldiers!' And with that he fired the fatal shot. The other white M.P., standing near-by, shot the Negro to death. After the shooting, whole companies at Fort Bragg not involved in the affair—their Negro officers included—were forced to stand all night with their hands above their heads while armed military policemen patrolled the camp.

This affair occurred before the war. Today, with national unity desperately needed, racial tensions have increased rather than abated. The N.A.A.C.P. [National Association for the Advancement of Colored People] urged the War Department to include in its military instructions courses on the racial implications in the war, believing that such instructions were greatly needed to counteract racial bigotry. The suggestion was courteously but firmly turned down. Meanwhile, friction between white and Negro troops reached a critical stage at Fort Dix, in New Jersey, which certainly suggests that the problem is not sectional. . . .

'It is all right to be loyal if it is encouraged,' ran a letter to the editor of Harlem's *Amsterdam-Star News*. 'But I fail to see where America is doing anything to encourage the loyalty of black men. . . . Remember, that which you [Negroes] fail to get now you won't get after the war.' That comment appeared one week after Pearl Harbor. The issue of the paper that published this comment contained twenty articles by staff writers which dealt critically with the treatment of Negroes. Two weeks later, sixty prominent Negroes met in New York City in a conference called by the N.A.A.C.P. and the National Urban League to consider the Negro's part in the war effort. The group passed with only five dissenting votes a resolution introduced by Judge William H. Hastie, then civilian aide to the Secretary of War, that 'the colored people are not wholeheartedly and unreservedly all out in support of the present war effort.' Walter White, executive secretary of the N.A.A.C.P., attributed this country-wide apathy of Negroes to discrimination in the Army, Navy, and Air Corps, and especially in the war industries.

The First World War

This situation has its roots in the very immediate past. In the first World War Negroes at once sought to participate as soldiers. With full consciousness of their duties as citizens and with the desire to act the rôles of men, they gladly bore their share of the war effort. W.E.B. Du Bois, then the acknowledged leader of the Negro community, articulated the race's view toward the conflict in his now famous 'Close Ranks' statement to the nation as well as to certain skeptical Negroes:

> We of the colored race have no ordinary interest in the outcome. That which the German power represents spells death to the aspirations of Negroes and all dark races for equality, freedom, and democracy. Let us not hesitate. Let us, while this war lasts, forget our special grievances and close ranks shoulder to shoulder with our own white fellow-citizens and the allied nations who are fighting for democracy. We make no ordinary sacrifice, but we make it gladly and willingly with our eyes lifted to the hills.

This stirred Negroes in 1918. The conditions facing Negroes did not cause any lag when the call for volunteers was heard. Also, more than two million Negroes were registered under the Selective Service Law, and more than three hundred thousand were called. To the number drafted throughout the country were added 37,723, representing the Negro regulars and National Guard members. About two hundred thousand saw service in France, fifty thousand in actual combat. The fighting units constituted the 92d and 93d Divisions. To the 92d was attached the 367th United States Infantry, popularly known as the 'Buffaloes,' while the 15th Regiment (the New York National Guard) was part of the 93d. Two Negroes, Henry Johnson and Needham Roberts, were the first American privates to receive the *Croix de Guerre*, the French award for bravery.

Not until the war was over did the full measure of ill-treatment meted out to the Negro troops come to light and then only after Du Bois had visited Europe in 1919 to attend the Pan-African Congress. Documentary evidence of the discriminatory conditions faced by Negro troops was published by *The Crisis* magazine. One section alone will illustrate the attitude of the American high command, a memorandum called 'Secret Information Concerning Black American Troops.' It began with this statement:

> It is important for French officers who have been called upon to exercise command over black American troops, or to live in close contact with them, to have an exact idea of the position occupied by Negroes in the United States. The information set forth in the

following communication ought to be given to these officers and it is to their interest to have these matters known and widely disseminated. It will devolve likewise on the French Military Authorities, through the medium of Civil Authorities, to give information on this subject to the French population residing in the cantonments occupied by American colored troops.

Here are a few typical passages:

We must prevent the rise of any pronounced degree of intimacy between French officers and black officers. We may be courteous and amiable with these last, but we cannot deal with them on the same plane as with the white American officers without deeply wounding the latter. We must not eat with them, must not shake hands or seek to talk or meet with them outside of the requirements of military service. . . .

Make a point of keeping the native cantonment population from 'spoiling' the Negroes. [White] Americans become greatly incensed at any public expression of intimacy between white women and black men. . . .

The increasing number of Negroes in the United States (about 15,000,000) would create for the white race in the Republic a menace of degeneracy were it not that an impassable gulf has been made between them. . . .

While these were the conditions abroad, the Negro civil population was the victim of some of the bloodiest race riots in American history. Even regiments in training in the United States were forced to undergo indignities and violence. . . .

At the close of the war, administration leaders began a campaign to convince Negroes that no great change in their traditional position in America could be expected. With such a government policy, Negroes became the victims of new outrages throughout the country. Even the Ku Klux Klan was revived. In view of these events, Du Bois was forced to confess that he was less sure today than then of the soundness of his war attitude. 'I did not realize the full horror of war and its wide impotence as a method of social reform,' he wrote sadly. 'I doubt if the triumph of Germany in 1918 could have had worse results than the triumph of the Allies. Possibly passive resistance by my twelve millions to war activity might have saved the world for black and white. . . .'

Little Change

Today, the prejudice shown by Army officials seems very little different from that of yesterday. Reports have trickled back from England—to illustrate—that the American high command is attempting to impose various forms of segregation and discrimination on the Negro troops. The British liberal *New Statesman and Nation* reports examples of discrimination and even assault against Negro soldiers. A British soldier wrote to complain that in a certain English port, Negroes were barred from a well-known restaurant. He said English soldiers were instructed not to eat and drink with Negroes, and restaurant employees were told to bar them. 'I have met [white] Southerners,' an English writer said, 'who seemed rational enough until the Negro problem was mentioned, and who would then show a terrified, lynching spirit, which was about the ugliest thing imaginable.' He also noticed that they 'took it for granted that it is their duty to interfere if they see black troops with white girls.' A most recent episode involves a Southern white soldier who was invited to an English home, and created a scene when he discovered that a fellow guest was an American Negro soldier. He attacked the Negro in the presence of the guests, ruining the evening for everybody. . . .

From all reports, Negro troops are very popular with the English people, who have arranged many entertainments for them—much to the disgust and indignation of some white Americans. This very spirit in certain unrelaxing whites is what caused a bloody race riot in the United States, when two thousand whites engaged in pitched battle with five hundred Negroes to prevent them from occupying the Sojourner Truth Homes, a Detroit housing project built with public funds for Negro war workers. Immediately, this occurrence was seized upon by Axis agents to stir up racial strife and disrupt war production. Mob rule gripped one of the country's principal arteries of war industry, and demonstrated the federal government's weakness on the race issue.

A firm stand by the government on racial questions, would be translated into acts by the humblest white citizen in America— not to mention the white troops abroad. More important, though, is the fact that native Fascists, prodded by Axis agents, defied the government in Detroit. This riot was perhaps one of the most successful acts of sabotage during this war. At secret meetings, Ku Kluxers received orders to keep the Negro workers from entering their new homes. The F.B.I. investigation revealed surprising scope to Ku Klux Klan activities in Detroit, even to boring from within labor's ranks, and to links with Axis agents. The National Workers' League, a pro-Nazi group whose officials were later indicted, cooperated with the Klan in preparing and staging the subsequent riot in which scores of people were injured.

Minorities Are Vital

Today, however, the importance of millions of Negroes is being increasingly recognized in administration circles—to wage total war, a total population must be set in motion. The President wrote the N.A.A.C.P. convention in the summer of 1942: 'I note with satisfaction that the theme of your significant gathering read, "Victory Is Vital to Minorities." This theme might well be reversed and given to the nation as a slogan. For today, as never before, "Minorities Are Vital to Victory."' The status of the Negro in 1942 is considerably different from that of 1917. For one thing, his opportunities are definitely broadening, but only under public pressure. For example, an aviation unit was established at Tuskegee, though there is provision to train only a dozen Negro pilots a year. With few exceptions, the officer personnel is Negro. The ranking administrative officer is Lieutenant Colonel Benjamin O. Davis, Jr., a graduate of West Point in 1936, son of Brigadier General Benjamin O. Davis, first and only Negro general. This fact, incidentally, reminds me that in the last war, to prevent the promotion that was rightfully due him, the ranking Negro officer, Colonel Charles Young, was retired on the pretext that he suffered from high blood pressure. To prove that he could withstand the rigors of a military campaign, he rode horseback from Chillicothe, Ohio, to Washington, D.C.!

Decidedly on the credit side of the ledger has been the partial removal of a long-standing discrimination in the Navy. It recently agreed to enlist Negro 'reservists,' a step forward, since it hitherto admitted Negroes only in the most menial capacities. Unfortunately, this development was marred by official Jim Crow, Negroes having been placed in distinct units separate from the whites. At the outbreak of the war abroad, there were about fourteen thousand Negro soldiers in the Regular Army, whereas only about four thousand of some hundred and forty thousand enlisted men in the Navy were Negroes. The draft brought many hundreds of thousands into the Army. The War Department has announced that at full strength there will be three hundred and seventy-five thousand Negro soldiers in the Army. However, the Army's more liberal policy toward Negroes has not been duplicated by the Navy—This is, however, somewhat like a choice between the frying pan and the fire. The Army is training several thousand Negro officers, but the Navy has made no provision for training officer material. A high degree of morale has been attained at the Army's Officer-Candidate Infantry School at Fort Benning. Here—on Talmadge's Georgia soil—white and Negro candidates attend the same classes, eat in the same mess hall, sleep in the same barracks, and generally fraternize together. There have been no racial incidents. Encouraging too was the launching of the merchant ship *Booker T. Washington* with a mixed crew of Chinese, Filipinos, Negroes, and whites, and with a Negro captain, Hugh Mulzac, in full charge of operations. Incidentally, a former British seaman, he sailed his first ship in the United States under the colors of Marcus Garvey's Black Star Line.

Black Support and White Prejudice

These things represent progress. Witness the acts of Negroes. During a drive in Austin, Texas, three Negro brothers—Arthur, Felix, and Osle Jackson—each bought twenty thousand dollars' worth of war bonds. Eddie Anderson, the Negro comedian known as 'Rochester,' invested his earnings in a San Diego parachute factory—and significantly enough, employs Negro, Mexican, and white workers. Two song writers, Andy Razaf and Eubie Blake, turned out a patriotic song called 'We Are Americans Too,' which is currently popular in Negro communities. While pro-Axis agitators shout, the masses of Harlem seek to be included in the war program and confidently carry out the tasks assigned them. For instance, the Negro community has shown better discipline during the city-wide blackout tests than any other area, according to the city officials. Said Newbold Morris, President of the City Council, 'If you give Harlem a chance, the people will respond.'

Listen to the simple faith of a Negro youngster. Alice Godwin, a Harlem high-school student, wrote the following composition in her French class:

> I am a member of a race without a chance to do what it wants to do and without liberty in the whole world. I have been told that this war is a war for liberty for everybody. That is the reason this war is important to me. . . . It is with great fear that I consider my future under the heel of Hitler. He has said, hasn't he, that I am only half of a human creature?. . . I shall be glad to wear old shoes not in style. These things are very little compared with the suffering in a world under Hitler. Each little sacrifice I make, I make joyously. It is for a new world, tomorrow, isn't it?

Hope among Negroes rides high. But a minority of vocal whites are determined that the Negro shall not advance. When white liberals and the federal administration appease such elements, the Negro's thinking is confused and his morale lowered. The almost insurmountable prejudice of employers and backward labor unions is no abstraction—but a solid fact the Negro faces day after day. He well knows there are white men in America who would rather lose the war—even their own freedom—than see any change in the racial *status quo*. This attitude has received provocative encouragement from Axis sources.

VIEWPOINT 3

"The consensus of opinion among the law-enforcement officers of this State is that there is more potential danger among the group of Japanese who are born in this country than from the alien Japanese."

Japanese Americans Constitute a Dangerous Security Threat

Earl Warren (1891–1974)

Japanese immigration to the United States was virtually extinguished by immigration laws passed in 1924. The 1940 census counted almost 127,000 Japanese Americans living in the United States, most of whom lived in the Pacific coastal states of California, Washington, and Oregon. Of these, 47,000 were "Issei," or first generation Japanese immigrants, all of whom were aliens barred by federal law from U.S. citizenship. The remaining 80,000 were "Nisei" (second generation) and "Sansei" (third generation) Japanese Americans who, unlike their Issei parents, were American citizens by virtue of being born in the United States.

After war was declared on Japan in December 1941, the U.S. government took several immediate steps to protect America's security against suspected spying and sabotage. The Department of Justice rounded up three thousand aliens it believed were dangerous, half of whom were Japanese. In a step that caused much economic hardship for Japanese Americans, the Treasury Department froze the bank accounts of all aliens from enemy countries and closed down American branches of Japanese banks. These steps did not go far enough, in the opinion of many political leaders in the region. Columnists, radio commentators, and others

Earl Warren, in House Select Committee Investigating National Defense Migration, *National Defense Migration: Hearings on H.R. 113*, 77th Cong., 2nd sess., February 21 & 23, 1942, pp. 11010–18.

called for, among other measures, the deportation of all Japanese residents. Some officials of the U.S. military agreed with these assessments and pressed for the authority to detain and evacuate all Japanese Americans. On February 19, 1942, President Franklin D. Roosevelt issued Executive Order 9066, which authorized the U.S. Army to exclude "any or all persons" from vital "military areas." While not mentioning Japanese Americans by name, its ramifications were felt most by that group.

One of the supporters of sweeping security measures against Japanese Americans was California attorney general Earl Warren. Warren is remembered for his tenure as chief justice on the Supreme Court from 1953 to 1969, during which he became famous as a defender of civil liberties. In 1942, however, appearing before a congressional committee that was holding hearings on the national security problems created by enemy aliens, he argued that Japanese Americans, both citizen and alien, posed a serious security threat to the state of California. He contends that Japanese American citizens who were born in America constitute an even greater threat than the older generation of Japanese aliens.

For some time I have been of the opinion that the solution of our alien enemy problem with all its ramifications, which include the descendants of aliens, is not only a Federal problem but is a military problem. We believe that all of the decisions in that regard must be made by the military command that is charged with the security of this area. I am convinced that the fifth-column activities of our enemy call for the participation of people who are in fact American citizens, and that if we are to deal realistically with the problem we must realize that we will be obliged in time of stress to deal with subversive elements of our own citizenry.

If that be true, it creates almost an impossible situation for the civil authorities because the civil authorities cannot take protective measures against people of that character. We may suspect their loyalty. We may even have some evidence or, perhaps, substantial evidence of their disloyalty. But until we have the whole pattern of the enemy plan, until we are able to go into court and beyond the exclusion of a reasonable doubt establish the guilt of those elements among our American citizens, there is no way that civil government can cope with the situation.

On the other hand, we believe that in an area, such as in California, which has been designated as a combat zone, when things have happened such as have happened here on the coast, something should be done and done immediately. We believe that any delay in the adoption of the necessary protective measures is to invite disaster. It means that we, too, will have in California a Pearl Harbor incident.

I believe that up to the present and perhaps for a long time to come the greatest danger to continental United States is that from well organized sabotage and fifth-column activity.

Opportunities for Sabotage

California presents, perhaps, the most likely objective in the Nation for such activities. There are many reasons why that is true. First, the size and number of our naval and military establishments in California would make it attractive to our enemies as a field of sabotage. Our geographical position with relation to our enemy and to the war in the Pacific is also a tremendous factor. The number and the diversification of our war industries is extremely vital. The fire hazards due to our climate, our forest areas, and the type of building construction make us very susceptible to fire sabotage. Then the tremendous number of aliens that we have resident here makes it almost an impossible problem from the standpoint of law enforcement.

A wave of organized sabotage in California accompanied by an actual air raid or even by a prolonged black-out could not only be more destructive to life and property but could result in retarding the entire war effort of this Nation far more than the treacherous bombing of Pearl Harbor.

I hesitate to think what the result would be of the destruction of any of our big airplane factories in this State. It will interest you to know that some of our airplane factories in this State are entirely surrounded by Japanese land ownership or occupancy. It is a situation that is fraught with the greatest danger and under no circumstances should it ever be permitted to exist. . . .

In order to advise the committee more accurately on this subject I have asked the various district attorneys throughout the State to submit maps to me showing every Japanese ownership and occupancy in the State. Those maps tell a story, a story that is not very heartening to anyone who has the responsibility of protecting life and property either in time of peace or in war.

To assume that the enemy has not planned fifth column activities for us in a wave of sabotage is simply to live in a fool's paradise. These activities, whether you call them "fifth column activities" or "sabotage" or "war behind the lines upon civilians," or whatever you may call it, are just as much an integral part of Axis warfare as any of their military and naval operations. When I say that I refer to all of the Axis powers with which we are at war.

It has developed into a science and a technique that has been used most effectively against every nation with which the Axis powers are at war. It has been developed to a degree almost beyond the belief of our American citizens. That is one of the reasons it is so difficult for our people to become aroused and appreciate the danger of such activities. Those activities are now being used actively in the war in the Pacific, in every field of operations about which I have read. They have unquestionably, gentlemen, planned such activities for California. For us to believe to the contrary is just not realistic.

Unfortunately, however, many of our people and some of our authorities and, I am afraid, many of our people in other parts of the country are of the opinion that because we have had no sabotage and no fifth column activities in this State since the beginning of the war, that means that none have been planned for us. But I take the view that that is the most ominous sign in our whole situation. It convinces me more than perhaps any other factor that the sabotage that we are to get, the fifth column activities that we are to get, are timed just like Pearl Harbor was timed and just like the invasion of France, and of Denmark, and of Norway, and all of those other countries.

Invisible Deadline for Sabotage

I believe that we are just being lulled into a false sense of security and that the only reason we haven't had disaster in California is because it has been timed for a different date, and that when that time comes if we don't do something about it it is going to mean disaster both to California and to our Nation. Our day of reckoning is bound to come in that regard. When, nobody knows, of course, but we are approaching an invisible deadline.

The Chairman [Rep. John H. Tolan]: On that point, when that came up in our committee hearings there was not a single case of sabotage reported on the Pacific coast, we heard the heads of the Navy and the Army, and they all tell us that the Pacific coast can be attacked. The sabotage would come coincident with that attack, would it not?

Attorney General Warren: Exactly.

The Chairman: They would be fools to tip their hands now, wouldn't they?

Attorney General Warren: Exactly. If there were sporadic sabotage at this time or if there had been for the last 2 months, the people of California or the Federal authorities would be on the alert to such an extent that they could not possibly have any real fifth column activities when the M-day comes. And I think that that should figure very largely in our conclusions on this subject.

Approaching an invisible deadline as we do, it seems to me that no time can be wasted in making the protective measures that are essential to the security of this State. And when I say "this State" I mean all of the coast, of course. I believe that Oregon and Washington are entitled to the same sort of consideration as the zone of danger as California. Perhaps our danger is intensified by the number of our industries and the number of our aliens, but it is much the same. . . .

American-Born Japanese

I want to say that the consensus of opinion among the law-enforcement officers of this State is that there is more potential danger among the group of Japanese who are born in this country than from the alien Japanese who were born in Japan. That might seem an anomaly to some people, but the fact is that, in the first place, there are twice as many of them. There are 33,000 aliens and there are 66,000 born in this country.

In the second place, most of the Japanese who were born in Japan are over 55 years of age. There has been practically no migration to this country since 1924. But in some instances the children of those people have been sent to Japan for their education, either in whole or in part, and while they are over there they are indoctrinated with the idea of Japanese imperialism. They receive their religious instruction which ties up their religion with their Emperor, and they come back here imbued with the ideas and the policies of Imperial Japan.

While I do not cast a reflection on every Japanese who is born in this country—of course we will have loyal ones—I do say that the consensus of opinion is that taking the groups by and large there is more potential danger to this State from the group that is born here than from the group that is born in Japan.

Mr. Arnold [Rep. Laurence F. Arnold]: Let me ask you a question at this point.

Attorney General Warren: Yes, Congressman.

Mr. Arnold: Do you have any way of knowing whether any one of this group that you mention is loyal to this country or loyal to Japan?

Attorney General Warren: Congressman, there is no way that we can establish that fact. We believe that when we are dealing with the Caucasian race we have methods that will test the loyalty of them, and we believe that we can, in dealing with the Germans and the Italians, arrive at some fairly sound conclusions because of our knowledge of the way they live in the community and have lived for many years. But when we deal with the Japanese we are in an entirely different field and we cannot form any opinion that we believe to be sound. Their method of living, their language, make for this difficulty. Many of them who show you a birth certificate stating that they were born in this State, perhaps, or born in Honolulu, can hardly speak the English language because, although they were born here, when they were 4 or 5 years of age they were sent over to Japan to be educated and they stayed over there through their adolescent period at least, and then they came back here thoroughly Japanese. . . .

I had together about 10 days ago about 40 district attorneys and

Enemy Aliens

In response to a request by California attorney general Earl Warren for written appraisals of the problem of "enemy aliens" in California, city officials of Madera, California, sent him a February 18, 1942, letter, reprinted here, in which they differentiate between Japanese, Italian, and German aliens.

Dear Sir: The Japanese question on the Pacific coast appears to the officials of this community to have two things to be considered. One is that if we leave the Japanese loose they will be in position to do, and many of them will do, terrific damage if they get an opportunity. It is impossible for the police officials of the community to tell which Japanese are dangerous and which are not. For this reason, although it will work injustices to some persons, the only safe procedure would be to take up all Japanese and intern them. There are only two possible objections to this course. One is the size of the job. The size of any job is always immaterial if the need is great enough, and it would appear that the need here is great enough. The other objection is that we need the Japanese to produce vegetables. There are many large farmers in this community capable of developing vegetable growing on a large scale, providing they are asked to do the job. They have both the experience and the implements. A discussion with some of these leading farmers is that they believe the job can be done without the Japs.

The general feeling about the Italians is that they are well assimilated, and we do not regard even the Italian aliens as alien in fact. We also know that loyal Italians would quickly disclose anything they might discover, if others of their race are inclined to get on the wrong side of the picture. This is not true with the Japs. We feel it is safe to let the Italians continue their normal life in this community.

So far as we know, there are no German aliens in this community. If there are any, they are unknown to the officials and they are probably regarded as nationals of this country.

This letter is the result of a discussion on the part of the police force with the city attorney and mayor, and has been signed by all the parties as representing their concurring opinion.

Sincerely,

> John G. Gordon, *Mayor.*
> Sherwood Green, *City Attorney.*
> Walter E. Thomas, *Chief of Police.*

about 40 sheriffs in the State to discuss this alien problem. I asked all of them collectively at that time if in their experience any Japanese, whether California-born or Japan-born, had ever given them any information on subversive activities or any disloyalty to this country. The answer was unanimously that no such information had ever been given to them.

Now, that is almost unbelievable. You see, when we deal with the German aliens, when we deal with the Italian aliens, we have many informants who are most anxious to help the local authorities and the State and Federal authorities to solve this alien problem. They come in voluntarily and give us information. We get none from the other source. . . .

Concerns over Vigilantism

There is one thing that concerns us at the present time. As I say, we are very happy over the order of the President yesterday [Executive Order 9066]. We believe that is the thing that should be done, but that is only one-half of the problem, as we see it. It is one thing to take these people out of the area and it is another thing to do something with them after they get out. Even from the small areas that they have left up to the present time there are many, many Japanese who are now roaming around the State and roaming around the Western States in a condition that will unquestionably bring about race riots and prejudice and hysteria and excesses of all kind.

I hate to say it, but we have had some evidence of it in our State in just the last 2 or 3 days. People do not want these Japanese just loaded from one community to another, and as a practical matter it might be a very bad thing to do because we might just be transposing the danger from one place to another.

So it seems to me that the next thing the Government has to do is to find a way of handling these aliens who are removed from any vital zone.

In the county of Tulare at the present time and in the county of San Benito and in other counties there are large numbers of the Japanese moving in and sometimes the suggestion has come from the place that they leave, that they ought to go to this other community. But when they go there they find a hostile situation. We are very much afraid that it will cause trouble unless there is a very prompt solution of this problem.

My own belief concerning vigilantism is that the people do not engage in vigilante activities so long as they believe that their Government through its agencies is taking care of their most serious problem. But when they get the idea that their problems are not understood, when their Government is not doing for them the things that they believe should be done, they start taking the law into their own hands.

That is one reason why we are so happy that this committee is out here today because we believe that it will help us solve this problem quickly, which is just as important as to solve it permanently. . . .

Japanese Land Ownership

Now, gentlemen, I have some maps which show the character of the Japanese land ownership and possessory interests in California. I will submit them at the time I submit a formal statement on the subject. These maps show to the law enforcement officers that it is more than just accident, that many of those ownerships are located where they are. We base that assumption not only upon the fact that they are located in certain places, but also on the time when the ownership was acquired.

It seems strange to us that airplane manufacturing plants should be entirely surrounded by Japanese land occupancies. It seems to us that it is more than circumstance that after certain Government air bases were established Japanese undertook farming operations in close proximity to them. You can hardly grow a jackrabbit in some of the places where they presume to be carrying on farming operations close to an Army bombing base.

Many of our vital facilities, and most of our highways are just pocketed by Japanese ownerships that could be of untold danger to us in time of stress.

So we believe, gentlemen, that it would be wise for the military to take every protective measure that it believes is necessary to protect this State and this Nation against the possible activities of these people.

VIEWPOINT 4

"We didn't want to be treated as a special group of enemy aliens and as descendants of enemy aliens. We want to be treated as Americans."

Japanese Americans Do Not Constitute a Dangerous Security Threat

Michio Kunitani (dates unknown)

Following the Japanese attack on Pearl Harbor, fears of Japanese attack and sabotage prompted much concern in the United States, especially in the states of California, Oregon, and Washington, where most Japanese Americans lived. In late February and early March 1942, a special committee of the House of Representatives investigating "National Defense Migration" (commonly called the Tolan Committee after its chairman, Democrat John H. Tolan of Oakland, California) held public hearings in Los Angeles, San Francisco, Portland, and Seattle on the "Problems of Evacuating Enemy Aliens and Others from Prohibited Military Zones." The hearings took place shortly after President Franklin D. Roosevelt issued Executive Order 9066, which authorized the U.S. Army to exclude "any or all persons" from vital "military areas," but before the army began to carry out such evacuations. Many of the witnesses, including California attorney general Earl Warren, testified in favor of mass evacuation of all Japanese citizens and noncitizens for security reasons.

The following viewpoint is excerpted from the statements of Michio Kunitani, one of fifteen Japanese Americans to testify before the committee. An American-born citizen who had renounced his Japanese citizenship, Kunitani spoke on behalf of the Nisei Demo-

Michio Kunitani, in House Select Committee Investigating National Defense Migration, *National Defense Migration: Hearings on H.R. 113*, 77th Cong., 2nd sess., February 21 & 23, 1942, pp. 11221–27.

cratic Club of Oakland, a political organization formed to promote political education and activism among Japanese American citizens. Kunitani, while not opposing mass evacuation per se, contends that Japanese Americans should not be treated different than other Americans because of their ethnic background. He disputes the conclusions of Warren and others that Japanese Americans are disloyal and constitute a security threat.

We come here as Americans prepared to take a frank attitude and make frank statements, and speak to the members of this committee here just as people probably would in the cloakroom of the House of Representatives. . . .

We come here as Americans, not by virtue of our birth in America, but by virtue of the social and cultural forces in America. We come here to be treated as Americans and we want to live as Americans in America.

As I say, we are Americans, not by the mere technicality of birth, but by all the other forces of sports, amusements, schools, churches, which are in our communities and which affect our lives directly.

Some of us are Yankee fans; some of us are Dodger fans; some like to sip beer; some like to go up to the Top of the Mark once in a while; we enjoy Jack Benny; we listen to Beethoven, and some of us even go through the Congressional Record. That is something.

The main idea that our group wanted to present here today was that we didn't want to be treated as a special group of enemy aliens and as descendants of enemy aliens. We want to be treated as Americans, or as other groups, such as Italians, Yugoslavs, or Finns.

It seems that among the reasons put forth by the committee, and the witnesses who testified this morning, and last Saturday, on why they thought that we should be treated as a special group were the following:

No. 1. Our physical characteristics.

No. 2. The question of dual citizenship.

No. 3. The vague question of Shintoism and national religion.

No. 4. The question of the language schools which many of us have attended.

Suggested Policies for Evacuation

Our group is in favor of evacuation if the military authorities of the United States deem it necessary. But if we do evacuate we think certain considerations should be taken into account:

No. 1. If we are evacuated we would like to have food, shelter, and clothing, whether it be in North Dakota, Arizona, or Florida.

No. 2. We think some plan should be instituted so that the evacuees can participate positively in the defense effort and that we can, by our efforts in some way help gain a quicker victory for the anti-Fascist forces.

No. 3. We want the evacuees who are in the various professions, such as doctors, opticians, lawyers, and so on, to continue to act in that capacity.

The Question of Loyalty

I would like to touch on the question of loyalty. There has been a hue and cry by a lot of the people in California that there has been no anti-Fascist action on the part of any Japanese group. I would like to refute that statement right here and now.

Our organization, since the Democratic campaign of 1938, has come out on numerous occasions against shipments of oil and scrap iron to the Fascist war lords of Japan, and we opposed aggression in Ethiopia. Our records are filled with communications to our Congressmen, even to our Representative, who happens to be Mr. Tolan, urging them to vote against such measures in Congress.

I want to touch upon the question of the language schools. I would like to point out to the members of the committee that our parents, most of them, have had very little education. You will find in any group, whether they be Jews, Yugoslavs, Finns, Danes, or Japanese, that the people who do migrate to other lands are usually those who have not had economic security in their native lands and, therefore, have come to new areas in order to gain a livelihood. Most of our parents fall into that category.

They set up these language schools for various reasons.

No. 1. They thought that since they enjoyed the fruits of American life that they should contribute something to America. They thought that the fine parts of Japanese culture could be integrated into American life and that the second generation of Japanese, if they were able to read and write, could thereby discover the better side of Japanese culture and they could give that as their contribution to America and, if they could do that, the parents would die happy.

No. 2. This so-called indoctrination on the part of our parents hasn't been only along Japanese lines, but it has also followed American lines. We had 500 students registered at the University of California last semester. That is the largest enrollment of any minority group in the State of California. The record will also show a large number of Japanese students attending universities and high schools.

There is another reason why a study of the Japanese language is encouraged and that is because a knowledge of the Japanese language is essential to the economic picture into which the Japanese man or woman has to fit. At least, in this generation most of our employers happen to be Japanese.

Discrimination and Its Effects

We were discriminated against in private industry and, therefore, the only other channel into which the Japanese people could gain an economic livelihood was in the Japanese group. It was essential for us to learn the Japanese language so that we could converse intelligently with our employers.

Another point that I want to bring out is that there aren't very many Japanese in the civil service of the Federal Government, or in the State and local governments. That those who are working for the Federal Government are in there because they are discriminated against in private industry. It is usually in the case of professional workers rather than, we will say, those who fall in the category of laborers.

Another point I want to bring out is that the time spent in language schools amounts to about an hour a day, maybe two or three times a week.

Most of the time of the Japanese student is spent in the public schools. He spends from 6 to 8 hours in public schools. After school he goes into the extra-curricular activity of the public schools. His Sundays and Saturdays are taken up by participation in athletic events, Boy Scout activities, and such.

The time element there is not present in which the young Japanese could be indoctrinated with Shintoism or anything else. . . .

Another point is this: Most of the second generation Japanese do not know the language sufficiently to be indoctrinated. In fact, most of our homes are places where, after dinner, we don't congregate around the living room, or at the dinner table and talk. Usually after 6 or 6:30 it is: "Well, I have to go to the basketball game," or "I have to go to a show."

That point is well brought out by the fact that the Army had to hire Japanese students to teach Japanese enrollees the Japanese language. That has been the case at Camp Roberts and at Fort Ord. It bears out my point that most of the Japanese, the young Japanese, don't know the language at all. . . .

Dual Citizenship

Now, I want to touch on the question of dual citizenship. I do not know very much about its history and background, but I can present my case in point.

Loyal Americans

Gordon K. Chapman spent twenty years as a Presbyterian missionary in Japan and later worked closely with Japanese Americans in California and other coastal states. In the following passages from his statement before the Tolan Committee, he argues that neither the aging first generation of Japanese Americans nor the Americanized younger generation pose subversive threats to the United States.

It is the considered opinion of the writer that the Federal Bureau of Investigation was doing an excellent piece of work in uncovering subversive activity and apprehending potentially dangerous Japanese. This conclusion is based on observation and some contact with Federal Bureau of Investigation agents in various places. The present evacuation from "prohibited zones" is working great hardship on a people who are in the main loyal and is accomplishing little or nothing as a defense measure. It would have been better to have left these aliens in all places except those in close proximity to strategic installations. While our inland churches had made plans to house and provide some measure of work for such evacuées, these plans were largely hampered because of the opposition to further influx of Japanese into most communities. It is the opinion of the writer that any and all plans which make a special class of the Japanese and provide restrictions from which Germans and Italians are exempt are manifestly unfair and contrary to American principles and ideals. Any scheme for the control of enemy aliens and other potentially dangerous persons should be equally applicable to Germans and Italians. Long and wide experience with American citizens of Japanese race has convinced the writer that they have become more thoroughly Americanized than is the case with the children of certain other racial groups. And it is true that these young people of Japanese parentage have again and again demonstrated their loyal Americanism. . . .

The writer personally knows many who have become intensely anti-Japanese because of their experiences when they visited the native land of their parents. As the President of a Japanese-American citizen league said to the writer last night: "We are striving to be loyal and cooperate with the Government in this time of crisis. We thought that this war was going to give us our great opportunity to prove our loyalty as American citizens, but now we are being discharged from the Army and made to feel that we are not wanted. If they don't want us to fight Japan, why don't they give us a crack at Hitler, etc." Any policy which involves racial discrimination at this time is likely to embitter a generation of fine young people who have proven that they can become loyal Americans and drink more deeply of our culture than is the case with many Mexicans, Italians, and certain other races.

I didn't even know that I was a citizen of Japan until I was about 17 years old, and a freshman in college. My father happened to tell me that I was a citizen of Japan. Therefore, I went through the legal channels and expatriated myself. . . .

Another thing I would like to point out to the members of the committee is the indivisibility of citizenship in the eyes of American law. If we are citizens here that is enough. I don't think all this cry about the question of dual citizenship is that important. I mean it doesn't play a major role in our lives.

Another thing in connection with dual citizenship that I would like to point out is that since the only other channel of expatriation has been closed to us by the closing of Japanese consulates, we favor the bill which was before Congress which provides that legal means be set up so that Japanese who have dual citizenship could expatriate themselves through American courts. Our organization is in favor of such a measure and we have written to our Congressman to support it.

Another thing I would like to point out, and it is probably a question you would ask me, is this: What about the recent raids by the F.B.I., when they found thousands of rounds of ammunition, sabers, binoculars, flashlights, and what not, in some of the homes, after the date set for turning in such contraband?

Our answer to that question is this: That our organization has instructed its members many times to tell their friends, and their parents, to surrender such things. I think most Japanese people have done this, and have carried out the regulation of the Department of Justice and the War Department in that connection.

Japanese in Defense Areas

Another thing I would like to point out is this: Which came first, the defense areas or the Japanese farms that are around the defense areas?

I would like to point out that agriculture was the first occupation open to the Japanese people. The people who came here first were agriculturalists. One-third of the present Japanese population in the United States is engaged in agricultural pursuits. It just happens that they have followed a pattern. It is a similar pattern in Des Moines, Iowa, in Jamestown, Va. as well as in California. It is a social pattern which is not peculiar to California, or to Washington. The fundamental basis is the same all over the United States. . . .

Another thing that I want to point out is that there is no conscious movement of Japanese to these areas. It is just simply a matter of following their occupations—farming. If it were third- or fourth-generation Japanese probably there might be—I mean if we found farms were around strategic areas, probably there would be a conscious effort by the Japanese to move around to certain areas, but I don't think at the present time, in this generation at least, there is any conscious movement on the part of the Japanese as a whole. . . .

Pearl Harbor

Another point I want to bring out is about Pearl Harbor. We hear lots about sabotage at Pearl Harbor.

Mr. Tolan pointed out frequently this morning, and this afternoon, that he heard of Army trucks put in the road. I don't know where Mr. Tolan got that information. I don't know whether that is true or not. I cannot say. I can only go on the Roberts report, which was the only official United States document put out, as to what happened at Pearl Harbor, and why things happened as they did. I think if you gentlemen look into the Roberts report again you will find that no mention was made of sabotage on the part of Japanese-Americans. They pointed out that 200 members operating out of the Japanese consulate were the most active participants in fifth column activities in Hawaii.

I mean to say the average Japanese in California isn't intelligent enough to go about and engage in fifth column activities. The odds are against him. He has an oriental face that can be easily detected.

I am not saying there wasn't any fifth column activity in Pearl Harbor on the part of Japanese, but I don't think there was wholesale fifth column activity on the part of the Japanese-Americans or the aliens in Pearl Harbor. . . .

Another point I want to make is this idea of hardship cases. I think Congressman Tolan pointed out numerous times this morning what should be done about hardship cases.

Our organization has a definite plan as to what should be done about such cases if evacuation is to be instituted here in California.

No. 1. Our prime purpose is that we should not be treated any differently than Italians, Germans, Finns, or Yugoslavs. We want to be treated equally.

No. 2. We think that the Federal authorities should handle such cases. We don't believe that local authorities have the time, or the money, to set up agencies to take care of such cases.

We believe that the Federal Security Administration, under the able direction of Paul G. McNutt, should take the matter into its hands. I don't think the Army and Navy should do it. They have a big fight on their hands outside. I think they would be willing to let civilian bureaus handle this job of hardship cases. We think that the United States Employment Service, or the State social security board, should take such cases and deal with them.

I do not think any individual in America has any idea as to the numerous problems which will arise when you transplant a whole economy from one area to another. There are so many variables involved that I do not think anybody could begin to comprehend them.

"At a time of threatened Japanese attack upon this country, the nature of our inhabitants' attachments to the Japanese enemy was consequently a matter of grave concern."

U.S. Security Policy Toward Japanese Americans Was Justified

Harlan F. Stone (1872–1946)

The wartime policy of exclusion and mass incarceration of Japanese Americans during World War II received several legal challenges that reached the Supreme Court. The first to be decided by the Supreme Court involved Gordon K. Hirabayashi, a student of the University of Washington and a Quaker who had received conscientious objector status before the attack on Pearl Harbor. He was convicted of violating military curfew orders that restricted all "enemy aliens" and all "persons of Japanese ancestry" on the West Coast to their residences at night and places of employment during the day. In June 1943 the Supreme Court unanimously affirmed his conviction for curfew violations. The decision, excerpted below, was written and delivered by Chief Justice Harlan F. Stone. Appointed to the Supreme Court by President Calvin Coolidge in 1925, Stone was elevated to be chief justice by President Franklin D. Roosevelt in 1941. In his court opinion Stone defends the government's policy toward Japanese Americans. He argues that the war powers of the national government and legitimate concerns about the security threat posed by Japanese Americans justified discriminatory government actions that in other circumstances might be considered unlawful and unconstitutional.

Harlan F. Stone, *Hirabayashi v. United States*, 320 U.S. (1943).

Appellant, an American citizen of Japanese ancestry, was convicted in the district court of violating the Act of Congress of March 21, 1942 . . . which makes it a misdemeanor knowingly to disregard restrictions made applicable by a military commander to persons in a military area prescribed by him as such, all as authorized by an Executive Order of the President.

The questions for our decision are whether the particular restriction violated, namely that all persons of Japanese ancestry residing in such an area be within their place of residence daily between the hours of 8:00 p.m. and 6:00 a.m., was adopted by the military commander in the exercise of an unconstitutional delegation by Congress of its legislative power, and whether the restriction unconstitutionally discriminated between citizens of Japanese ancestry and those of other ancestries in violation of the Fifth Amendment.

The indictment is in two counts. The second charges that appellant, being a person of Japanese ancestry, had on a specified date, contrary to a restriction promulgated by the military commander of the Western Defense Command, Fourth Army, failed to remain in his place of residence in the designated military area between the hours of 8:00 o'clock p.m. and 6:00 a.m. The first count charges that appellant, on May 11 and 12, 1942, had, contrary to a Civilian Exclusion Order issued by the military commander, failed to report to the Civil Control Station within the designated area, it appearing that appellant's required presence there was a preliminary step to the exclusion from that area of persons of Japanese ancestry.

Appellant asserted that the indictment should be dismissed because he was an American citizen who had never been a subject of and had never borne allegiance to the Empire of Japan, and also because the Act of March 21, 1942, was an unconstitutional delegation of Congressional power. On the trial to a jury it appeared that appellant was born in Seattle in 1918, of Japanese parents who had come from Japan to the United States, and who had never afterward returned to Japan; that he was educated in the Washington public schools and at the time of his arrest was a senior in the University of Washington; that he had never been in Japan or had any association with Japanese residing there.

The evidence showed that appellant had failed to report to the Civil Control Station on May 11 or May 12, 1942, as directed, to register for evacuation from the military area. He admitted failure to do so, and stated it had at all times been his belief that he would be waiving his rights as an American citizen by so doing. The evidence also showed that for like reason he was away from his place of residence after 8:00 p.m. on May 9, 1942. The jury returned a verdict of guilty on both counts and appellant was sentenced to imprisonment for a term of three months on each, the sentences to run concurrently. . . .

Executive Order 9066

On December 8, 1941, one day after the bombing of Pearl Harbor by a Japanese air force, Congress declared war against Japan. . . . The President promulgated Executive Order No. 9066. . . . The Order recited that "the successful prosecution of the war requires every possible protection against espionage and against sabotage to national-defense material, national-defense premises, and national-defense utilities. . . ." By virtue of the authority vested in him as President and as Commander in Chief of the Army and Navy, the President purported to "authorize and direct the Secretary of War, and the Military Commanders whom he may from time to time designate, whenever he or any designated Commander deems such action necessary or desirable, to proscribe military areas in such places and of such extent as he or the appropriate Military Commander may determine, from which any or all persons may be excluded, and with respect to which, the right of any person to enter, remain in, or leave shall be subject to whatever restrictions the Secretary of War or the appropriate Military Commander may impose in his discretion."

On February 20, 1942, the Secretary of War designated Lt. General J.L. DeWitt as Military Commander of the Western Defense Command, comprising the Pacific Coast states and some others, to carry out there the duties prescribed by Executive Order No. 9066. On March 2, 1942, General DeWitt promulgated Public Proclamation No. 1. The proclamation recited that the entire Pacific Coast "by the geographical location is particularly subject to attack, to attempted invasion by the armed forces of nations with which the United States is now at war, and, in connection therewith, is subject to espionage and acts of sabotage, thereby requiring the adoption of military measures necessary to establish safeguards against such enemy operations." It stated that "the present situation requires as a matter of military necessity the establishment in the territory embraced by the Western Defense Command of Military Areas and Zones thereof;" it specified and designated as military areas certain areas within the Western Defense Command; and it declared that "such persons or classes of persons as the situation may require" would, by subsequent proclamation, be excluded from certain of these areas, but might be permitted to enter or remain in certain others, under regulations and restrictions to be later prescribed. Among the military areas so designated by Public Proclamation No. 1 was Military Area No. 1, which embraced, besides the southern part of Arizona, all the coastal region of the three Pacific Coast states, including the City of Seattle, Washington, where appellant resided. . . .

WESTERN DEFENSE COMMAND AND FOURTH ARMY WARTIME CIVIL CONTROL ADMINISTRATION
Presidio of San Francisco, California
April 1, 1942

INSTRUCTIONS TO ALL PERSONS OF

JAPANESE

ANCESTRY

Living in the Following Area:

All that portion of the City and County of San Francisco, State of California, lying generally west of the north-south line established by Junipero Serra Boulevard, Worchester Avenue, and Nineteenth Avenue, and lying generally north of the east-west line established by California Street, to the intersection of Market Street, and thence on Market Street to San Francisco Bay.

All Japanese persons, both alien and non-alien, will be evacuated from the above designated area by 12:00 o'clock noon Tuesday, April 7, 1942.

No Japanese person will be permitted to enter or leave the above described area after 8:00 a. m., Thursday, April 2, 1942, without obtaining special permission from the Provost Marshal at the Civil Control Station located at:

1701 Van Ness Avenue
San Francisco, California

The Civil Control Station is equipped to assist the Japanese population affected by this evacuation in the following ways:

1. Give advice and instructions on the evacuation.
2. Provide services with respect to the management, leasing, sale, storage or other disposition of most kinds of property including: real estate, business and professional equipment, buildings, household goods, boats, automobiles, livestock, etc.
3. Provide temporary residence elsewhere for all Japanese in family groups.
4. Transport persons and a limited amount of clothing and equipment to their new residence, as specified below.

The Following Instructions Must Be Observed:

1. A responsible member of each family, preferably the head of the family, or the person in whose name most of the property is held, and each individual living alone, will report to the Civil Control Station to receive further instructions. This must be done between 8:00 a. m. and 5:00 p. m., Thursday, April 2, 1942, or between 8:00 a. m. and 5:00 p. m., Friday, April 3, 1942.

2. Evacuees must carry with them on departure for the Reception Center, the following property:
   (a) Bedding and linens (no mattress) for each member of the family;
   (b) Toilet articles for each member of the family;
   (c) Extra clothing for each member of the family;
   (d) Sufficient knives, forks, spoons, plates, bowls and cups for each member of the family;
   (e) Essential personal effects for each member of the family.

All items carried will be securely packaged, tied and plainly marked with the name of the owner and numbered in accordance with instructions received at the Civil Control Station.

The size and number of packages is limited to that which can be carried by the individual or family group.

No contraband items as described in paragraph 6, Public Proclamation No. 3, Headquarters Western Defense Command and Fourth Army, dated March 24, 1942, will be carried.

3. The United States Government through its agencies will provide for the storage at the sole risk of the owner of the more substantial household items, such as iceboxes, washing machines, pianos and other heavy furniture. Cooking utensils and other small items will be accepted if crated, packed and plainly marked with the name and address of the owner. Only one name and address will be used by a given family.

4. Each family, and individual living alone, will be furnished transportation to the Reception Center. Private means of transportation will not be utilized. All instructions pertaining to the movement will be obtained at the Civil Control Station.

Go to the Civil Control Station at 1701 Van Ness Avenue, San Francisco, California, between 8:00 a. m. and 5:00 p. m., Thursday, April 2, 1942, or between 8:00 a. m. and 5:00 p. m., Friday, April 3, 1942, to receive further instructions.

J. L. DeWITT
Lieutenant General, U. S. Army
Commanding

SEE CIVILIAN EXCLUSION ORDER NO. 5

Detailed instructions for the mass evacuation of Japanese Americans were posted on April 1, 1942, in San Francisco, California, and other communities.

Appellant does not deny that he knowingly failed to obey the curfew order as charged in the second count of the indictment, or that the order was authorized by the terms of Executive Order No. 9066, or that the challenged Act of Congress purports to punish with criminal penalties disobedience of such an order. His contentions are only that Congress unconstitutionally delegated its legislative power to the military commander by authorizing him to impose the challenged regulation, and that, even if the regulation were in other respects lawfully authorized, the Fifth Amendment prohibits the discrimination made between citizens of Japanese descent and those of other ancestry.

It will be evident from the legislative history that the Act of March 21, 1942, contemplated and authorized the curfew order which we have before us. The bill which became the Act of March 21, 1942, was introduced in the Senate on March 9th and in the House on March 10th at the request of the Secretary of War who, in letters to the Chairman of the Senate Committee on Military Affairs and to the Speaker of the House, stated explicitly that its purpose was to provide means for the enforcement of orders issued under Executive Order No. 9066. This appears in the committee reports on the bill, which set out in full the Executive Order and the Secretary's letter. . . . And each of the committee reports expressly mentions curfew orders as one of the types of restrictions which it was deemed desirable to enforce by criminal sanctions. . . .

The Chairman of the Senate Military Affairs Committee explained on the floor of the Senate that the purpose of the proposed legislation was to provide means of enforcement of curfew orders and other military orders made pursuant to Executive Order No. 9066. He read General DeWitt's Public Proclamation No. 1, and statements from newspaper reports that "evacuation of the first Japanese aliens and American-born Japanese" was about to begin. He also stated to the Senate that "reasons for suspected widespread fifth-column activity among Japanese" were to be found in the system of dual citizenship which Japan deemed applicable to American-born Japanese, and in the propaganda disseminated by Japanese consuls, Buddhist priests and other leaders, among American-born children of Japanese. Such was stated to be the explanation of the contemplated evacuation from the Pacific Coast area of persons of Japanese ancestry, citizens as well as aliens. Congress also had before it the Preliminary Report of a House Committee investigating national defense migration, of March 19, 1942, which approved the provisions of Executive Order No. 9066, and which recommended the evacuation, from military areas established under the order, of all persons of Japanese ancestry, including citizens. The proposed legislation provided criminal sanctions for violation of orders, in terms broad enough to include the curfew order now before us, and the legislative history demonstrates that Congress was advised that curfew orders were among those intended, and was advised also that regulation of citizen and alien Japanese alike was contemplated.

The conclusion is inescapable that Congress, by the Act of March 21, 1942, ratified and confirmed Executive Order No. 9066. . . . And so far as it lawfully could, Congress authorized and implemented such curfew orders as the commanding officer should promulgate pursuant to the Executive Order of the President. The question then is not one of congressional power to delegate to the

President the promulgation of the Executive Order, but whether, acting in co-operation, Congress and the Executive have constitutional authority to impose the curfew restriction here complained of. We must consider also whether, acting together, Congress and the Executive could leave it to the designated military commander to appraise the relevant conditions and on the basis of that appraisal to say whether, under the circumstances, the time and place were appropriate for the promulgation of the curfew order and whether the order itself was an appropriate means of carrying out the Executive Order for the "protection against espionage and against sabotage" to national defense materials, premises and utilities. For reasons presently to be stated, we conclude that it was within the constitutional power of Congress and the executive arm of the Government to prescribe this curfew order for the period under consideration and that its promulgation by the military commander involved no unlawful delegation of legislative power.

Executive Order No. 9066, promulgated in time of war for the declared purpose of prosecuting the war by protecting national defense resources from sabotage and espionage, and the Act of March 21, 1942, ratifying and confirming the Executive Order, were each an exercise of the power to wage war conferred on the Congress and on the President, as Commander in Chief of the armed forces, by Articles 1 and 2 of the Constitution. . . .

We have no occasion to consider whether the President, acting alone, could lawfully have made the curfew order in question, or have authorized others to make it. For the President's action has the support of the Act of Congress, and we are immediately concerned with the question whether it is within the constitutional power of the national government, through the joint action of Congress and the Executive, to impose this restriction as an emergency war measure. The exercise of that power here involves no question of martial law or trial by military tribunal. . . .

Appellant has been tried and convicted in the civil courts and has been subjected to penalties prescribed by Congress for the acts committed.

Government War Powers

The war power of the national government is "the power to wage war successfully." It extends to every matter and activity so related to war as substantially to affect its conduct and progress. The power is not restricted to the winning of victories in the field and the repulse of enemy forces. It embraces every phase of the national defense, including the protection of war materials and the members of the armed forces from injury and from the dangers which attend the rise, prosecution and progress of war. . . .

Since the Constitution commits to the Executive and to Congress the exercise of the war power in all the vicissitudes and conditions of warfare, it has necessarily given them wide scope for the exercise of judgment and discretion in determining the nature and extent of the threatened injury or danger and in the selection of the means for resisting it. . . .

Proper Security Measures

In the 1944 case of Korematsu v. United States, *Hugo Black, an associate justice on the Supreme Court from 1937 to 1971, defended the government's actions against charges of racism. Fred Korematsu was a welder who refused to leave his home in San Leandro, California, following a military order excluding "all persons of Japanese ancestry" from the area.*

It is said that we are dealing here with the case of imprisonment of a citizen in a concentration camp solely because of his ancestry, without evidence or inquiry concerning his loyalty and good disposition towards the United States. Our task would be simple, our duty clear, were this a case involving the imprisonment of a loyal citizen in a concentration camp because of racial prejudice. Regardless of the true nature of the assembly and relocation centers—and we deem it unjustifiable to call them concentration camps with all the ugly connotations that term implies—we are dealing specifically with nothing but an exclusion order. To cast this case into outlines of racial prejudice, without reference to the real military dangers which were presented, merely confuses the issue. Korematsu was not excluded from the Military Area because of hostility to him or his race. He *was* excluded because we are at war with the Japanese Empire, because the properly constituted military authorities feared an invasion of our West Coast and felt constrained to take proper security measures, because they decided that the military urgency of the situation demanded that all citizens of Japanese ancestry be segregated from the West Coast temporarily, and finally, because Congress, reposing its confidence in this time of war in our military leaders—as inevitably it must—determined that they should have the power to do just this. There was evidence of disloyalty on the part of some, the military authorities considered that the need for action was great, and time was short. We cannot—by availing ourselves of the calm perspective of hindsight—now say that at that time these actions were unjustified.

Where, as they did here, the conditions call for the exercise of judgment and discretion and for the choice of means by those branches of the Government on which the Constitution has placed the responsibility of war-making, it is not for any court to sit in review of the wisdom of their action or substitute its judgment for theirs.

The actions taken must be appraised in the light of the conditions with which the President and Congress were confronted in the early months of 1942, many of which, since disclosed, were then peculiarly within the knowledge of the military authorities. . . .

That reasonably prudent men charged with the responsibility of our national defense had ample ground for concluding that they must face the danger of invasion, take measures against it, and in making the choice of measures consider our internal situation, cannot be doubted.

The challenged orders were defense measures for the avowed purpose of safeguarding the military area in question, at a time of threatened air raids and invasion by the Japanese forces, from the danger of sabotage and espionage. As the curfew was made applicable to citizens residing in the area only if they were of Japanese ancestry, our inquiry must be whether in the light of all the facts and circumstances there was any substantial basis for the conclusion, in which Congress and the military commander united, that the curfew as applied was a protective measure necessary to meet the threat of sabotage and espionage which would substantially affect the war effort and which might reasonably be expected to aid a threatened enemy invasion. The alternative which appellant insists must be accepted is for the military authorities to impose the curfew on all citizens within the military area, or on none. In a case of threatened danger requiring prompt action, it is a choice between inflicting obviously needless hardship on the many, or sitting passive and unresisting in the presence of the threat. We think that constitutional government, in time of war, is not so powerless and does not compel so hard a choice if those charged with the responsibility of our national defense have reasonable ground for believing that the threat is real. . . . At a time of threatened Japanese attack upon this country, the nature of our inhabitants' attachments to the Japanese enemy was consequently a matter of grave concern. Of the 126,000 persons of Japanese descent in the United States, citizens and noncitizens, approximately 112,000 resided in California, Oregon and Washington at the time of the adoption of the military regulations. Of these approximately two-thirds are citizens because born in the United States. Not only did the great majority of such persons reside within the Pacific Coast states but they were concentrated in or near three of the large cities, Seattle, Portland and Los Angeles, all in Military Area No. 1.

Japanese Solidarity

There is support for the view that social, economic and political conditions which have prevailed since the close of the last century, when the Japanese began to come to this country in substantial numbers, have intensified their solidarity and have in large measure prevented their assimilation as an integral part of the white population. In addition, large numbers of children of Japanese parentage are sent to Japanese language schools outside the regular hours of public schools in the locality. Some of these schools are generally believed to be sources of Japanese nationalistic propaganda, cultivating allegiance to Japan. Considerable numbers, estimated to be approximately 10,000, of American-born children of Japanese parentage have been sent to Japan for all or a part of their education.

Dual Citizenship

Congress and the Executive, including the military commander, could have attributed special significance, in its bearing on the loyalties of persons of Japanese descent, to the maintenance by Japan of its system of dual citizenship. Children born in the United States of Japanese alien parents, and especially those children born before December 1, 1924, are under many circumstances deemed, by Japanese law, to be citizens of Japan. No official census of those whom Japan regards as having thus retained Japanese citizenship is available, but there is ground for the belief that the number is large.

The large number of resident alien Japanese, approximately one-third of all Japanese inhabitants of the country, are of mature years and occupy positions of influence in Japanese communities. The association of influential Japanese residents with Japanese Consulates has been deemed a ready means for the dissemination of propaganda and for the maintenance of the influence of the Japanese Government with the Japanese population in this country.

As a result of all these conditions affecting the life of the Japanese, both aliens and citizens, in the Pacific Coast area, there has been relatively little social intercourse between them and the white population. The restrictions, both practical and legal, affecting the privileges and opportunities afforded to persons of Japanese extraction residing in the United States, have been sources of irritation and may well have tended to increase their isolation, and in many instances their attachments to Japan and its institutions.

Viewing these data in all their aspects, Congress and the Executive could reasonably have concluded that these conditions have encouraged the continued attachment of members of this group to Japan and Japanese institutions. These are only some of the many considerations which those charged with the responsibility for the national defense could take into account in determining the nature and extent of the danger of espionage and sabotage, in the event of invasion or air raid attack. The extent of that danger could be definitely known only after the event and after it was too late to meet it. Whatever views we may entertain regarding the loyalty to this country of the citizens of Japanese ancestry, we cannot reject as unfounded the judgment of the military authorities and of Congress that there were disloyal members of that population, whose number and strength could not be precisely and quickly ascertained. We cannot say that the war-making branches of the Government did not have ground for believing that in a critical hour such persons could not readily be isolated and separately dealt with, and constituted a menace to the national defense and safety, which demanded that prompt and adequate measures be taken to guard against it.

Appellant does not deny that, given the danger, a curfew was an appropriate measure against sabotage. It is an obvious protection against the perpetration of sabotage most readily committed during the hours of darkness. If it was an appropriate exercise of the war power its validity is not impaired because it has restricted the citizen's liberty. Like every military control of the population of a dangerous zone in wartime, it necessarily involves some infringement of individual liberty, just as does the police establishment of fire lines during a fire, or the confinement of people to their houses during an air raid alarm—neither of which could be thought to be an infringement of constitutional right. Like them, the validity of the restraints of the curfew order depends on all the conditions which obtain at the time the curfew is imposed and which support the order imposing it.

The Fifth Amendment and Race

But appellant insists that the exercise of the power is inappropriate and unconstitutional because it discriminates against citizens of Japanese ancestry, in violation of the Fifth Amendment. The Fifth Amendment contains no equal protection clause and it restrains only such discriminatory legislation by Congress as amounts to a denial of due process. . . . Congress may hit at a particular danger where it is seen, without providing for others which are not so evident or so urgent. . . . Distinctions between citizens solely because of their ancestry are by their very nature odious to a free people whose institutions are founded upon the doctrine of equality. For that reason, legislative classification or discrimination based on race alone has often been held to be a denial of equal protection. . . . We may assume that these considerations would be controlling here were it not for the fact that the danger of espionage and sabotage, in time of war and of threatened invasion, calls upon the military authorities to scrutinize every relevant fact bearing on the loyalty of populations in the danger areas. Because racial discriminations are in most circumstances irrelevant and therefore prohibited, it by no means follows that, in dealing with the perils of war, Congress and the Executive are wholly precluded from taking into account those facts and circumstances which are relevant to measures for our national defense and for the successful prosecution of the war, and which may in fact place citizens of one ancestry in a different category from others. . . . The adoption by Government, in the crisis of war and of threatened invasion, of measures for the public safety, based upon the recognition of facts and circumstances which indicate that a group of one national extraction may menace that safety more than others, is not wholly beyond the limits of the Constitution and is not to be condemned merely because in other and in most circumstances racial distinctions are irrelevant. . . .

Protection Against Sabotage

Here the aim of Congress and the Executive was the protection against sabotage of war materials and utilities in areas thought to be in danger of Japanese invasion and air attack. We have stated in detail facts and circumstances with respect to the American citizens of Japanese ancestry residing on the Pacific Coast which support the judgment of the war-waging branches of the Government that some restrictive measure was urgent. We cannot say that these facts and circumstances, considered in the particular war setting, could afford no ground for differentiating citizens of Japanese ancestry from other groups in the United States. The fact alone that attack on our shores was threatened by Japan rather than another enemy power set these citizens apart from others who have no particular associations with Japan. . . .

The Constitution as a continuously operating charter of government does not demand the impossible or the impractical. The essentials of the legislative function are preserved when Congress authorizes a statutory command to become operative, upon ascertainment of a basic conclusion of fact by a designated representative of the Government. . . . The present statute, which authorized curfew orders to be made pursuant to Executive Order No. 9066 for the protection of war resources from espionage and sabotage, satisfies those requirements. Under the Executive Order the basic facts, determined by the military commander in the light of knowledge then available, were whether that danger existed and whether a curfew order was an appropriate means of minimizing the danger. Since his findings to that effect were, as we have said, not without adequate support, the legislative function was performed and the sanction of the statute attached to violations of the curfew order.

"Our wartime treatment of the Japanese and the Japanese-Americans on the West Coast was a tragic and dangerous mistake."

U.S. Military Policy Toward Japanese Americans Was Not Justified

Eugene V. Rostow (b. 1913)

The evacuation and incarceration of Japanese Americans during World War II has received much subsequent criticism on the grounds that it violated the Constitution and curtailed the civil liberties of Japanese Americans, two-thirds of whom were U.S. citizens. One of the earliest critiques of this episode was a 1945 article in *Harper's Magazine*, reprinted here, written by Eugene V. Rostow. He condemns the internment of Japanese Americans as a "tragic and dangerous mistake" and argues that Supreme Court rulings affirming the internment create precedents that endanger the civil liberties of all Americans. Then a professor of law at Yale Law School, Rostow had served in the U.S. State Department as a legal adviser and later was on the staff of President John F. Kennedy.

As time passes, it becomes more and more plain that our wartime treatment of the Japanese and the Japanese-Americans on the West Coast was a tragic and dangerous mistake. That mistake is a threat to society, and to all men. Its motivation and its impact on our system of law deny every value of democracy.

An Incredible Story

In the perspective of our legal tradition, the facts are almost incredible.

During the bleak spring of 1942, the Japanese and the Japanese-Americans who lived on the West Coast of the United States were taken into custody and removed to camps in the interior. More than one hundred thousand men, women, and children were thus exiled and imprisoned. More than two-thirds of them were American citizens.

These people were taken into custody as a military measure on the ground that espionage and sabotage were especially to be feared from persons of Japanese blood. The whole group was removed from the West Coast because the military authorities thought it would take too long to conduct individual investigations on the spot. They were arrested without warrants and were held without indictment or a statement of charges, although the courts were open and freely functioning. They were transported to camps far from their homes, and kept there under prison conditions, pending investigations of their "loyalty." Despite the good intentions of the chief relocation officers, the centers were little better than concentration camps.

If the evacuees were found "loyal," they were released only if they could find a job and a place to live, in a community where no hoodlums would come out at night to chalk up anti-Japanese slogans, break windows, or threaten riot. If found "disloyal" in their attitude to the war, they were kept in the camps indefinitely—although sympathy with the enemy is no crime in the United States (for white people at least) so long as it is not translated into deeds or the visible threat of deeds. On May 1, 1945, three years after the program was begun, about 70,000 persons were still in camps. While it is hoped to have all these people either free, or in more orthodox confinement, by January 1, 1946, what is euphemistically called the Japanese "relocation" program will not be a closed book for many years.

The Supreme Court

The original program of "relocation" was an injustice, in no way required or justified by the circumstances of the war. But the

Supreme Court, in three extraordinary decisions, has upheld its main features as constitutional. This fact converts a piece of wartime folly into national policy—a permanent part of the law—a doctrine enlarging the power of the military in relation to civil authority. It is having a sinister impact on the minority problem in every part of the country. It is giving aid to reactionary politicians who use social division and racial prejudice as their tools. The precedent is being used to encourage attacks on the civil rights of both citizens and aliens. As Mr. Justice [Robert] Jackson has said, the principle of these decisions "lies about like a loaded weapon ready for the hand of any authority that can bring forward a plausible claim of an urgent need." All in all, the case of the Japanese-Americans is the worst blow our liberties have sustained in many years. Unless repudiated, it may support devastating and unforeseen social and political conflicts.

Enemy Aliens

What was done in the name of military precaution on the West Coast was quite different from the security measures taken in Hawaii or on the East Coast, although both places were active theaters of war in 1942.

On the East Coast enemy aliens were controlled without mass arrests or evacuations, despite their heavy concentration in and near shipping and manufacturing centers. Aliens had been registered, and the police had compiled information about fascist sympathizers, both aliens and citizens. "On the night of December 7, 1941," Attorney General [Francis] Biddle reported, "the most dangerous of the persons in this group were taken into custody; in the following weeks a number of others were apprehended. Each arrest was made on the basis of information concerning the specific alien taken into custody. We have used no dragnet techniques and have conducted no indiscriminate, large-scale raids." General regulations were issued, somewhat restricting the freedom of all enemy aliens over fourteen years of age. They were forbidden to enter military areas; they had to get the District Attorney's permission before traveling; they were forbidden to own or use firearms, cameras, short-wave radio sets, codes, ciphers, or invisible ink. This control plan kept security officers informed, but otherwise allowed the aliens almost their normal share in the work and life of the community.

Enemy aliens under suspicion, and those who violated the regulations, were subject to summary arrest, and were then promptly examined by one of the special Alien Enemy Hearing Boards. These boards could recommend that the individual alien be interned, paroled, or released unconditionally. The examinations were smoothly conducted, and they did nothing to lower prevailing standards of justice. Of the 1,100,000 enemy aliens in the country, 9,080 had been examined by the end of June 1943, about 4,000 of them being then interned. By June 30, 1944, the number interned had been reduced to approximately 2,500.

In Hawaii a different procedure was followed, but one less drastic than the evacuation program pursued on the West Coast, although Hawaii was certainly a more active theater of war. Immediately after Pearl Harbor, martial law was installed in Hawaii, and the commanding general assumed the role of military governor. Yet, although about one-third the population of Hawaii is of Japanese descent, and although the tension was great after the Pearl Harbor raid, there was no mass roundup on the islands. Fewer than 800 Japanese aliens were sent to the mainland for internment, and fewer than 1,000 persons of Japanese ancestry, 912 of them being citizens, were sent to relocation centers on the mainland. Many of the latter group were families of interned aliens, transferred voluntarily. Those arrested in Hawaii were taken into custody on the basis of individual suspicion, resting on previous examination or observed behavior. Even under a regime of martial law, men were arrested as individuals, and not because of the color of their skins. Safety was assured without mass arrests, or needless hardship.

On the West Coast the security program was something else again. Immediately after Pearl Harbor there were no special regulations for persons of Japanese extraction. Known enemy sympathizers among the Japanese, like white traitors and enemy agents, were arrested. There was no sabotage by persons of Japanese ancestry. There was no reason to suppose that the 112,000 persons of Japanese descent on the West Coast, less than 2 per cent of the population, constituted a greater menace than such persons in Hawaii, where they were 32 per cent of the population.

After a month's silence, the organized minority whose business it has been to exploit racial tensions on the West Coast went to work. They had strong support in the Hearst press and its equivalents. Politicians, fearful of an unknown public opinion, spoke out for white supremacy. West Coast Congressional delegations led by Senator Hiram Johnson urged the administration to exclude all persons of Japanese blood from the coast states. Anti-Oriental spokesmen appeared before special hearings of the Tolan Committee, and explained the situation as they conceived it to Lieutenant General J.L. DeWitt, commanding the Western Defense Command. Tension was intensified, and doubters, worried about the risks of another Pearl Harbor, remained silent, preferring too much caution to too little. An opinion crystallized in favor of evacuating the Japanese.

After some hesitation, General DeWitt proposed the policy of exclusion on grounds of military need. The War Department backed him up. No one in the government took the responsibility for opposing or overruling him.

Despite the nature of the emergency, the Army's lawyers wanted more legal authority before action was taken. The President issued an Executive Order in February 1942, and in March Congress passed a statute, authorizing military commanders to designate "military areas" and to prescribe the terms on which any persons could enter, leave, or remain in such areas. A policy of encouraging the Japanese to move away individually had shown signs of producing confusion. It was therefore decided to establish a compulsory system of detention in camps, to simplify the process of resettlement, and to afford the fullest measure of security.

Weak Evidence

The history of law affords nothing more fantastic than the evidence which is supposed to justify this program. General DeWitt's final recommendation to the Secretary of War, dated February 14, 1942, but not made public until early in 1944, explains the basis of his decision.

"In the war in which we are now engaged," he said, "racial affinities are not severed by migration. The Japanese race is an enemy race and while many second and third generation Japanese born on United States soil, possessed of United States citizenship, have become 'Americanized,' the racial strains are undiluted." From the premise of a war of "races," the general had no difficulty reaching his conclusion. There is "no ground for assuming," he said, that Japanese-Americans will not turn against the United States. So much for the idea that men are presumed innocent until proved guilty, and that American citizens stand on an equal footing before the law without regard for race, color, or previous condition of servitude! "It therefore follows," the general added, "that along the vital Pacific Coast over 112,000 potential enemies, of Japanese extraction, are at large today. There are disturbing indications that these are organized and ready for concerted action at a favorable opportunity. The very fact that no sabotage has taken place to date is a disturbing and confirming indication that such action will be taken."

There was somewhat more evidence than the absence of sabotage to prove its special danger. The Japanese lived closely together, often concentrated around harbors and other strategic areas. Japanese clubs and religious institutions played an important part in their segregated social life. Japanese language schools existed, to preserve for the American born something of the cultural heritage of Japan. The Japanese government, like that of many other countries, asserted a doctrine of nationality different from our own, which gave rise to possible claims of dual citizenship. Thus a long-standing conflict in international law, involving many countries other than Japan, was invoked to cast special doubt on the loyalty of American citizens of Japanese descent.

Much of the suspicion inferentially based on these statements disappears on closer examination. In many instances the concentration of Japanese homes around strategic areas had come about years before, and for entirely innocent reasons. Japanese cannery workers, for example, had had to live on the waterfront in order to be near the plants in which they worked. Japanese truck gardeners had rented land in the industrial outskirts of large cities to be close to their markets. They had rented land for gardening under high tension lines—regarded as a very suspicious circumstance—because the company could not use the land for other purposes; the initiative in starting this practice had come from the utility companies, not from the Japanese.

Despite discrimination against the Japanese, many had done well in America. They were substantial property owners. Their children participated normally and actively in the schools and universities of the West Coast. Their unions and social organizations had passed resolutions of loyalty in great number, before and after Pearl Harbor. It is difficult to find real evidence that either religious or social institutions among the Japanese had successfully fostered Japanese militarism or other dangerous sentiments. The Japanese language schools, which the Japanese-Americans themselves had long sought to put under state control, seem to represent little more than the familiar desire of many immigrant groups to keep alive the language and tradition of the "old country"; in the case of Japanese-Americans, knowledge of the Japanese language was of particular economic importance, since so much of their working life was spent with other Japanese on the West Coast.

Some Elements Were Suspect

Some elements among the Japanese were, of course, suspect. They were known to the authorities, who had for several years been checking on the Japanese-American population. Many had been individually arrested immediately after Pearl Harbor, and the others were under constant surveillance.

It is also true that a considerable percentage of the evacuees later gave negative answers to loyalty questions in the questionnaires they were asked to fill out while in camps. Many of those answers were expressly based upon the treatment the individuals had received; the same shock of evacuation and confinement undoubtedly was responsible indirectly for many more. Basically, however, the issue of abstract loyalty is irrelevant. Disloyalty, even in the aggravated form of enthusiastic verbal support for the Axis cause, is not a crime in the United States. At most, it is a possible ground for interning enemy aliens. Citizens must do more than talk or think disloyal thoughts before being arrested and jailed.

Apart from the members of the group known to be under suspicion, there was no evidence beyond the vaguest fear to connect the Japanese on the West Coast with the unfavorable military events of 1941 and 1942. Both at Pearl Harbor and in sporadic attacks on the West Coast the enemy had shown that he had knowledge of our dispositions. There was some signaling to enemy ships at sea, both by radio and by lights, along the West Coast. There were several episodes of shelling the coast by submarine—although two of the three such cases mentioned by General DeWitt as tending to create suspicion of the Japanese-Americans took place *after* their removal from the coast. (These were the only such items in his report which were not identified by date.) And those subsequently arrested as Japanese agents in the Pearl Harbor area were all white men.

The most striking comment on the quality of the evidence produced by General DeWitt to support his proposal was made by Solicitor General Fahy, whose job it was to defend the general's plan before the Supreme Court. He relied upon the general's report "only to the extent that it relates" statistics and other details concerning the actual evacuation and the events which took place after it. But the briefs that he himself presented were identical in the substance of their argument. The Japanese-Americans were an unknown, unknowable, foreign group, living together, and moving in mysterious ways, inscrutable to puzzled white men. Therefore, let them be imprisoned; let their property be taken into custody, sold off at bargain prices, dissipated, and lost; let their roots be torn up, let their children suffer the irreparable shock of life in a concentration camp; let their relation to society be distorted by the searing memory of humiliation, rejection, and punishment.

The evidence supports one conclusion only: the dominant element in the development of our relocation policy was race prejudice, not a military estimate of a military problem.

Changing War Conditions

By the time the issues raised by this program reached the Supreme Court, the crisis which was supposed to justify it had passed. The first cases came up in June 1943, the second and third in December 1944. The course of the war had changed completely; the Japanese were no longer prowling off California, but fighting defensively among the islands of the Western Pacific.

The problem presented to the Supreme Court was thus completely different from that which confronted worried soldiers, legislators, and executive officials in the melancholy months after

Pearl Harbor. Invalidation of the relocation scheme would do no possible harm to the prosecution of the war. The Supreme Court could afford to view the issues in perspective, giving full weight to its own special responsibilities for the development of constitutional law as a whole.

Moreover, the issue for the court was infinitely more complex than that which faced General DeWitt in 1942. The court had to decide not only whether General DeWitt had acted within the scope of his permissible authority, but whether it should validate what had been done. As many episodes in our constitutional history attest, those are different issues. The court could not escape the fact that it was the Supreme Court, arbiter of a vast system of customs, rules, habits, and relationships. Its decision inevitably would have far-reaching effects—on the power of the military, on our developing law of emergencies, on the future of those demagogues and political groups which live by attacking minorities, and on the future decision of cases in lower courts and police stations, involving the rights of citizens and aliens, the availability of habeas corpus, and like questions.

The question of how and on what grounds the Supreme Court should dispose of the cases also was one of broad political policy. Would a repudiation of Congress, the President, and the military in one aspect of their conduct of the war affect the people's will to fight? Would it create a campaign issue for 1944? Would it affect the power and prestige of the Supreme Court as a political institution?

In a bewildering and unimpressive series of opinions, relieved only by the dissents of Justice [Owen] Roberts and Justice [Frank] Murphy in one of the three cases—*Korematsu* v. *United States*—the court chose to assume that the main issues did not exist. In avoiding the risks of overruling the government on an issue of war policy, it weakened society's control over military power—one of the controls on which the whole organization of our society depends. It failed to uphold the most ordinary rights of citizenship, making Japanese-Americans into second-class citizens, who stand before the courts on a different legal footing from other Americans. It accepted and gave the prestige of its support to dangerous racial myths about a minority group, in arguments which can easily be applied to any other minority in our society.

The reasoning of the court was simple and direct. The problem was the scope of the war power of the national government. Both Congress and the executive seemed to have decided that special measures were required because espionage and sabotage were especially to be feared from persons of Japanese descent on the West Coast in the spring of 1942. It was not the job of the Supreme Court to decide such questions for itself. Its task was that of judicial review—to uphold the judgment of the officers directly responsible for fighting the war if, the court said, there was "any substantial basis" in fact for the conclusion that protective measures were necessary.

The Legalization of Racism

Frank Murphy, an associate justice of the Supreme Court from 1940 to 1949, wrote a concurring opinion in the 1943 case of Hirabayashi v. United States. *A year later, however, he was one of three justices to dissent from the similar case of* Korematsu v. United States, *arguing that the blanket exclusion of all Japanese from prescribed areas was racist and unconstitutional. Parts of his dissenting opinion in the 1944 case are reprinted here.*

This exclusion of "all persons of Japanese ancestry, both alien and non-alien," from the Pacific Coast area on a plea of military necessity in the absence of martial law ought not to be approved. Such exclusion goes over "the very brink of constitutional power" and falls into the ugly abyss of racism. . . .

The main reasons relied upon by those responsible for the forced evacuation . . . do not prove a reasonable relation between the group characteristics of Japanese Americans and the dangers of invasion, sabotage and espionage. The reasons appear, instead, to be largely an accumulation of much of the misinformation, half-truths and insinuations that for years have been directed against Japanese Americans by people with racial and economic prejudices—the same people who have been among the foremost advocates of the evacuation. A military judgment based upon such racial and sociological considerations is not entitled to the great weight ordinarily given the judgments based upon strictly military considerations. Especially is this so when every charge relative to race, religion, culture, geographical location, and legal and economic status has been substantially discredited by independent studies made by experts in these matters. . . .

No adequate reason is given for the failure to treat these Japanese Americans on an individual basis by holding investigations and hearings to separate the loyal from the disloyal, as was done in the case of persons of German and Italian ancestry. . . .

I dissent, therefore, from this legalization of racism. Racial discrimination in any form and in any degree has no justifiable part whatever in our democratic way of life. It is unattractive in any setting but it is utterly revolting among a free people who have embraced the principles set forth in the Constitution of the United States. All residents of this nation are kin in some way by blood or culture to a foreign land. Yet they are primarily and necessarily a part of the new and distinct civilization of the United States. They must accordingly be treated at all times as the heirs of the American experiment and as entitled to all the rights and freedoms guaranteed by the Constitution.

Two propositions which the court accepted as "facts" were held to afford a sufficiently "rational basis" for military decision. The first was that in time of war "residents having ethnic affiliations with an invading enemy may be a greater source of danger than those of different ancestry"—a doctrine which belongs with the race theories of the Nazis and, moreover, is contrary to the experience of American society in both our World Wars. (The weight of scientific evidence is that the most important driving urge of such minority groups is to conform, not to rebel.) The second was that on the West Coast in 1942 there was no time to isolate and examine the suspected Japanese on an individual basis—although of the 110,000 persons subject to the exclusion orders, 43 per cent were over fifty or under fifteen years old; they had lived in California without committing sabotage for five months after Pearl Harbor; in the country as a whole, thousands of aliens were examined individually without substantial delay; and in Britain 74,000 enemy aliens were checked in a few months.

By accepting the military judgment on these two points, without any evidence in the record to back it up, without requiring any testimony from the military, and even without adequate discussion by the court itself, the court has taken "judicial notice" of doubtful and controversial propositions of fact, as if they were as well-established as the census statistics or the tide tables. The court could have sent the cases back for a full trial on the justification for General DeWitt's decision. Instead, it upheld his ruling. Thus it created a profound question as to the position of the military power in our public life.

War Powers of the American Government

The conception of the war power under the American Constitution rests on the experience of the Revolution and the Civil War. It rests on basic political principles which men who had endured those times of trouble had fully discussed and carefully set forth. The chief architects of the conception were men of affairs who had participated in war, and had definite and well-founded ideas about the role of the professional military mind in the conduct of war.

The first and dominating principle of the war power under the Constitution is that the Commander-in-Chief of the armed forces must be a civilian, elected and not promoted to his office. In no other way can the subordination of the military to the civil power be assured. And in every democracy, the relationship between civil and military power is the crucial issue—the issue on which its capacity to survive in time of crisis ultimately depends.

The second principle governing the war power in a democracy is that of responsibility. Like every other officer of government, soldiers must answer for their decisions to the nation's system of law, and not to the Chief of Staff alone. Where military decisions lead to conflicts between individuals and authority—as in the Japanese exclusion program—the courts must adjudicate them. It is essential to every democratic value in society that official action, taken in the name of the war power, should be held to standards of responsibility under such circumstances. The courts have not in the past, and should not now, declare such problems to be beyond the reach of judicial review. The present Supreme Court is dominated by the conviction that in the past judicial review has unduly limited the freedom of administrative action. But surely the right answer to bad law is good law, rather than no law at all. The court must review the exercise of military power in a way which permits ample freedom to the executive, yet assures society as a whole that appropriate standards of responsibility have been met.

The issue for judicial decision in these cases is not lessened or changed by saying that the war power includes any steps required to win the war. The problem is still one of judgment as to what helps win a war. Who is to decide whether there was a sensible reason for doing what was done? Is it enough for the general to say that when he acted, he honestly thought it was a good idea to do what he did?

Unless the courts require a showing, in cases like these, of an intelligible relationship between means and ends, society has lost its basic protection against the abuse of military power. The general's good intentions must be irrelevant. There should be evidence in court that his military judgment had a suitable basis in fact.

The history of this question in the Supreme Court is unmistakable. The earlier decisions of the court had vigorously asserted that "what are the allowable limits of military discretion, and whether or not they have been overstepped in a particular case, are judicial questions"; and that there must be evidence enough to satisfy the court as to the need for the action taken. They had made it clear that the law is not neutral in such issues, but has a positive preference for protecting civil rights where possible, and a long-standing suspicion of the military mind when acting outside its own sphere.

Yet in the Japanese-American cases there was literally no evidence whatever by which the court might test the responsibility of General Dewitt's action. Dozens of Supreme Court decisions had said that the court would not pass on serious constitutional questions without a record before it, establishing the essential facts. Those cases were all ignored. One hundred thousand persons were sent to concentration camps on a record which wouldn't support a conviction for stealing a dog.

The earlier cases not only established the rule that there must be an independent judicial examination of the justification for a military act. They went much further. They declared a simple rule-of-thumb as a guide in handling cases involving military discretion, in which the military undertook to arrest, hold, or try people. So long as the civil courts were open and functioning, the Supreme Court had previously held, there could be no military necessity for allowing generals to hold, try, or punish people. The safety of the country could be thoroughly protected against treason, sabotage, and like crimes by ordinary arrest and trial in the civil courts, unless the courts were shut by riot, invasion, or insurrection.

That was the moral of the great case of *Ex Parte Milligan*, decided in 1866. *Ex Parte Milligan* is a monument in the democratic tradition, and until now it has been the animating force in this branch of our law. . . .

Yet in the cases of the Japanese-Americans the Supreme Court held the precedent of *Ex Parte Milligan* inapplicable. The reasoning is extraordinarily dangerous. The Japanese-Americans, the court said, were detained by a civilian agency, not by the Army. The program was not exclusively a matter for military administration, and it was enforceable under a statute by ordinary criminal remedies. Therefore, it did not present the question of the power of military tribunals to conduct trials under the laws of war.

But the Japanese-Americans were ordered detained by a general, purporting to act on military grounds. The military order was enforceable, on pain of imprisonment. While a United States marshal, rather than a military policeman, assured obedience to the order, the ultimate sanction behind the marshal's writ is the same as that of the military police: the bayonets of United States troops. It is hardly a ground for distinction that the general's command was backed by the penalty of civil imprisonment, or that he obtained civilian aid in running the relocation camps. The starting point for the entire program was a military order, which had to be obeyed.

In *Ex Parte Milligan* the Supreme Court had said that the military could not constitutionally arrest, nor could a military tribunal constitutionally try, civilians charged with treason and conspiracy to destroy the state by force, at a time when the civil courts were open and functioning. Yet under the plan considered in the Japanese-American cases, people not charged with crime are imprisoned without even a military trial, on the ground that they have the taint of Japanese blood. It would seem clear that if it is illegal to arrest and confine people after an unwarranted military trial, it is surely even more illegal to arrest and confine them without any trial at all. But the Supreme Court says that the issues of the *Milligan* case were not involved in this case because the evacuees were committed to camps by military orders, not by military tribunals, and because their jailers did not wear uniforms!

There are, then, two basic constitutional problems concealed in the court's easy dismissal of *Ex Parte Milligan:* the arrest, removal, and confinement of persons without trial, pending examination of their loyalty; and the indefinite confinement of persons found to be disloyal. On both counts, at least as to citizens, the moral of *Ex Parte Milligan* is plain.

As for the Japanese *aliens* involved in the evacuation program, the constitutional problem is different. In time of war, the government possesses great powers over enemy aliens, which are to be exercised, the courts say, for the "single purpose" of preventing enemy aliens from aiding the enemy. They may be interned if dangerous and their property in the United States may be taken into custody. Yet they are entitled to our general constitutional protections of individual liberty—to trial by jury, the writ of habeas corpus, and the other basic rights of the person. Is it permissible to intern all the Japanese who live on the West Coast, but to allow German and Italian aliens, and Japanese who live elsewhere, general freedom? Surely the control and custody of enemy aliens in wartime should be reasonably equal and even-handed.

Five Dangerous Propositions

The Japanese exclusion program rests on five propositions of the utmost potential menace:

1. Protective custody, extending over three or four years, is a permitted form of imprisonment in the United States.

2. Political opinions, not criminal acts, may contain enough danger to justify such imprisonment.

3. Men, women, and children of a given racial group, both Americans and resident aliens, can be presumed to possess the kind of dangerous ideas which require their imprisonment.

4. In time of war or emergency the military—perhaps without even the concurrence of the legislature—can decide what political opinions require imprisonment, and which groups are infected with them.

5. The decision of the military can be carried out without indictment, trial, examination, jury, the confrontation of witnesses, counsel for the defense, the privilege against self-incrimination, or any of the other safeguards of the Bill of Rights.

The idea of punishment only for individual criminal behavior is basic to all systems of civilized law. A great principle was never lost so casually. Mr. Justice [Hugo] Black's comment was weak to the point of impotence: "Hardships are a part of war, and war is an aggregation of hardships." It was an answer in the spirit of cliché: "Don't you know there's a war going on?" It ignores the rights of citizenship, and the safeguards of trial practice which have been the historical attributes of liberty.

We believe that the German people bear a common political responsibility for outrages secretly committed by the Gestapo and the SS. What are we to think of our own part in a program which violates every principle of our common life, yet has been approved by the President, Congress, and the Supreme Court?

Three chief forms of reparation are available, and should be pursued. The first is the inescapable obligation of the federal government to protect the civil rights of Japanese-Americans against organized and unorganized hooliganism. If local law enforcement fails, federal prosecutions under the national Civil Rights Act should be undertaken.

Secondly, generous financial indemnity should be sought. Apart from the sufferings of their imprisonment, the Japanese-Americans have sustained heavy property losses from their evacuation.

Finally, the basic issues should be presented to the Supreme Court again, in an effort to obtain a prompt reversal of these wartime cases. The Supreme Court has often corrected its own errors in the past, especially when that error was occasioned by the excitement of a tense moment. After the end of the Civil War, several earlier decisions were reversed by *Ex Parte Milligan*. The famous flag-salute case of 1940 has recently been overruled in the decision of *West Virginia* v. *Barnett*. Similar public expiation in the case of the Japanese-Americans would be good for the court, and for the country.

CHAPTER 5

Historians Debate the "Good War"

Chapter Preface

World War II has frequently been called (both with and without irony) the "Good War" by Americans who remember it or who write about it. Beyond being a "just" war in which America fought on the right side, World War II was, in the memories of many Americans who lived through it, a golden age of national unity and accomplishment—a time when through selflessness, grit, and technical inventiveness, the United States was able to gain victory over its evil enemies.

Historians have identified several reasons why World War II, the most destructive war in human history, is often viewed as a good war. Its battles were fought far from America's shores, sparing the United States most of the war's brutality. The moral justification for fighting a war against Germany was strengthened by postwar revelations of the extent of the Holocaust that killed millions of Jews and other "undesirables." America emerged from World War II victorious over its enemies and relatively united at home—qualities that were conspicuously lacking in the nation's subsequent major military conflicts in Korea and, especially, Vietnam. In addition, historian Roger Daniels writes, World War II was

> a war that united, rather than divided, the American people; a war that ended the worst depression in our history; a war that set off a decades-long boom that transformed the economic and social life of the American people; a war that made the United States clearly and unmistakably the most powerful nation on earth. It reinforced Americans' notions about themselves as a "can do" people who could solve almost any problem. So, it is no wonder that, in retrospect, a kind of nostalgia has allowed Americans to think of it as the "good war."

Such a nostalgic view of World War II as a time when "everyone was united" and "things were better" distorts the past, according to historian Michael C.C. Adams, one of the authors included in this chapter. He insists that perceiving World War II as a good war allows people to gloss over the extreme human suffering and moral complexities of the conflict. It is the job of the American historian, Adams argues, to go beyond the nostalgic memories and motion picture depictions of the "Good War" and examine the event's harmful aspects, such as the mental and moral breakdown many American soldiers experienced in combat and the government's manipulation of media coverage during the war.

A different perspective on World War II is presented by the other contributor to this chapter, historian William O'Neill. His book *A Democracy at War* details many of the failures and shortcomings of the American war effort, ranging from the manufacture of submarine torpedoes that did not explode to the internment of Japanese Americans. However, in his conclusion, excerpted here, he contends that positive memories of World War II as a good war have much basis in fact. The United States, he asserts, was able to preserve its democratic institutions, rise above its ethnic divisions, and leave the world situation much better than it would have been had the nation stayed out of war. The two divergent views presented here reflect the complexity of judging World War II and its place in American history.

VIEWPOINT 1

"Americans could be proud of themselves, not only for winning the war but, by and large, for the way in which they won it."

World War II Was a Time of Noteworthy American Achievement

William L. O'Neill (b. 1935)

William L. O'Neill, a professor of history at Rutgers University, New Jersey, has written many books on American history, including *Feminism in America: A History* and *American High: The Years of Confidence, 1945–1960*. The following viewpoint is excerpted from his book *A Democracy at War: America's Fight at Home and Abroad in World War II*, in which he examines American society's response to the challenges of World War II. O'Neill concludes that, despite some lapses in America's military and political leadership, and despite the fact that the country did not entirely live up to its democratic ideals, Americans can and should take pride in the nation's overall record of accomplishment during World War II. He argues that most soldiers returned from the war better prepared for civilian life than before they left, that the American system of democracy was vindicated against the challenges of war and fascism, and that the war created a sense of national togetherness and cooperation. Arguing that "the great thing about democracy is that it self-corrects," O'Neill contends that even the country's lapses, such as its treatment of blacks and Japanese-Americans, were later corrected in social reforms, such as those resulting from the civil rights movement, that had roots in the expressed ideals and actual experiences of World War II.

A disaster for everyone else, World War II was experienced differently by the United States. Its worse feature, the 405,000 servicemen who died of all causes, was more than offset by population growth, the total number of Americans rising from 133.4 million in 1941 to 140 million in 1945, mainly through natural increase. Sixteen babies were born for every man who died in uniform. Further, they were born into a country whose people had gained much from military spending, mean family income rising by over 25 percent in constant dollars between 1941 and 1944, a remarkable accomplishment for a nation at war.

This is not to minimize the sorrow. For those deprived of a loved one, no amount of prosperity could serve as compensation. Many individuals suffered such devastating losses, and many neighborhoods and towns as well. However, most of the boys not only returned, but were better equipped for civilian life than when they left it, tempered by war, older than their years, determined to make up lost ground. Greatly aided by the GI Bill and the surge of postwar prosperity, which they profited from, but to which they also contributed, they would go to school or get jobs, marry, and settle down. A magnificent generation in war, they would be splendid in peacetime also.

Justice Was Served

Justice, too, would be served by the war. At the time, most Americans felt that victory had vindicated their democratic system and in many ways it had. To remain democratic, to the extent even of holding elections on schedule, while fighting a long and terrible war showed how committed Americans were to safeguarding their political rights. Moreover, American war aims were appropriate to a democracy, the nation asking for no territories, no indemnities, and, in a real sense, no revenge. America fought a generous war, and its benevolence extended afterward to rebuilding the economies of the states it had defeated as well as those of its allies. Americans could be proud of themselves, not only for winning the war but, by and large, for the way in which they won it.

America nevertheless failed to live up to its highest principles in very important ways, discriminating against refugees, Japanese-Americans, and blacks, while denying women full equality on the job and in the armed services. These faults were poorly understood at the time, and, except by the victims, too seldom censured. The experience was not wasted, even so. Blacks lost little time organizing after the war and 15 years later legalized segregation was everywhere under attack, with veterans playing a major part in its destruction. Immigration laws were revised, enabling many refugees to come here after the war ended. Ultimately even racial exclusion practices were struck down, opening the Promised Land to Hispanics and Asians on a scale undreamed of in the 1940s. Japanese-Americans had a long wait before the crime against them was acknowledged, but finally even this injustice was owned up to and restitution ordered by Congress. Women never got their due. When gender discrimination came under assault in the late 1960s it was for reasons unrelated to women's wartime contribution, which has never been sufficiently recognized.

That many wrongs were righted after the war does not excuse their commission. What it does show, however, is that American democracy was evolving. Wartime injustice was produced by the nation that was, not the nation that would be. Those Negroes and Japanese-Americans who fought for the chance to fight for their country were right, because the political system they defended with their lives was not so much an institution as a process. Jim Crow was legal in 1945, but in 20 more years it would be finished. The great thing about democracy is that it self-corrects, and in all these areas did.

Lessons of the War

Some valuable lessons were learned from the war, others quickly forgotten. The one that made the greatest impression was the danger of being unprepared and alone. When the Cold War developed, America would arm itself it to the teeth and form military alliances with dozens of countries. Though moderation would have been better still, this overreaction was certainly preferable to a feeble response. The lesson of the 1930s was learned at last, even if all too well.

The mobilization muddles were not taken to heart, or even remembered for long. Everyone knows the Army was large, but few that it was not large enough, and desperately short of Wacs [women]. The manpower crisis is little remembered, the failure to enact national service not at all. The resulting lack of rotation for combat troops figures only in history books. The cost of fighting two Pacific Wars instead of having a single strategy has never been conceded. There has never been, and never will be, a movie about strategic bombing that shows it didn't work.

The structural weaknesses of American democracy that gave isolationists almost a veto over national security affairs in the prewar era have not changed, either. This has nothing to do with civil rights and liberties, rather, it concerns the way decisions are made in a country where representatives run for office every two years, and in which the executive and legislative branches are frequently deadlocked. Public-opinion polls are more potent than ever. Congress remains reluctant to offend any interest group, or pass measures, however needed, that will cause inconvenience. The short term, even more than before, is what counts in Washington.

People Helping Each Other

One of the more striking aspects of the war was a generosity of spirit that it brought forth. Though government programs often fell short of need, volunteerism and individual effort took up much of the slack. While this side of the war is poorly documented, many remember it as a time when people helped each other out with car pools, block organizations, and simple neighborliness.

Before troops were shipped overseas, their wives often followed them from camp to camp, living in squalid conditions but sustained by each other, and sometimes by the kindness of strangers. Susan Keller, whose husband Dempsey was in Company K of the 84th Infantry Division, followed him to Louisiana, even though she had no car and an infant in arms and another on the way. The only place she could find to live was a single room with a family of five. The parents not only took Susan in but to the hospital when her second child was born, frequently looking after her children in addition to their own. Such experiences were far from rare. Americans were united in a common cause and had a sense of the country as being more than the sum of its interest groups. Whatever their faults, those Americans were, as Stephen Ambrose says, a "we" generation and knew it.

On V-J Day, Marjorie Haselton of Massachusetts wrote to her husband in China:

> You and I were brought up to think cynically of patriotism . . . by the bitter, realistic writers of the twenties and thirties. [But] this war has taught me—I love my country and I'm not ashamed to admit it anymore. . . . I am proud of the men of my generation. Brought up like you and I in false prosperity and then degrading depression, they have overcome these handicaps. And shown the world that America has something the world can never take away from us—a determination to keep our way of life. . . . Call it Yankee ingenuity or whatever you will, it still is the one force that won the war—the thing the enemy never believed we had. That is why, tonight, I am proud to be an American and married to one of its fighting men. . . . You proved that Americans may look soft and easy going, "spoiled" by the highest standard of living in the world, yet when the hour of need came you showed them we could take it—*and* dish it out.

On the same day, Rose McClain of Washington State wrote a less militant but equally heartfelt letter to her husband in the Pacific:

> Today I cried and thanked God for the end of this war and I

shall continue to pray that this shall be the end of war for all time. That our children will learn kindness, patience, honesty, and the depth of love and trust we have learned from all of this, without the tragedy of war. That they shall never know hate, selfishness and death from such as this has been.

Nancy Arnot Harjan was seventeen when the war ended. She had been doing her bit, giving blood, knitting scarves and caps for the servicemen, dancing with sailors at the USO, and bringing them home for dinner. On one level she knew that most of the warriors were boys like those she dated. Yet, on another level, as she later recalled:

I saw on the news films the Parisian people, with tears streaming down their faces, welcoming our GIs. They were doing what I wanted them to do. When the Holocaust survivors came out, I felt we were liberating them. When the GIs and the Russian soldiers met, they were all knights in shining armor, saving humanity. [Laughs.] I believed in that.

The embarrassed laughter is that of the adult recalling her naive youth, yet, what she remembered thinking then was, if not the entire truth about the war, certainly true enough.

The American Record

In a passage from his book A Democracy at War, *historian William L. O'Neill argues that Americans have little reason to feel ashamed of America's war record.*

Although no nation can come out of a long and brutal war with an unblemished record, Americans had little reason to feel ashamed. Except for the terror bombing of Germany and Japan, a big exception of course, America waged as humane a war as it could. And if its hands were not perfectly clean, one need only look at those of Germany and Japan and Russia to restore perspective. Fighting for their lives against cruel foes, Americans did what they had to do. For this the entire world, including the enemy peoples whose own freedom was thereby gained, remains in their debt. Americans spread democracy in the most unlikely places, where it remains a monument to their effort and their sacrifice.

Though an exciting time for girls like Nancy, the war years were hard on women separated from the men they loved. This was true even of college students, who had fewer problems than most. Katherine McReynolds was an undergraduate at the University of Missouri who, after the war had ended and she did not have to keep up a cheerful front, wrote to her future husband overseas:

> [Our housemother] thinks we all seem so mature. Why shouldn't
> we? Franny's Richard and June Digby's twin brother were killed.
> Meyer's fiance spent six months in a German prison camp. The
> rest of us have been worried sick and hopelessly lonesome for
> years. It's a wonder we aren't old women.

There is no way to factor these elements into a comprehensive
equation. How do we balance precious lives lost against those
precious new lives brought into the world even as the fighting
raged? The sum of human suffering, at home and on the battlefield, cannot be measured against the good times that got better
and better even as the casualties rose.

A World Made Better

All one can say in the end is that the war was, and remains,
well worth the effort and the heartbreak. As evidence, one has
only to imagine what kind of world we would live in today if
America had remained neutral. Russia might have survived in a
shrunken form, and Great Britain for a time also, but the rest of
Eurasia would have been enslaved by the Axis powers. The Holocaust would have gone on to its bitter end, and we can be sure
that a victorious Hitler, armed soon with atomic weapons and
ballistic missiles, would have caused additional havoc—dwarfing
that which was actually wreaked. The most to be hoped for in
that event would have been the world that George Orwell described in *1984*—at worst, no world at all.

By passing this greatest of all modern tests America also won
the right to become a better nation. Though social reform was not
why most servicemen took the risks they did, it would be one of
the outcomes. Some reforms, like the defeat of racial segregation,
would have roots in the war experience. Others would result
from the democratic impulse itself that the war had been fought
to preserve.

The Strengths of America

In a host of ways the war brought out, or underlined, the
strengths of America that far outweighed its defects. Family values were not just a political slogan but a fact of daily life. Most
people married for keeps. Fathers supported their children. The
war years were not an age of innocence. . . . Relations between the
Allies were strained, politicians often cynical, and individual selfishness remained about the same. But, more so than now, Americans accepted responsibility for their acts and did not uphold personal gratification as the be all and end all of life. They believed
in doing their duty, at home as at the front.

The most pluralistic of democracies, a Trans-National America,
as the social critic Randolph Bourne had called it, this country

proved that ethnic diversity enriched rather than weakened. Its fighting men met every test. Its leaders may have faltered, but did not fail. The people overcame their enemies, surmounting as well the difficulties presented by allies, a chaotic and divided government, among other faults, to gain what [Franklin] Roosevelt had promised would be "the inevitable triumph." "Sweet land of liberty," the children sang, and so it was, and so it would remain—thanks to a great generation.

VIEWPOINT 2

"World War II . . . has been converted over time from a complex, problematic event . . . to a simple, shining legend of the Good War."

World War II Had Many Negative Aspects for America

Michael C.C. Adams (b. 1945)

Michael C.C. Adams is a professor of history at Northern Kentucky University at Highland Heights. His books include *Our Masters, the Rebels*, a book on the Civil War, and *The Best War Ever: America and World War II*, from which the following viewpoint is excerpted. Adams argues that Americans have collectively forgotten many unpleasant realities of World War II in order to remember it as a golden age of national unity and accomplishment—a view of the "Good War" that he asserts is largely a myth. He argues that World War II resulted in more human costs and negative consequences for Americans than is commonly recognized, including family stress, racial discrimination, and military atrocities. Adams asserts that many of the problems Americans have associated with later wars and periods—such as psychiatric problems among soldiers and a rising divorce rate—were widespread during World War II.

All societies to some degree reinvent their pasts. This is not intended, not a pattern of deliberate lying; but too much has happened for it all to be retained in popular memory. Therefore, to make our understanding of history manageable, we try to retrieve from the huge clutter of the past only those events that seem to be particularly useful, interesting, or exciting. Usable historical events appear to offer helpful insights into how people of the past confronted problems or situations similar to our own.

Examples of functional and engaging past happenings are dramatic disasters, such as the sinking of the Titanic, which serve as warnings, or great triumphs, such as World War II. We tend to dwell on the victories because they make us feel good about ourselves. We see them as events that showcase our national strength, collective courage, idealism, and other desirable traits.

Sometimes we conjure up the past in such a way that it appears better than it really was. We forget ugly things we did and magnify the good things. This is wishful thinking, the desire to retell our past not as it was but as we would like it to have been. If the past is remolded too drastically, it ceases to be real history. It becomes what we call myth, or folklore, instead. One task of the historian is to try to keep our knowledge of the past as complete and accurate as possible so that our popular version does not depart too far from reality. If history becomes too mythologized, it may lose its value as a tool for understanding our course as a society. Adolf Hitler presented a deeply distorted view of Germany's history and role in the twentieth century. When this was accepted by his people, they embarked on a course leading to national disaster.

The influence of historians is, however, limited. Because they must be comprehensive in their treatment of the past and cannot simply choose to highlight the exciting and dramatic, their work often strikes people as boring and tedious. It cannot compete with modern vehicles of folklore history: film and television. In addition, historians, too, are victims of the immenseness of the past: they can never read, digest, and describe all there is to know about an event or character (there are one million documents in the Lyndon Baines Johnson Library alone). They must be highly selective in what they choose to present to us, so their picture is incomplete, a distortion to some degree. And as they are creatures of their time and place, members of the society as well as professional observers of it, their retelling of history will be molded partly by the same biases and constraints that shape the popular view. Then, through repetition, people come to believe that this partial portrait is the whole landscape of history, and what is forgotten will be thought never to have existed.

The Best War Ever

Such a process happened with World War II, which has been converted over time from a complex, problematic event, full of nuance and debatable meaning, to a simple, shining legend of the Good War. For many, including a majority of survivors from the era, the war years have become America's golden age, a peak in the life of society when everything worked out and the good guys definitely got a happy ending. It was a great war. For Americans it was the best war ever.

This was the film age, and the script could have been written in Hollywood. The original villains were the Nazis and the Fascists, many of whom obligingly dressed in black. They bullied the weak-willed democratic politicians who tried to buy them off, which gave us the word *appeasement* as a catchall term of contempt for anyone who suggests a diplomatic solution to potential international aggression. The bad guys then took the first rounds, driving opponent after opponent out of the fighting. The Americans gave material aid to their cousins, the British, who finally fought pluckily with their backs to the wall, until the United States was brought into the fighting by the treacherous Japanese, who crippled the Pacific fleet at Pearl Harbor.

For a while, it looked grim all over, but then the Allies fought back, their victories culminating in the unconditional surrender of all enemy nations, who were then made over in our image. America emerged from the war strong, united, prosperous, and the unrivaled and admired leader of the free world. . . .

The idea that World War II was the best war America had is not entirely off the mark; like any enduring myth, it rests on a solid core of credible argument. America cemented its final rise to world power with relatively light losses: about 300,000 Americans died; a further 1 million were wounded, of whom 500,000 were seriously disabled. Tragic as these figures are, they are dwarfed by those for other belligerents. The Japanese lost 2.3 million, Germany about 5.6 million, China perhaps as many as 10 million, and the Soviet Union a staggering 20 million. Put another way, the death rate in the American Civil War of 1861–65 was 182 per ten thousand population. For World War II, the proportion of Americans killed was 30 per ten thousand.

Of the major belligerents, the United States was alone in enjoying a higher standard of living as a result of the war. Following the lean Depression years, the gross national product for 1940 was $97 billion. By 1944 it had reached $190 billion. The average gross weekly wage rose from $25.20 in 1940 to $43.39 in 1945, an increase of 72 percent. The United States was unique among the principal combatants in being neither invaded nor bombed, and most people, in or out of uniform, never saw a fighting front. As a result, the war was for many a prosperous, exciting, even safe change from the "ruined and colorless landscape of the Depression," as Russell Baker, a writer who grew up in the 1930s,

The Myth of National Unity

Historians Kenneth Paul O'Brien and Lynn Hudson Parsons, in their introduction to the book The Home-Front War, *argue that Americans were not as united in their purpose as some remember.*

Government-sponsored hoopla and economic expansion provided the seeds for what Michael C.C. Adams calls the "myth" about the war. As he [in *The Best War Ever*] describes the myth: "Everyone was united: there were no racial or gender tensions, no class conflicts. Things were better, from kitchen gadgets to public schools. Families were well adjusted; kids read a lot and respected their elders." To help Americans believe in this version of the war years, Hollywood created film after film reinforcing the view. Few in the movie capital wished to challenge the prevailing mythology being orchestrated by government propagandists who made unity in the war one of their major themes.

In reality, of course, America was hardly united, at least not to the extent remembered. Beneath the veneer of national compliance, a black market flourished in rationed goods. When African Americans and women were employed in jobs that had been the traditional preserve of white males, hostility often resulted, sometimes even violence. The same boom that brought endless jobs also brought widespread distress. Small manufacturers found themselves without the raw materials to make goods. Appliance and auto dealers discovered they had no products to sell. If the bureaucracy grew dramatically in Washington, services often suffered on other levels, as many civil servants were enticed into factory work by the higher wages paid by contracts for war production. The same was true for teachers. Local medical care became a problem as nurses and doctors, desperately needed by the armed forces, left their home communities. Family life changed. Fewer men were home to gather around holiday tables. Even those families fortunate enough to have adult men at home often had to adjust to midnight shifts and 52-hour workweeks. Leisure itself became a problem as well. The traditional twentieth-century American pressure valve, the privately owned and operated automobile, was effectively put to rest by gasoline and tire rationing, the 35 mile-per-hour speed limit, and the ban on pleasure driving. Then there were those young teenagers, many of whom left schools for either the service or war work in 1944 and 1945. Others were thought to be seen running wild in the streets, leading to a chorus of complaints about rising rates of juvenile delinquency.

termed the decade. "It was," he remembered, "a season of bread lines, soup kitchens, hobo jungles, bandits riding the highways." The Depression had been a lonely time; people struggled in isolation for survival, and some committed suicide. There was, said Baker, a felt loss of love and security. World War II for a time gave Americans a sense of belonging, of community, as they were caught up in the war fever.

Most of us still agree that nazism was an evil so monstrous that the war in Europe had to be fought. "Unlike Vietnam—the war that dominated our children's lives," said 1940s veteran Roger Hilsman, "World War II was a 'good' war. Hitler was a maniacal monster, and young as we were, we saw this and understood its implications." Hilsman was correct about the need to fight. Yet he was writing with the benefit of hindsight. This is problematic, and it gives us a window through which to begin exploring what is wrong with the myth.

At the time, many Americans didn't fully understand the threat of Hitler; they wanted to beat the Japanese first because they hated them more (a 1942 poll showed 66 percent of Americans wanting the Pacific war to have priority). The Pacific campaigns were fought with a mutual ferocity that culminated in the Japanese kamikaze attacks and the Allied incendiary and atomic bombings of Japan's major cities. Many Americans of the war generation like to divorce the atom bombings from the conflict, seeing them as the curtain raiser on the nuclear age rather than the last act of our best war. But they were in fact the final destructive episode in a fight that, as historian John Ellis said, was won and lost by brute force.

Reality and Myth

Here is the point. To make World War II into the best war ever, we must leave out the area bombings and other questionable aspects while exaggerating the good things. The war myth is distorted not so much in what it says as in what it doesn't say. Combat in World War II was rarely glamorous. It was so bad that the breakdown rate for men consistently in action for twenty-eight days ran as high as 90 percent. Soldiers of all nations performed deeds of courage, but they also shot prisoners, machine-gunned defenseless enemies in the water or in parachutes, and raped women, including their own military personnel. And they had nightmares afterward about what they had seen and done. About 25 percent of the men still in the hospital from the war are psychiatric cases.

Posttraumatic stress disorder no more originated with Vietnam than did napalm. This terrible weapon, a jellied gasoline that burns its victims, was invented by American scientists during

World War II and used in all major combat zones, along with phosphorous, another flesh-searing load for bombs and shells. On all battlefronts where there were perceived ethnic differences, the war was fought without many rules. Russians and Germans butchered each other indiscriminately. The Japanese abused Allied prisoners and were in turn often seen as subhuman "gooks."

Contrary to the popular myth that dumps all negatives on Vietnam, the worst war we had, there was significant discrimination in the armed forces during World War II. Many soldiers didn't know what the war was about, and some resented their war-long terms of service, feeling they were doing everybody's fighting. The majority of returning soldiers got no parades. James Jones, a veteran, noted that wounded men repatriated to the United States were treated as though diseased, and people rushed to wash their hands after greeting them. Civilians feared that the GIs would think the country owed them a living, while veterans felt that "when you come back they treat you just like scum." Said this anonymous soldier: "If you ever get the boys all together they will probably kill all the civilians."

America's industrial output to sustain the war was prodigious. As indicators, 86,000 tanks, 296,000 planes, and 71,000 warships were produced. Many of these were of sound design and quality. Others were not. For economy and swiftness, many American aircraft carriers had unarmored flight decks, which made them vulnerable to airborne attacks. American torpedoes were of poor quality initially, until Axis designs were copied. The "mulberries," floating artificial harbors used to assist the British-American Normandy landings, functioned poorly, and the American one at Omaha Beach was wrecked by high seas. Although Joe DeChick, a local talk-show host, recently called the B-17 Flying Fortress a "lean, mean fighting machine" that "was virtually invincible," it suffered heavy losses in raids over Germany until it could be protected by new, long-range fighter planes.

After the initial post–Pearl Harbor burst of unity and willing sacrifice, Americans showed the average amount of selfishness and cupidity. Politics became politics again. The administration collected gossip about General Douglas MacArthur's sex life to use if he ran for president on the Republican ticket. And innuendos about homosexuality helped to force Sumner Welles out of the State Department when it was decided he was too pro-Soviet. Labor-management disputes continued. Merchant seamen, taking badly needed supplies to the troops on Guadalcanal, turned back when they were refused extra pay. An elderly gentleman on a bus in Viola, Kentucky, home of a munitions plant, hit a female passenger with his umbrella when she said she hoped the war wouldn't end until she had worked long enough to buy a refrigerator.

The war massively altered the face of American society. Small farmers and storeowners went under, while big businesses became great corporations. Fed by the emergency, the federal bureaucracy mushroomed from 1 million to 3.8 million. Most people paid income tax for the first time. Millions of Americans moved, usually to the cities, which experienced considerable racial tension and some violence as ethnic groups were thrown together. The stress of social change also showed up in a record number of hospital admissions for patients suffering from psychoses. Family dislocation came to be a concern: with fathers in the armed forces and mothers working, kids seemed to go wild, and people worried about juvenile delinquency. In a 1946 opinion poll, a majority of adults said adolescent behavior had degenerated during the war; only 9 percent thought it had improved. And people may now think that marriages were more sacred back then, but marital strain led to a record high 600,000 divorces in 1946.

Americans may have been better educated then, too, but a 1942 poll showed that 59 percent of them couldn't locate China, a major ally, on the map. In the same year, Philip Wylie, a disillusioned federal official, published *Generation of Vipers*, a book cataloguing America's ills. The list is startlingly modern. Young people, he said, could no longer think because education failed to challenge them—and nobody flunked. They listened to radio and watched movies instead of reading books. Teachers who were intellectually demanding got fired. Consumerism and uncritical boosterism were pervasive, making discussion of social issues like pollution, urban congestion, drug addiction, and materialism impossible. Many of Wylie's strictures were ignored at the time and have been forgotten since.

Censorship

The selective process by which only positive aspects of the war received mainstream attention began during the conflict itself—one of the most censored events in modern history. Every nation rigorously edited the news. No Japanese or American newspaper, for example, carried a single report of atrocities by their own military, though there were in fact many. The beating and even killing of African-American soldiers by other U.S. service personnel also went undisclosed. Canadian correspondent Charles Lynch spoke for the whole international press corps when he said of the reporters: "We were cheerleaders." Perhaps, he thought, this was necessary for national survival in a total war. But "it wasn't good journalism. It wasn't journalism at all."

The U.S. military censored all reports from the front, and those who broke the rules were sent home. In America, the Office of Censorship vetted public and private communications, while the

Office of Facts and Figures, and later the Office of War Information, published propaganda in support of the war effort. The result was a cleaned-up, cosmetically-enhanced version of reality. The war, said writer Fletcher Pratt, was reported like a polite social function. "The official censors pretty well succeeded in putting over the legend that the war was won without a single mistake by a command consisting exclusively of geniuses." When Walter Cronkite filed a report that the Eighth Air Force had blindly bombed Germany through solid cloud cover, challenging the myth that all American bombing was pinpoint accurate and hit only military targets, his copy was held up. A combat photographer who recorded the murder of SS soldiers by their American guards was told the film couldn't be screened because of technical difficulties. And when Eric Sevareid tried to broadcast descriptions of faceless, limbless boys in military hospitals, the censors told him to write about new miracle drugs and medical instruments instead.

But the news wasn't manipulated only by the censors. John Steinbeck, a tough-minded writer who exposed human misery during the Depression, admitted that as a war reporter he deliberately slanted his stories to omit anything that might shock civilians. He didn't report on the rotten conditions suffered by the infantry or on homosexual activity in the military.

Censorship in the interests of military security, even protection of civilian morale, has its purpose. But the image-making went beyond this. Generals, even whole branches of the service like the paratroops and the Marine Corps, employed platoons of public relations officers and advertising agencies to make sure they looked good. General Douglas MacArthur was a notorious publicity hound. During the first months of 1942, when the Japanese were smashing his defenses in the Philippines, he still found time to publish 140 press releases. Manufacturing an enemy body count is usually associated with Vietnam, but for one two-year period in the Pacific war, MacArthur reported 200,000 Japanese killed for 122 Allied losses. After he was driven from the Philippines, the general became famous for the line, "I shall return." But this sound bite was manufactured from his speeches by staffers. When he did return, the dramatic scenes of him wading ashore were filmed several times on different beaches to get the right effect. . . .

One of the most popular mantel ornaments of the 1940s was a set of three brass monkeys, one covering its eyes, another its ears, a third its mouth. Called See No Evil, Hear No Evil, and Speak No Evil, they represented a quite common approach to life. When the Pentagon released candid photographs of American corpses after the battle for Tarawa in the Pacific, it received piles of abusive mail demanding that such obscene disclosures be stopped. After disfigured soldiers from the plastic surgery hospital in Pasadena, California, were allowed to go downtown, the local paper got letters asking, "Why can't they be kept on their own grounds and off the streets?" An army survey of GI sexual practices overseas, including statistics on pregnancies caused, was kept secret for forty years after the war out of fear about public reaction. . . .

The Problem of Myths

To the degree that America has simplified the complex experience of World War II, it is left with an incomplete and therefore misleading legacy. . . .

The ultimate problem of powerful myths about an idealized past is that they postulate a golden age, when things were better than they are now, a peak of efficiency from which the country has declined and which it must refoster if it is to prosper. In short, America's future lies in reclaiming its past. It is understandable that Americans should see the 1940s as this golden age. As a result of the war, America became prosperous and powerful. But no magic formula produced this scenario; it was a unique situation, produced largely by the fact that America alone of the great world powers was not a battleground. These circumstances cannot be recreated.

This is just as well, for the image of this golden age is highly selective. It leaves out the fact that America of the 1940s was wracked by change and troubled by many of the same problems that vex it now. It faced a rising divorce rate, juvenile delinquency, declining educational standards, and a loss of the traditional verities. And it did not always manage to resolve these difficulties. Americans do themselves a disservice when they assume that their predecessors did everything better than they do. Usually, those who want to return to the past are those who know too little about it. The war created problems that are even now not fully resolved, such as what to do about nuclear weapons and their threat to the future of humanity. The war highlighted racism in the culture and guaranteed that the issue of civil rights would be on the national agenda in the decades following 1945.

The past and its legacies are complex. We should consider all the ramifications of the war, not just the glorious and dramatic moments captured for us in Hollywood movies. The war was not a discrete event that ended when the last enemy surrendered unconditionally, leaving America the most powerful superpower in the world. The war was a profoundly disturbing moment in the flow of history, the after effects of which, like waves radiating out from a pebble dropped in water, continue now.

For Discussion

Chapter One

1. Does Franklin D. Roosevelt, in either his 1939 speech on American neutrality or his 1940 speech in favor of Lend-Lease, leave open the possibility that the United States *might* enter the war? In light of the fact that the United States ultimately entered World War II, are charges by his opponents that he misled the American public legitimate? Explain your answer.

2. What harmful effects might a peacetime military draft have on the United States, according to Maxwell S. Stewart? Does Freda Kirchwey share Stewart's concerns? What reasons does she give for supporting a draft? Whose argument is more persuasive? Why?

3. What harms do Arthur H. Vandenberg, Robert M. Hutchins, and Norman Thomas predict will befall the United States if it enters a state of war? Do you believe that Hutchins's suggested course of action for the United States, along with the claim he makes in the last sentence of his viewpoint, is realistic? Why or why not?

4. Does Norman Thomas express agreement with the logic of the opening arguments of Stanley High? Do you believe both authors would agree with the concluding sentences of the viewpoint by Arthur H. Vandenberg? Explain your answer.

Chapter Two

1. Of the arguments of George C. Marshall, Henry L. Stimson, and Charles Sweeny concerning a possible cross-Channel invasion, which could be classified as arguments of military strategy? Which could be classified as arguments of diplomatic concerns? Which arguments address both military and diplomatic issues?

2. Do the viewpoints by Henry Morgenthau Jr. and the State Department express fundamental differences on the goals of U.S. policy in Germany, or merely on the means to attain them? Do they present differing views as to whether the German people as a whole were to blame for World War II? Explain your answers.

3. The State Department memorandum on the Soviet Union was written in early 1942, while John Hickerson's analysis dates from early 1945. What was the position of the Soviet Union in the war at each time, and how might changes in that position account for the two opinions regarding U.S. policy toward that nation?

4. What moral and military arguments does the *Christian Century* present in criticizing the use of the atomic bomb? Do you believe the arguments of Henry L. Stimson to be an adequate defense of what the United States did? Why or why not?

Chapter Three

1. Would Leon Henderson's arguments have been enough to convince you to pay higher taxes or forgo certain consumer goods? What parts of his speech do you find especially persuasive? What parts do you find unpersuasive? Explain your answers.

2. Can the arguments made by the editors of *Consumer's Research Bulletin* be dismissed as personal attacks on Leon Henderson and other government officials? Why or why not?

3. Warren H. Atherton represents himself as speaking for American soldiers and veterans, while the Chamber of Commerce represents businesses. What reasons might the authors have for emphasizing or deemphasizing the interests of their respective constituencies while making statements to the general public in a congressional hearing?

4. Can Edith N. Rogers be described as a supporter of women's rights and/or of feminism based on her presented arguments concerning women in the military? Based on her opposition to the arguments of Clare Hoffman? Why or why not?

5. Judging from clues in the viewpoint by Patricia Davidson Guinan, what is her target audience? Does it overlap at all or much with the professional women addressed by Minnie L. Maffett? In what ways are their arguments tailored for their respective audiences?

Chapter Four

1. Does J. Saunders Redding argue that the struggle for black equality should be stopped for the duration of the war? Do you agree or disagree with such a position? Why? Would the general climate of black opinion, as reported by Roi Ottley, make such a position practical? Explain.

2. Under what conditions does Michio Kunitani support mass evacuation of Japanese Americans in the interests of national security? Does Earl Warren convincingly describe a situation in which these conditions are met? Why or why not?

3. Eugene V. Rostow argues that "the dominant element in the development of our relocation policy was race prejudice, not a military estimate of a military problem." Can evidence be found in the viewpoints by Earl Warren and Harlan F. Stone to support Rostow's contention, or were there legitimate national security concerns behind the decision to relocate Japanese Americans? Explain your answer.

Chapter Five

1. Could the viewpoints by Michael C.C. Adams and William L. O'Neill be accurately described as being analogous to one person seeing the glass half empty, the other seeing the glass half full? Explain your answer.

2. What does Michael C.C. Adams believe to be the primary duty of historians? Do you agree? Why or why not?

Appendix

The Atlantic Charter

In August 1941 President Franklin D. Roosevelt and Prime Minister Winston S. Churchill of Great Britain held a secret three-day conference on a ship off the coast of Newfoundland, Canada. At the meeting's conclusion they issued the Atlantic Charter, a joint declaration of common objectives for the postwar world. The text of the charter follows:

The President of the United States of America and the Prime Minister, Mr. Churchill, representing His Majesty's Government in the United Kingdom, being met together, deem it right to make known certain common principles in the national policies of their respective countries on which they base their hopes for a better future for the world.

First, their countries seek no aggrandizement, territorial or other;

Second, they desire to see no territorial changes that do not accord with the freely expressed wishes of the peoples concerned;

Third, they respect the right of all peoples to choose the form of government under which they will live; and they wish to see sovereign rights and self-government restored to those who have been forcibly deprived of them;

Fourth, they will endeavor, with due respect for their existing obligations, to further the enjoyment by all states, great or small, victor or vanquished, of access, on equal terms, to the trade and to the raw materials of the world which are needed for their economic prosperity;

Fifth, they desire to bring about the fullest collaboration between all nations in the economic field with the object of securing, for all, improved labor standards, economic advancement, and social security;

Sixth, after the final destruction of the Nazi tyranny, they hope to see established a peace which will afford to all nations the means of dwelling in safety within their own boundaries, and which will afford assurance that all the men in all the lands may live out their lives in freedom from fear and want;

Seventh, such a peace should enable all men to traverse the high seas and oceans without hindrance;

Eighth, they believe that all of the nations of the world, for realistic as well as spiritual reasons, must come to the abandonment of the use of force. Since no future peace can be maintained if land, sea, or air armaments continue to be employed by nations which threaten, or may threaten, aggression outside of their frontiers, they believe, pending the establishment of a wider and permanent system of general security, that the disarmament of such nations is essential. They will likewise aid and encourage all other practicable measures which will lighten for peace-loving peoples the crushing burden of armaments.

Chronology

1933	Franklin D. Roosevelt is inaugurated as president of the United States; Adolf Hitler is named chancellor of Germany.
March 7, 1936	Germany reoccupies the Rhineland in open defiance of the Treaty of Versailles.
July 7, 1937	Fighting breaks out between Chinese and Japanese troops in Beijing; the clash ultimately erupts into full-scale war between China and Japan that continues until 1945.
October 5, 1937	President Franklin Roosevelt deplores "international lawlessness" in his "quarantine speech" in Chicago.
September 29, 1938	Great Britain, France, and Germany sign the Munich Pact, which transfers the Sudetenland from Czechoslovakia to Germany; British prime minister Neville Chamberlain declares that the agreement will bring "peace in our time."
March 1939	Germany takes the rest of Czechoslovakia; Chamberlain abandons an appeasement policy towards Germany and declares that Britain and France will defend Poland against attack.
August 23, 1939	Hitler and Soviet leader Joseph Stalin agree to a nonaggression pact; Poland is divided between Germany and the Soviet Union in a secret protocol.
September 1, 1939	Germany invades Poland.
September 3, 1939	Great Britain and France declare war on Germany.
September 5, 1939	President Roosevelt officially proclaims America neutral.
November 4, 1939	Roosevelt signs the Neutrality Act of 1939, which revises American neutrality laws to permit Germany's enemies to buy American goods on a "cash and carry" basis.
May 1940	President Roosevelt requests more defense spending and calls for the manufacturing of fifty thousand airplanes a year.
May 10, 1940	Winston S. Churchill becomes Britain's new prime minister, replacing Neville Chamberlain.
June 3, 1940	The War Department of the United States authorizes the release of surplus and outdated war materials to Great Britain.

June 22, 1940	France surrenders to Germany.
July 26, 1940	The U.S. government takes steps to restrict exports of aviation fuel and scrap metal to Japan.
August 8–October 31, 1940	Germany tries and fails to subdue Great Britain with air attacks in the Battle of Britain.
September 3, 1940	Great Britain and the United States announce the "destroyers-for-bases" deal, in which the United States lends Great Britain fifty destroyers in exchange for the right to construct U.S. military bases on British possessions in the Western Hemisphere.
September 16, 1940	Roosevelt signs into law America's first peacetime compulsory military service.
September 27, 1940	Germany, Italy, and Japan sign a ten-year pact pledging mutual defense assistance.
October 30, 1940	President Roosevelt, campaigning for a third term, declares in a Boston speech that "your boys aren't going to be sent into any foreign wars."
November 2, 1940	President Roosevelt defeats Republican Wendell Willkie in the presidential election.
December 1940	Roosevelt proposes a program of "Lend-Lease" aid to a beleaguered Great Britain, calls for the United States to be an "arsenal of democracy," and establishes the Office of Production Management to coordinate defense production.
January 6, 1941	Roosevelt enunciates the "four freedoms" in his annual message to Congress.
February–May 1941	The Battle of the Atlantic rages as German submarines sink British ships; America expands its naval patrols in the North Atlantic.
March 11, 1941	Congress passes the Lend-Lease Act, enabling Roosevelt to aid nations, including Great Britain, deemed by the president to be vital to America's defense.
March 27, 1941	After secretly meeting in Washington for two months, American, British, and Canadian military representatives draw up plans of military cooperation "should the United States be compelled to resort to war."
April 11, 1941	The Office of Price Administration and Civilian Supply is established.
May 1941	The United States begins sending Lend-Lease supplies to China.
June 22, 1941	Germany invades the Soviet Union; Roosevelt promises U.S. aid to the Soviets.
June 25, 1941	President Roosevelt signs Executive Order 8802 banning discrimination in employment in defense

	industries and creating the Fair Employment Practices Commission to enforce the ban.
July 1941	American troops are stationed in Iceland.
July 25, 1941	Responding to Japan's military occupation of the French colony of Indochina, President Roosevelt freezes all Japanese assets in the United States and places Gen. Douglas MacArthur in charge of defending the Philippines.
August 9–12, 1941	Roosevelt and Churchill meet off the coast of Newfoundland, Canada, and draft the Atlantic Charter.
August 18, 1941	By a vote of 203-202, the House of Representatives votes to extend the army service of draftees for eighteen months.
September 11, 1941	President Roosevelt delivers his "shoot on sight" address announcing that navy ships are to aggressively defend themselves against attacks by Axis ships and submarines.
October 31, 1941	The *Reuben James,* an American destroyer patrolling the Atlantic, becomes the first armed American ship to be destroyed by a German submarine.
November 1941	Talks between the United States and Japan break down as the two sides reject each other's peace proposals.
December 7, 1941	Japanese forces bomb Pearl Harbor, Hawaii, and launch offensives in Hong Kong and the Philippines.
December 8, 1941	Congress declares war on Japan by votes of 82-0 and 388-1.
December 11, 1941	Germany and Italy declare war on the United States.
December 23, 1941	Representatives of labor and management sign a "no-strike" pledge.
January 1, 1942	Twenty-six Allied countries sign the United Nations Declaration pledging no "separate armistice or peace with the enemies."
January 12, 1942	National War Labor Board is established with the power to settle labor disputes with arbitration.
January 16, 1942	Roosevelt establishes the War Production Board to mobilize national resources for war.
February 19, 1942	Roosevelt signs Executive Order 9066 authorizing the military to prescribe defense zones from which to exclude suspected enemy aliens; the order is used to authorize the military evacuation and internment of 120,000 Japanese Americans by September.
March 1942	Gen. Louis Hershey rules that a conscientious objector to military conscription must have a belief

	in God, not just express adherence to "ethical imperatives."
April 1942	President Roosevelt proposes that salaries should be limited to $25,000 after taxes "insofar as practicable."
	The U.S. Navy agrees to accept blacks for positions other than messman.
April 9, 1942	American and Filipino soldiers besieged on the Bataan Peninsula in the Philippines surrender to the Japanese; thousands of prisoners perish on the subsequent Bataan Death March (a forced march to Japanese prison camps).
April 18, 1942	U.S. bombers, led by Col. James Doolittle, bomb Tokyo, Japan.
June 1942	The Civilian Conservation Corps becomes one of several New Deal agencies to be abolished during the course of the war.
June 4, 1942	America's naval victory over Japan in the Battle of Midway marks a turning point in the war for both nations.
June 12, 1942	President Roosevelt asks Americans to conserve rubber for the war effort.
July 23, 1942	Attorney General Francis Biddle indicts twenty-six "native fascists" under the Espionage Act of 1917; no convictions are obtained.
August 7, 1942	In America's first major offensive in the Pacific, U.S. Marines land at Guadalcanal in the Solomon Islands; the Japanese finally evacuate the island on February 8, 1943, after killing seven thousand Americans and losing thirty thousand of their own soldiers.
November 8, 1942	Operation Torch begins as British and American troops invade North Africa; all German troops in Africa surrender by May 13, 1943.
November 24, 1942	Rabbi Stephen S. Wise holds a news conference in Washington, D.C., detailing Germany's mass murder plans for European Jews.
December 1942	The government announces that the first war bond drive nets $12.9 billion.
December 6, 1942	The Manzanar riot, the most serious outbreak of violence in a Japanese American internment camp, takes place.
1943	Major strikes in the coal and rubber industries put nearly half a million workers on the picket lines in these crucial industries at various times during the year; Congress responds by passing legislation authorizing the federal government to seize and run essential wartime industries.

	The U.S. Army reaches its peak personnel strength of 8.3 million.
January 1943	Roosevelt and Churchill announce the "unconditional surrender" formula at the Casablanca Conference, precluding any possibility for a negotiated settlement to end the war.
	The U.S. Army announces that a special Japanese American combat unit, the 442nd Regimental Combat Team, is to be organized.
	To conserve fuel, all pleasure driving is banned in the United States for the duration of the war.
January 31, 1943	German forces surrender to the Russians at Stalingrad.
April 1943	A secret laboratory, part of the Manhattan Project, is established in Los Alamos, New Mexico, for the design and manufacture of atomic weapons.
April 8, 1943	Roosevelt orders a freeze on wages, prices, and salaries.
April–May 1943	The bombing campaign against Germany by Great Britain and the United States reaches its peak.
May 28, 1943	Former senator and Supreme Court justice James Byrnes is placed in charge of the new Office of War Mobilization.
June 1943	In *Hirabayashi v. United States*, the Supreme Court in a 9-0 vote upholds the constitutionality of the internment of Japanese Americans.
	"Zoot-suit" riots flare in Los Angeles, California, when sailors and soldiers attack Mexican Americans.
June 20–21, 1943	A major race riot erupts in Detroit; twenty-five blacks and nine whites die.
July 10, 1943	The Allies begin invasion of Europe in Sicily; their victory brings about the fall of Italian dictator Benito Mussolini.
August 11–24, 1943	Meeting at the First Quebec Conference, Roosevelt and Churchill reaffirm plans for a cross-Channel invasion of Normandy (Operation Overlord) and set a target date of May 1, 1944.
September 8, 1943	Italy announces surrender to invading Allies, who nonetheless meet continued stiff resistance from German forces.
October 19–30, 1943	Moscow Conference of Foreign Ministers marks the first three-way meeting of representatives of the United States, Great Britain, and the Soviet Union; the countries pledge support for a future "general international organization."

November 28–December 1, 1943	Roosevelt, Churchill, and Stalin meet at Teheran, Iran; the United States and Great Britain promise a major invasion of Europe; the Soviet Union reaffirms its promise to join the war against Japan after Germany's surrender.
December 28, 1943	President Roosevelt declares at a press conference that "Dr. Win-the-War" must replace "Dr. New Deal."
January 26, 1944	Roosevelt creates the War Refugee Board.
June 6, 1944	D-Day; Allied forces under Gen. Dwight D. Eisenhower launch a cross-Channel invasion of Normandy, France (Operation Overlord).
June 22, 1944	President Roosevelt signs the GI Bill of Rights, providing for educational benefits and relocation allowances for World War II veterans.
July 1–20, 1944	Delegates from forty-four nations meet at Bretton Woods, New Hampshire, to plan the monetary and economic foundations of the postwar world economy.
July 20, 1944	Hitler survives an assassination attempt.
August 25, 1944	Paris is liberated by the Allies.
September 11–16, 1944	At the Second Quebec Conference, Churchill and Roosevelt tentatively accept the Morgenthau Plan, which would make Germany an agricultural nation (but the plan is later dropped).
October 20, 1944	American forces invade Leyte, the first step in retaking the Philippines.
November 7, 1944	President Roosevelt is elected to a fourth term.
December 12, 1944	The German counteroffensive (Battle of the Bulge) begins.
January 12, 1945	The Soviets begin a major offensive against Poland and Germany.
January 20, 1945	Nearly all Japanese Americans in relocation centers are permitted to leave.
February 7–12, 1945	Roosevelt, Churchill, and Stalin meet at Yalta; the Soviets agree to enter the war in the Pacific; the three leaders sign a Declaration on Liberated Europe.
February 7–April 26, 1945	Allied forces launch a final drive against Germany.
Spring 1945	American B-29 bombers drop thousands of tons of incendiary bombs on Tokyo, Yokohama, and other Japanese cities.
April 1945	Allied forces liberate Nazi concentration camps at Buchenwald, Dachau, and Bergen-Belsen.
April 12, 1945	President Roosevelt dies at Warm Springs, Georgia; Vice President Harry S. Truman becomes president.

April 25, 1945	The United Nations founding conference opens in San Francisco.
April 30, 1945	Adolf Hitler commits suicide.
May 8, 1945	Allies designate this date as V-E (Victory in Europe) Day.
July 16, 1945	An atomic bomb is successfully exploded in New Mexico.
July 17–August 2, 1945	Truman, Stalin, and Churchill (later replaced by new British prime minister Clement C. Attlee) meet at Potsdam, Germany, to discuss the occupation of Germany and the war against Japan.
July 26, 1945	The United States, Britain, and China issue the Potsdam Declaration sending an ultimatum to surrender to Japan.
August 6, 1945	The United States drops an atomic bomb on Hiroshima, Japan.
August 8, 1945	The Soviet Union declares war on Japan.
August 9, 1945	A second atomic bomb is dropped on Nagasaki, Japan.
August 15, 1945	V-J (Victory over Japan) Day is declared the day after Japan surrenders.
September 2, 1945	Final Japanese surrender terms are signed aboard the battleship *Missouri*.

Annotated Bibliography

Henry H. Adams. *Harry Hopkins: A Biography.* New York: Putnam, 1977. A biography of a key Roosevelt associate who ran Lend-Lease, coordinated Allied strategy, and accompanied the president to the "Big Three" wartime conferences.

Gar Alperovitz. *Atomic Diplomacy.* New York: Simon & Schuster, 1965. A highly critical account of the decision to drop the atomic bomb that argues that the bomb was used on Japan to keep the Soviet Union out of the Pacific war and to convince them to leave Eastern Europe.

Stephen E. Ambrose. *The Supreme Commander: The War Years of General Dwight D. Eisenhower.* Garden City, NY: Doubleday, 1970. The best single-volume biography of the wartime career of the commander of the D-Day invasion.

Jervis Anderson. *A. Philip Randolph: A Biographical Portrait.* New York: Harcourt Brace Jovanovich, 1973. A sympathetic biography of the black union and civil rights leader who exerted great pressure on the Roosevelt administration to assure blacks access to defense work and to desegregate the military during World War II.

Leonard Baker. *Roosevelt and Pearl Harbor.* New York: Macmillan, 1970. A journalist's account of the Roosevelt administration from Roosevelt's January 1941 inauguration through the December 7, 1941, bombing of Pearl Harbor.

Charles A. Beard. *President Roosevelt and the Coming of the War, 1941.* New Haven, CT: Yale University Press, 1948. A critical study of Roosevelt's diplomacy that accuses the president of maneuvering the United States into World War II.

Francis Biddle. *In Brief Authority.* Garden City, NY: Doubleday, 1948. The autobiography of the attorney general during World War II who presided over the internment of Japanese Americans and who was deeply involved in a number of civil rights issues.

Jim Bishop. *FDR's Last Year.* New York: Morrow, 1974. A grim account of the final months of the life of President Roosevelt with emphasis on his poor health, his election to a fourth term, the Yalta Conference, and his death.

John Morton Blum. *V Was for Victory: Politics and American Culture During World War II.* New York: Harcourt Brace Jovanovich, 1976. An acclaimed cultural and social history of the American home front during the war.

David Brinkley. *Washington Goes to War.* New York: Knopf, 1988. An engaging account of the growth of Washington, D.C., and the federal government bureaucracy during World War II.

A. Russell Buchanan, ed. *The United States and World War II: Military and Diplomatic Documents.* Columbia: University of South Carolina Press, 1972. A collection of official reports, writings, and diplomatic documents of World War II.

Russell D. Buhite and David W. Levy, eds. *FDR's Fireside Chats.* Norman: University of Oklahoma Press, 1992. Complete texts and objective commentary on President Roosevelt's radio addresses to the nation before and during World War II.

James MacGregor Burns. *Roosevelt: The Soldier of Freedom.* New York: Harcourt Brace Jovanovich, 1970. An essentially sympathetic portrait of President Franklin D. Roosevelt as a war leader.

James F. Byrnes. *Speaking Frankly.* New York: Harper, 1947. The autobiography of a key Roosevelt administration official during World War II.

Bruce Catton. *The War Lords of Washington.* Westport, CT: Greenwood Press, 1969. A reprint of a history published shortly after World War II that is part personal reminiscence and part firsthand account of the development of wartime bureaucracies by a confidant of Donald Nelson of the War Production Board.

Mark Chadwin. *The Hawks of World War II.* Chapel Hill: University of North Carolina Press, 1968. A study of the efforts of private citizens, often working in collaboration with the Roosevelt administration, to influence public opinion and steer the United States into World War II.

William Henry Chamberlin. *America's Second Crusade.* Chicago: Regnery, 1950. A history of American policy making during World War II from the standpoint of a conservative critic of the Roosevelt administration.

Winston S. Churchill. *The Second World War.* Vol. 1, *The Gathering Storm.* Vol. 2, *Their Finest Hour.* Vol. 3, *The Grand Alliance.* Vol. 4, *The Hinge of Fate.* Vol. 5, *Closing the Ring.* Vol. 6, *Triumph and Tragedy.* Boston: Houghton Mifflin, 1948–53. An epic account of the Second World War written by the British prime minister who led his country from 1940 to 1945.

Diane Shaver Clemens. *Yalta.* New York: Oxford University Press, 1970. A revisionist history of the Yalta Conference that places a good share of the blame for a divided Europe on the United States.

J. Garry Clifford and Samuel R. Spenser Jr. *The First Peacetime Draft.* Lawrence: University Press of Kansas, 1986. A thorough account of the passage of the 1940 Burke-Wadsworth Act, including material on the critical efforts of private citizens to secure this legislation.

Wayne S. Cole. *Charles A. Lindbergh and the Battle Against American Intervention in World War II.* New York: Harcourt Brace Jovanovich, 1974. A portrait of the most important spokesman of the isolationist America First Committee and his efforts to keep the United States out of World War II.

Wayne S. Cole. *Roosevelt and the Isolationists, 1932–1945*. Lincoln: University of Nebraska Press, 1983. A comprehensive history of the hot-and-cold relationship between President Roosevelt and the leading isolationists in Congress.

Richard Collier. *1940: The World in Flames*. New York: Penguin, 1979. A popular account of the first full year of World War II in Europe, Asia, and North and South America.

John Costell. *Virtue Under Fire: How World War II Changed Our Social and Sexual Attitudes*. Boston: Little, Brown, 1985. A sociological account of the impact of World War II on basic American values and practices.

Robert Dallek. *Franklin D. Roosevelt and American Foreign Policy, 1932–1945*. New York: Oxford University Press, 1981. The best single-volume history of the full range of Roosevelt's foreign policy and one that is essentially in agreement with the efforts of the president.

Roger Daniels. *Prisoners Without Trial: Japanese-Americans in World War II*. New York: Hill and Wang, 1993. A careful and critical study of Japanese American internment during World War II.

Roger Daniels, ed. *American Concentration Camps: A Documentary History of the Relocation and Incarceration of Japanese-Americans, 1942–1945*. New York: Garland Press, 1989. An important source of primary documents relating to the internment of Japanese Americans during World War II.

Richard E. Darilek. *A Loyal Opposition in Time of War: The Republican Party and the Politics of Foreign Policy from Pearl Harbor to Yalta*. Westport, CT: Greenwood Press, 1976. A history of Republican Party participation in foreign policy debates during World War II.

Kenneth S. Davis. *FDR: Into the Storm, 1937–1940*. New York: Random House, 1993. A critical and comprehensive portrait of Franklin Roosevelt on the eve of American entry into World War II that concludes that the president was too hesitant to engage the Axis powers.

John Diggins. *Mussolini and Fascism: The View from America*. Princeton, NJ: Princeton University Press, 1972. A disturbing history of the American fascination with fascism, especially on the part of intellectuals, and a commentary on the possibilities for fascism in America.

Robert Divine. *Roosevelt and World War II*. Baltimore: Johns Hopkins University Press, 1969. Essays on Franklin Roosevelt's foreign policy leadership, including pre-1941 issues, the making of the United Nations, and Soviet-American relations during the war.

Robert Divine, ed. *Causes and Consequences of World War II*. Chicago: Quadrangle, 1969. A collection of essays on major issues and debates surrounding World War II.

Justus Doenecke. *Anti-Intervention: A Bibliographical Introduction to Isolationism and Pacifism from World War I to the Early Cold War*. New York:

Garland Press, 1987. A detailed survey of the literature relating to all varieties of American anti-interventionism.

Ray Douglas. *The World War, 1939–1945: The Cartoonists' Vision.* London: Routledge, 1990. A narrative account dotted with a series of insightful cartoons from the major countries involved in the war.

John Dower. *War Without Mercy: Race and Power in the Pacific War.* New York: Pantheon Books, 1986. A disturbing study of the Pacific conflict and how it was, on both sides, rooted in racial hatred and beliefs of ethnic superiority.

Dwight D. Eisenhower. *Crusade in Europe.* Garden City, NY: Doubleday, 1948. World War II as seen through the eyes of its most famous general and a future U.S. president.

John Ellis. *The Sharp End: The Fighting Man in World War II.* New York: Scribner, 1980. A study of the experiences of the frontline soldier in all theaters of the war that covers everything from induction and training to discipline and morale.

Thomas R. Fehrenbach. *FDR's Undeclared War, 1939–1941.* New York: David McKay, 1967. A sympathetic portrait of a president seeking to lead a reluctant nation into what both he and the author perceive to be a necessary war.

George Feifer. *Tennozan: The Battle of Okinawa and the Atomic Bomb.* New York: Ticknor & Fields, 1992. An account of the costly American invasion of Okinawa and its effect on the decision to drop atomic bombs on Hiroshima and Nagasaki.

Herbert Feis. *The A-Bomb and the End of World War II.* Princeton, NJ: Princeton University Press, 1966. A study of the decision to use the atomic bomb against Japan that stresses the importance of ending the war quickly but concludes that a desire to impress the Soviet Union did play a role in American thinking.

George Q. Flynn. *The Mess in Washington.* Westport, CT: Greenwood Press, 1979. A thoroughly researched account of the efforts to mobilize the civilian economy during World War II that focuses on the work of the War Production Board.

Frank Freidel. *Franklin D. Roosevelt: A Rendezvous with Destiny.* Boston: Little, Brown, 1990. A distillation of previous scholarship into a single volume by one of the major biographers of Franklin Roosevelt.

Paul Fussell. *Wartime: Understanding and Behavior in the Second World War.* New York: Oxford University Press, 1989. An examination of the emotional and psychological factors affecting the attitudes of soldiers and others during World War II by a World War II veteran and literary critic.

John Lewis Gaddis. *The United States and the Origins of the Cold War.* New York: Columbia University Press, 1972. An examination of the World War II alliance between the United States and the Soviet Union and how it eventually led to the Cold War.

Herbert Garfinkel. *When Negroes March.* New York: Atheneum, 1969. A study of the March on Washington Movement led by A. Philip Randolph during World War II and the attitudes of African Americans toward the war.

Martin Gilbert. *The Holocaust: The History of the Jews in Europe During the Second World War.* New York: Holt, Rinehart, and Winston, 1985. An exhaustive history of the mass killing of European Jews based on both eyewitness accounts and secondary literature.

Sherna Berger Gluck. *Rosie the Riveter Revisited: Women, the War, and Social Change.* Boston: Twayne, 1987. A history of female defense workers in California that places their labors in the context of the working lives of women from the 1930s through the 1950s.

Doris Kearns Goodwin, *No Ordinary Time: Franklin and Eleanor Roosevelt: The Home Front in World War II.* New York: Simon & Schuster, 1994. An intimate look at the Roosevelt family during World War II that captures many details of the history of the period.

Kent Roberts Greenfield. *American Strategy in World War II: A Reconsideration.* Westport, CT: Greenwood Press, 1963. An assessment by the chief historian of the Department of the Army of American military strategy and Roosevelt's performance as commander in chief.

Ross Gregory. *America 1941: A Nation at the Crossroads.* New York: Free Press, 1989. An entertaining and instructive social and political history of a transforming year in the life of the United States that culminated with American entry into World War II.

Mark Jonathan Harris, Franklin D. Mitchell, and Steven J. Schechter. *The Homefront: America During World War II.* New York: Putnam, 1984. An evocative oral history based on the recollections of thirty-seven ordinary Americans who experienced a new commitment to national unity because of World War II.

Jeffrey Hart. *From This Moment On: America in 1940.* New York: Crown, 1987. A series of riveting biographical and social portraits that provides a snapshot of a country on the eve of war.

Susan M. Hartmann. *The Home Front and Beyond: American Women in the 1940s.* Boston: Twayne, 1982. A history of a decade of change for women, who were caught between traditional ideas of women's roles and wartime demands for work.

Max Hastings. *Overlord: D-Day and the Battle for Normandy.* New York: Simon & Schuster, 1984. A superb account of the strategy and tactics of the actual campaign that stresses Allied matériel superiority and the professionalism of the German soldier.

George C. Herring Jr. *Aid to Russia, 1941–1946: Strategy, Diplomacy, and the Origins of the Cold War.* New York: Columbia University Press, 1973. A detailed study of the interaction of strategy, diplomacy, and political influences that shaped American policy on aid to the Soviet Union during World War II.

John Hersey. *Hiroshima.* New York: Knopf, 1946. An acclaimed account of the atomic bombing of the Japanese city and its immediate aftermath.

Roy Hoopes. *Americans Remember the Homefront: An Oral Narrative of the World War II Years in America.* New York: Hawthorn Books, 1977. Memories of famous as well as obscure Americans of World War II.

Akira Iriye. *Power and Culture.* Cambridge, MA: Harvard University Press, 1981. An examination and reinterpretation of Japanese American relations and their cultural context.

Manfred Jonas. *Isolationism in America, 1935–1941.* Ithaca, NY: Cornell University Press, 1966. A critical study of isolationist politicians, intellectuals, and pamphleteers in the years immediately preceding American entry into World War II.

John Keegan. *The Second World War.* New York: Viking, 1989. A compelling account of the conflict that divides the story into categories of narrative, strategic analysis, battles, and general themes of war, including supply and production.

George F. Kennan. *Memoirs, 1925–1950.* Boston: Little, Brown, 1967. Brilliant memoirs of an American diplomat and expert on Russia who was skeptical of the U.S.-Soviet wartime alliance.

Lee Kennett. *G.I.:The American Soldier in World War II.* New York: Scribner, 1987. A study that focuses on the American draftee, favors the infantry, and is replete with both anecdotal and sociological material.

Warren F. Kimball. *The Juggler.* Princeton, NJ: Princeton University Press, 1991. A collection of essays by a veteran Roosevelt scholar on various aspects of Roosevelt's diplomacy during World War II.

Gabriel Kolko. *The Politics of War, 1943–1945.* New York: Random House, 1968. A revisionist history of World War II diplomacy that stresses the economic factors behind American decisions.

Eric Larrabee. *Commander in Chief: Franklin Delano Roosevelt, His Lieutenants, and Their War.* New York: Harper and Row, 1987. A comprehensive, collective portrait of American military leadership that concentrates on President Roosevelt's relationship with eight key military subordinates, including Generals George C. Marshall, Dwight D. Eisenhower, Douglas MacArthur, and Joseph W. Stilwell.

Joseph P. Lash. *Roosevelt and Churchill, 1939–1941: The Partnership That Saved the West.* New York: Norton, 1976. A highly laudatory account of the pre–Pearl Harbor relationship between the two men who would ultimately guide the Allies to victory.

William Leahy. *I Was There.* New York: McGraw-Hill, 1950. The memoirs and frank opinions of the chairman of the Joint Chiefs of Staff during World War II.

William M. Leary, ed. *We Shall Return! MacArthur's Commanders and the Defeat of Japan.* Lexington: University Press of Kentucky, 1988. Essays by nine respected scholars on Douglas MacArthur's top lieutenants.

Ralph B. Levering. *American Opinion and the Russian Alliance, 1939–1945.* Chapel Hill: University of North Carolina Press, 1976. A pioneering history of the shifts in American opinion toward the Soviet Union from hostility to warm friendship (especially among educated Americans) during World War II, and then away from that friendship as the Cold War loomed.

Richard R. Lingeman. *Don't You Know There's a War On? The American Home Front, 1941–1945.* New York: Putnam, 1970. A popular social history of the American World War II home front.

Walter Lippmann. *U.S. War Aims.* Boston: Little, Brown, 1944. Policy prescriptions from America's most prominent political columnist during World War II.

William R. Louis. *Imperialism at Bay, 1941–1945.* New York: Oxford University Press, 1977. An examination of the crucial differences between the United States and Great Britain concerning Britain's desire to keep its empire and the efforts of the Roosevelt administration to end European imperialism in general.

John Lukacs. *1945: The Year Zero.* Garden City, NY: Doubleday, 1978. A series of compelling portraits of the key players, including Churchill, Roosevelt, Stalin, Hitler, and Truman, as World War II ended and the Cold War began.

Robert James Maddox. *The United States and World War II.* Boulder, CO: Westview Press, 1992. A concise, general account of America's involvement in the war.

William Manchester. *American Caesar: Douglas MacArthur, 1880–1964.* Boston: Little, Brown, 1978. A biography of the celebrated and controversial general.

Bill Mauldin. *Up Front.* New York: Holt, 1945. A collection of famous "Willie and Joe" cartoons, plus interpretive text, about the experiences of American soldiers in World War II.

Phillip McGuire, ed. *Taps for a Jim Crow Army: Letters from Black Soldiers in World War II.* Lexington: University Press of Kentucky, 1993. A collection of letters written by black soldiers, many with bitter descriptions of experiences of racial discrimination.

Charles Mee. *Meeting at Potsdam.* New York: M. Evans, 1975. The best account of the last wartime meeting of the leaders of the United States, Great Britain, and the Soviet Union.

Ruth Milkman. *Gender at Work: The Dynamics of Job Segregation by Sex During World War II.* Chicago: University of Illinois Press, 1987. A careful analysis of the influx of working women into the automobile and electrical manufacturing industries that challenges the argument that these women were anxious to return to the role of housewife following World War II.

Walter Millis. *This Is Pearl!* New York: Morrow, 1947. A journalistic account of the bombing of Pearl Harbor.

Ted Morgan. *FDR: A Biography*. New York: Simon & Schuster, 1985. A solid and readable single-volume biography of President Franklin Roosevelt.

Samuel Eliot Morison. *The Two-Ocean War: A Short History of the United States Navy in the Second World War*. Boston: Little, Brown, 1963. The condensed version of the author's official *History of U.S. Naval Operations in World War II*, focusing on the most important battles and campaigns.

Arthur D. Morse. *While Six Million Died: A Chronicle of American Apathy*. Woodstock, NY: Overlook Press, 1983. A highly critical account of the failures of the Roosevelt administration and of the United States in general in responding to the Holocaust.

Kenneth Paul O'Brien and Lynn Hudson Parsons, eds. *The Home-Front War*. Westport, CT: Greenwood Press, 1995. Papers by nine historians examine how World War II affected American society.

Raymond G. O'Connor. *Diplomacy for Victory: FDR and Unconditional Surrender*. New York: Norton, 1971. An account of Roosevelt's decision to announce the unconditional surrender formula and an argument against the notion that this decision prolonged World War II either in Europe or in the Pacific.

Thomas D. Parrish. *Roosevelt and Marshall: Partners in Politics and War*. New York: Morrow, 1989. A judicious account of the sometimes uneasy relationship between President Franklin D. Roosevelt and George C. Marshall, U.S. Army chief of staff.

James T. Patterson. *Mr. Republican: A Biography of Robert A. Taft*. Boston: Houghton Mifflin, 1972. A sympathetic portrait of a leading Republican isolationist.

Amos Perlmutter. *FDR and Stalin: A Not So Grand Alliance, 1943–1945*. Columbia: University of Missouri Press, 1993. A highly critical account of Roosevelt's diplomacy that concentrates on the major wartime conferences and the second-front issue.

Geoffrey Perret. *Days of Sadness, Years of Triumph: The American People, 1939–1945*. New York: Coward, Cabell & Geoghegen, 1973. An often colorful social history of American life for the 90 percent of Americans who experienced the war at home, away from the battlefields.

Richard Polenberg. *War and Society: The United States, 1941–1945*. Philadelphia: Lippincott, 1972. A brief general social history of the impact of World War II on many aspects of American life.

Gordon W. Prange. *At Dawn We Slept: The Untold Story of Pearl Harbor*. New York: McGraw-Hill, 1981. A voluminous account of the Japanese attack that triggered American entry into World War II.

Ernie Pyle. *Here Is Your War*. New York: Holt, 1943. A collection of the author's popular newspaper columns describing the North African campaign.

Richard Rhodes. *The Making of the Atomic Bomb*. New York: Simon & Schuster, 1986. A very detailed yet highly compelling account of the Manhattan Project.

Eleanor Roosevelt. *This I Remember*. New York: Harper, 1949. The second volume of the memoirs of the First Lady that includes her experiences in World War II.

Louis Ruchames. *Race, Jobs, and Politics: The FEPC*. New York: Columbia University Press, 1953. A well-documented account of the federal Fair Employment Practices Commission and an evaluation of its services during and immediately following World War II.

Bruce Russett. *No Clear and Present Danger*. New York: Harper, 1972. A brief revisionist account of American entry into World War II that seeks to make the case that the United States would have benefited from staying out of the war.

Keith Sainsbury. *The Turning Point: Roosevelt, Stalin, Churchill, and Chiang Kai-shek, 1943: The Moscow, Cairo, and Teheran Conferences*. New York: Oxford University Press, 1985. A British historian's treatment of the often discordant purposes of the Allies as evidenced at the major wartime conferences.

Ronald Schaffer. *Wings of Judgment*. New York: Oxford University Press, 1985. An examination of American bombing campaigns in World War II and the moral issues they raise.

Lois Scharf. *ER: First Lady of American Liberalism*. Boston: Twayne, 1987. A brief and largely sympathetic biography of Eleanor Roosevelt and her efforts to make sure that the war was fought for liberal purposes.

Paul Schroeder. *The Axis Alliance and Japanese-American Relations, 1941*. Ithaca, NY: Cornell University Press, 1958. A diplomatic history of U.S.-Japanese relations prior to Pearl Harbor that is highly critical of American policy making.

Michael Sherry. *The Rise of American Air Power: The Creation of Armageddon*. New Haven, CT: Yale University Press, 1987. A survey of pre–World War II American thinking on the subject of air power and an analysis of American bombing campaigns against Germany and Japan.

Martin J. Sherwin. *A World Destroyed: The Atomic Bomb and the Grand Alliance*. New York: Knopf, 1975. A history of the Manhattan Project and the efforts of the Roosevelt administration to keep this work a secret from not just Germany and Japan, but the Soviet Union as well.

Robert Shogan and Tom Craig. *The Detroit Race Riots*. Philadelphia: Chilton Books, 1964. A compelling narrative account of the most serious and bloody race riots in the United States during World War II.

Bradley F. Smith. *The Shadow Warriors: OSS and the Origins of the CIA*. New York: Basic Books, 1983. A monumental study of the World War II American spy organization and its controversial leader, William Donovan.

Ronald Spector. *Eagle Against the Sun: The American War with Japan*. New York: Free Press, 1985. An account of the Pacific war that is critical of Gen. Douglas MacArthur.

Mark A. Stoler. *The Politics of the Second Front*. Westport, CT: Greenwood Press, 1977. A study of American military planning and diplomacy from 1941 to 1943.

I.F. Stone. *The War Years, 1939–1945*. Boston: Little, Brown, 1988. A collection of wartime articles by the famous Washington investigative journalist, frequently focusing on how big business used the war for private gain.

A.J.P. Taylor. *The Origins of the Second World War*. New York: Atheneum, 1961. A controversial revisionist history that contends that Hitler did not seek war during the years between his coming to power in 1933 and the start of World War II in 1939.

Studs Terkel. *"The Good War": An Oral History of World War II*. New York: Pantheon Books, 1984. More than a hundred oral accounts of World War II, including those of Americans, Japanese, Germans, civilians, POWs, entertainers, government officials, military officers, and enlisted soldiers.

Christopher Thorne. *Allies of a Kind: The United States, Britain, and the War Against Japan*. New York: Oxford University Press, 1978. A history of the often complicated alliance between the two nations (as well as with France, Australia, New Zealand, and the Netherlands) and their varying goals in the war with Japan.

John Toland. *Infamy: Pearl Harbor and Its Aftermath*. Garden City, NY: Doubleday, 1982. A history of the background of the bombing of Pearl Harbor that argues for the possibility that the Roosevelt administration knew in advance of the Japanese attack.

John Toland. *The Rising Sun: The Decline and Fall of the Japanese Empire*. New York: Random House, 1970. An account of the war from the perspective of Japanese troops.

Barbara Tuchman. *Stilwell and the American Experience in China*. New York: Macmillan, 1970. A compelling biography of the American general who tried to preside over the Allied war effort in Burma and China and to work with Chinese leader Chiang Kai-shek.

William M. Tuttle. *Daddy's Gone to War: The Second World War in the Lives of America's Children*. New York: Oxford University Press, 1993. A valuable and moving account based on archival research and on more than two thousand solicited inquiries concerning the impact of the war and of absent fathers on the lives of children.

Jonathan G. Utley. *Going to War with Japan, 1937–1941*. Knoxville: University of Tennessee Press, 1985. A history of pre–World War II U.S.-Japanese relations that is critical of American diplomacy.

Frederick S. Voss. *Reporting the War: The Journalistic Coverage of World War II*. Washington, DC: Smithsonian Institution Press, 1994. An examination of the reporters and photographers who covered World War II, including a chapter on black newspapers and their coverage of the war.

Donald Cameron Watt. *How War Came: The Immediate Origins of the Second World War, 1938–1939.* New York: Pantheon Books, 1989. A diplomatic history of the crucial eleven months between the Munich agreement and the Nazi invasion of Poland.

Doris Weatherford. *American Women and World War II.* New York: Facts On File, 1990. A thoroughly documented study of the issues women faced during this time, including women in the military, industrial workers, and mothers.

Sumner Welles. *The Time for Decision.* New York: Harper, 1944. Memoirs and prescriptions for the future by the State Department undersecretary and President Roosevelt's special representative in Europe.

Wendell Willkie. *One World.* New York: Simon & Schuster, 1943. A plea for the United States to join a new world organization, written by the defeated Republican presidential candidate of 1940, who undertook an international goodwill tour for his victorious opponent, President Franklin D. Roosevelt.

Allan M. Winkler, *Home Front U.S.A.: America During World War II.* Arlington Heights, IL: Harlan Davidson, 1986. A concise summary of how the war affected American domestic life.

Nancy Baker Wise and Christy Wise. *A Mouthful of Rivets: Women at Work in World War II.* San Francisco: Jossey-Bass, 1994. An oral history of women and their World War II experiences.

Lawrence Wittner. *Rebels Against War: The American Peace Movement, 1941–1960.* New York: Columbia University Press, 1969. A sympathetic treatment of the peace movement that seeks to dispel any notion that its members were naive in their commitment to pacifism.

Roberta Wohlstetter. *Pearl Harbor: Warning and Decision.* Stanford, CA: Stanford University Press, 1962. A detailed account of the background of the attack on Pearl Harbor that exonerates the Roosevelt administration by arguing that there was too much rather than too little intelligence information with which to make decisions.

Peter Wyden. *Day One: Before Hiroshima and After.* New York: Simon & Schuster, 1984. An account of the American scientists, politicians, and military personnel who were involved in the Manhattan Project, including Robert Oppenheimer and Gen. Leslie Groves.

David S. Wyman. *The Abandonment of the Jews: America and the Holocaust, 1941–1945.* New York: Pantheon Books, 1984. A comprehensive examination of what Americans did—and did not do—to rescue Jews from the Holocaust.

Robert H. Zeiger. *American Workers, American Unions, 1920–1985.* Baltimore: Johns Hopkins University Press, 1986. A general history of organized labor that includes much material on its activities during World War II.

278

Index